The Perplexity of a Muslim Woman

The Perplexity of a Muslim Woman

Over Inheritance, Marriage, and Homosexuality

By Olfa Youssef
Translated by Lamia Benyoussef

LEXINGTON BOOKS
Lanham • Boulder • New York • London

Published by Lexington Books
An imprint of The Rowman & Littlefield Publishing Group, Inc.
4501 Forbes Boulevard, Suite 200, Lanham, Maryland 20706
www.rowman.com

Unit A, Whitacre Mews, 26-34 Stannary Street, London SE11 4AB

British Library Cataloguing in Publication Information Available

Library of Congress Cataloging-in-Publication Data
The hardback edition of this book was previously catalogued by the Library of Congress as follows:

Names: Y?usuf, Ulfah author. | Zayzafoon, Lamia Ben Youssef, 1966- translator.
Title: The perplexity of a Muslim woman : over inheritance, marriage, and homosexuality / by Olfa
    Youssef ; translated by Lamia Benyoussef.
Other titles: ?Hayrat Muslimah. English
Description: Lanham : Lexington Books, 2017. | Includes bibliographical references and index.
Identifiers: LCCN 2016045727 (print) | LCCN 2016047582 (ebook)
Subjects: LCSH: Women (Islamic law) | Inheritance and succession (Islamic law) | Marriage (Islamic
    law) | Women in Islam.
Classification: LCC KBP526.32.Y87 A34 2017 (print) | LCC KBP526.32.Y87 (ebook) | DDC 342/
    .1670878—dc23 LC record available at http://lccn.loc.gov/2016045727

ISBN 978-1-4985-4169-5 (cloth : alk. paper)
ISBN 978-1-4985-4171-8 (pbk.: alk. paper)
ISBN 978-1-4985-4170-1 (electronic)

Printed in the United States of America

"None knows its interpretation but God"
(The Amramites [Āli 'Imrān] 3:7)
To my mother and father

Contents

Translator's Preface

This book translation project started in 2010 when I was invited to speak at a conference on critical theory and cultural production of African literature and cinema jointly held by Michigan State University and the University of Michigan.[1] As I researched the discrepancy between what was produced on North Africa at home and by the diaspora, I realized not only how little scholarly criticism produced in Arabic had been translated into English in the last twenty years in the field of Islamic Studies, but also how limited the dialogue between Maghrebi and sub-Saharan academics was in the absence of Arabic translation. That same fall, I gave a talk at the Middle Eastern Studies Association[2] in San Diego on the new school of Islamic psychoanalysis of Tunis represented by Fethī Benslāma, Rajā Benslāma, Olfa Youssef, and Amāl Grāmī. Questioning the relevance of Freudian or Lacanian approach to the field of Islamic Studies, the panel respondent rejected the insight of this new Tunisian school on the ground that psychoanalysis was a discipline primarily developed to treat individual mental illness in the West, and therefore, it could not be used to study the collective behavior of a people belonging to an entirely different culture. Although this line of criticism is not new, as seen in Marie-Cécile Ortigues and Edmond Ortigues's *Oedipe africain*,[3] it does raise new questions about the selective use of Western psychoanalysis in the Arabic and Islamic context by some postcolonial Arabic scholars. Why would for example Freud or Lacan be relevant to the study of mourning and narrative in the Middle Eastern novel[4] but not to the study of masculine power, gender, and divine law in the field of Islamic Studies? In addition, just as West African writers revised Western psychoanalysis to meet the needs of their cultural specificities, so did North African writers like Fethī Benslāma and Youssef in the context of Islamic Studies. As I argue elsewhere,[5] in his seminal work *Psychoanalysis and the Challenge of Islam*,

1

Benslāma does not blindly reproduce Freudian psychoanalysis in the Islamic context, but rather questions its premise concerning the castrating presence of the father. In lieu of the father-son conflict usually found in Freudian thought, Benslāma holds the father's absence as the primary trauma in the Muslim psyche, "from the story of Abraham's abandonment of Hagar and Ishmael in the desert, to Muhammad's status as an orphan and his symbolic abandonment (through death) by his biological and adoptive fathers."[6]

While Fethī Benslāma has subjected psychoanalysis to the challenge of Islam, in her book *Le Coran au risque de la psychanalyse* (*The Qur'an and the Challenge of Psychoanalysis*),[7]—not accidentally titled in reverse of Benslāma's work—Olfa Youssef (1966–) subjects Islam to the challenge of Arabic lexicography, Saussurean linguistics, and Lacanian psychoanalysis. Against nativist voices which exclude Western critical theory when it comes to revisiting and excavating Islam's sacred texts, Youssef suggests in *The Perplexity of a Muslim Woman: Over Inheritance, Marriage, and Homosexuality*[8] that if Islam is valid for any time and for any space as fervent Muslim disciples often proclaim, it is not because there is some eternal truth to be retrieved from the sacred text, but because it is an open or non-sutured text. It is thus the act of reinterpretation through a variety of methodologies that makes the Qur'anic text valid at any time and space, not the phallocentric readings and opinions of medieval Muslim religious scholars that have been institutionalized in many parts of the Muslim world as laws because believed to be sacred. As she excavates medieval religious polemics, she discloses how male bias, economic interest, and Jāhiliyyan[9] patriarchal culture framed the religious scholars' interpretation of Qur'anic verses in matters of inheritance, marriage, and homosexuality, showing in some cases that even when the Qur'anic text is clear, legal scholars dismissed the explicit ruling in God's text to resort to consensus (*ijmā'*) to protect their male interests, especially in matters of inheritance and marriage. Departing from essentialist readings of the Qur'an in the Hānafī, Mālikī, Shāfi'ī, and Hanbalī schools of Islamic jurisprudence which purport to interpret, translate, and explain divine truth to the ignorant Muslim masses, Youssef states in the preliminary pages of her book that knowledge of God's intent is impossible as attested in His statement "None knows its true interpretation but God" (The Amramites 3:7).

Born on 21 November 1966 in Sousse, Tunisia, Youssef studied at al Mahatta Elementary School and earned in 1983 her High School Diploma in Arts from Le Lycée de jeunes filles de Sousse with honors. She then joined the École Normale Supérieure of Sousse from which she graduated with a B.A. degree in Arabic Studies in 1987. Because she was Valedictorian throughout her undergraduate education, she received President Habīb Bourguība's Award in 1987. Within two years, she received the Certificat d'Aptitude à la Recherche in linguistics (1988) and the Agrégation in Arabic

Letters with Outstanding Distinction (1989) from the Faculty of Arts and Human Sciences of Tunis. In 2002, she became Docteur d'État in Arabic Letters and Civilization after successfully defending (also with Outstanding Distinction) a dissertation on "Polysemy in the Qur'an" at the Faculty of Arts and Letters of Manouba. A professor in Arabic Studies, she is currently holding a joint appointment in three Tunisian institutions of higher education: the Faculty of Arts and Letters of Manouba (since 1989), the Higher Institute of Languages of Tunis (since 2014), and the High Institute of Arts of Sousse (since 2007). Considered Tunisia's child prodigy throughout her educational career, she also served in key important administrative positions, namely the director of the Higher Institute for Children's Executives in Carthage (2003–2009) and the director of Tunisia's National Library Beit al Hikma (2009–2011). She also hosted several literary and educational programs on national TV such as "A Book in a Few Minutes" (1994–2004) to encourage literacy, "A One Hour Dialogue" (1994–1995 and 1997) to address the problems of the Tunisian youths, "Polemics" (2000–2001) which covered debates in literature, philosophy, and social sciences, "Themed Evenings" (2001) which discussed biographies and important historical events, "The Books of the Day" (2000–2001) that aimed at introducing to the layman key concepts in the social sciences, as well as some religious programs like "Biography of the Prophet" (2007), "Women in the Qur'an and the Sunna" (2008) and "Islam's Values" (2008). A public figure, she hosted a morning talk show on Jawhara FM Radio (2015–2016) and was frequently a guest-speaker at *France 24*, *Al Arabiya*, *Al Hurra*, and *Al Mayadeen*, not to mention numerous articles and interviews in the Arabic media.

Her publications covered a plethora of topics ranging from gender studies, society and education, religious thought, to the exchange between civilizations, with a particular leaning for psychoanalysis, sociology, and linguistics as methodological approaches. As Amin Tais judiciously argues in "Islamic Perspectives in Post-Revolutionary Tunisia," Youssef's most important "contribution" in the field of Islamic Studies is her introduction of the "methods of the new scholars" in the traditional field of interpreting the Qur'an and the hadiths: "She harnesses modern linguistics, semiology, and psychoanalysis to both deconstruct traditional interpretations and propose new avenues in reading the religious text."[10] If the notion of linguistic ambiguity is central to Youssef's text, it is because it is "the door through which she forcefully enters the debate room with traditionalist interpretations of Islam." For her, "all interpretations are relative, including the ones that have been accepted as authoritative within the four madhāhib (legal schools)."[11] Countering the simplistic yet confident explanations provided by fundamentalists on the Friday sermons or Islamic satellite channels, she argues that ambiguity is one of the characteristics of the Qur'anic text. Her first book chapter appeared in an edited volume entitled *Women and Memory: Tunisian*

Women in Public Life 1920–1960 (1992) which covered the testimonies of Tunisian women from different fields in the first half of the twentieth century.[12] It was followed by a co-authored book entitled *A Semiotic and Symbolic Study of Mahmoud al Messa'di's "The Dam"* (1994),[13] *Women Weak in Mind and Religion: Chapters in the Hadiths/a Psychanalytic and Psychological Approach* (2003),[14] *The Multiplicity of Meanings in the Qur'an: A Study of the Foundations of the Multiplicity of Meaning in Language through the Science of Interpreting the Qur'an* (2003),[15] *A Debate Between Lexicography and Linguistics Among Contemporary Arab Linguists* (1997), *Narrating about Women in the Qur'an and the Sunna* (1997),[16] *Perplexity of a Muslim Woman* (2008),[17] and *Desire: A Reading of Islam's Foundations* (2010).[18] After the 2011 Tunisian Revolution, she published *The Male is not like the Female: On Gendered Identity* (2013)[19] and a series of books called *Allahu A'lam* (God Knows Better) consisting of seven short books on contemporary controversies in the Muslim world: *On the Death Penalty* (2012),[20] *On Wine* (2012),[21] *On Homosexuality* (2012),[22] *On the Penalty for Theft* (2012),[23] *On Polygamy* (2012),[24] *On the Marriage of the Muslim Woman with a Man from the People of the Book* (2012).[25] Two of her books have recently been translated into French, *Sept controverses en Islam: Parlons-en* and *Désir: Des dimensions spirituelles et psychiques des pilliers de l'Islam*.[26] She is currently the most prolific and most well-known Tunisian scholar of Arabic expression. In Tunisia alone, *The Perplexity of the Muslim Woman*, for example, sold about fifteen thousand copies, which is a record for a Tunisian woman author (usually five hundred copies are printed and sold), not to mention pirated copies on the internet. The first edition of Youssef's recent 2014 book *The Male is not Like the Female* is already at its second edition. In recognition of her scholarly contributions, she has been the recipient of several national honor awards, namely the Zoubeidia Béchir Award from CREDIF for best Academic Arabic Scholarship, the Order of Merit from the Ministry of Culture (2002, 2008), the Order of Merit from the Ministry of Education (2007), and other awards from the city councils of several Tunisian towns like Nabeul (1999), Metouia (2004), and La Goulette (2004). In addition, she served on the jury of several prestigious book awards like the COMAR Book Prize for Best Tunisian Novel (2002, 2003, 2006, 2007, 2008, and 2010) and Tāhar al Haddād Book Award (1996).

Since the 14 January 2011 Revolution, which ousted former president Zīne El 'Ābidīne Ben Alī (1987–2011) and catapulted the rest of the Middle East into a series of political upheavals known as the Arab Spring, Youssef became, like most Tunisian academics in the humanities, a *Facebook* cyber activist, with about 182,000 followers from Tunisia and beyond, devoted fans but also fierce enemies who accuse her of insulting Islam and the Prophet, of usurping the male power of medieval scholars like Ibn Hanbal, and of collaborating with the former regime. On 23 October 2011, Tunisia held its first democratic elections for the National Constituent Assembly in charge of writing the country's new constitution. Although Ennahdha Islamist Party won the biggest number of seats in the 23 October 2011 elections, it did not have the required majority to control the assembly. To govern more smoothly, the party leader Rachid al Ghannoushi struck an alliance with two centrist parties, the Congress for the Republic Party of Moncef Marzūkī (CPR) and the Democratic Forum for Labor and Liberties of Mustapha Ben Ja'far (FDTL) to form the Troika coalition. Although the National Constituent Assembly was elected for one year, the Troika leadership breached its mandate and stayed three years in power. Under public pressure, notably the Bardo Sit-Ins launched in protest of the assassination of two opposition leaders,[27] the government of Alī La'rayedh was finally forced to step down in December 2013 in favor of an interim neutral government of technocrats who would lead the country in this difficult transition until the 2014 presidential elections.

If Youssef was a controversial figure before the 2011 Tunisian Revolution on religious grounds only, both admiration and criticism levied against her became increasingly divided across political and religious lines in its aftermath. In 2010, Youssef and a book cover of *Perplexity of the Muslim Woman* appeared in an ultra-conservative misogynist rap video clip that dismissed the secularism of Mustafa Kamāl, the reformist movements of Jamāl Eddīn al Afghānī, Muhammad 'Abdū, and Tāhar al Haddād, Arab nationalism, socialism, and Nasserism, and the feminism of Qāsim Amīn, Huda Sha'rāwī, and Youssef as viruses against Islam and the Ottoman Caliphate introduced by Zionists and Western colonial powers.[28] Other Tunisian scholars on the left of the political spectrum like Wassīm Jday[29] find the approach of Tunisian scholars like Youssef, Muhammad Tālbi, and Yusuf Saddīq to reform Muslim society and combat terrorism from within an Islamic perspective to be a futile exercise. For them, the seeds of fundamentalism are in the text itself not the interpretation. Instead they call for reform from within the principles delineated in the Universal Declaration of Human Rights.

On 7 August 2013, Youssef received a death threat that she would be assassinated on the anniversary of the Personal Status Code (13 August 2013) that former president Habib Bourguība (1956–1987) had promulgated on 13 August 1956 and which some Islamists still see today as anathema because it abolished polygamy and faith-based courts. She has been ever since under police protection even to go teach.[30] Although she voted for Nidā Tūnis Party of Bejī Caid Essebsī in the 2014 presidential elections to counter the Islamist threat, she has since withdrawn all her support for this party not just because of its alliance with some Islamists, but also because of its corruption and failure to pass any program that would address the urgent problems of unemployment, inflation, terrorism, regional disparities, and social injustice.

While some radical Salafists want to spill her blood because of her views on homosexuality, marriage, inheritance, apostasy in Islam, or because she cast doubt on the "sacred" authority of medieval male scholars, some secular centrist critics, especially from the former CPR[31] party of interim president Moncef Marzūkī (2011–2014), accuse her of collaboration with the Ben Alī regime. In July 2013, her name appeared among the list of Tunisian academics and public figures who were accused of having collaborated with Ben Alī in the infamous 2013 *Black Book*,[32] which interim president Marzūkī is reported to have published to discredit his political enemies.[33] In response to this accusation, Youssef struck back that, despite his many faults, "[Ben Alī was] more coherent and clear than Marzūkī."[34] Using the power of social media, she challenged him to show any evidence that she had praised or received bribes from Ben Alī. Even more, she shamed him for groveling at the feet of Islamists and sinking to become "a peddler of human rights" as seen in his "imprisonment of Jāber al Mājrī [for insults to the Prophet] while "shaking hands with terrorists and criminals."[35]

If the witch-hunts—in their religious or secular robes—against Youssef and many other Tunisian feminist activists in the aftermath of the January 2011 Revolution demonstrate anything, it is the vulnerability of all Tunisian women, who benefited to a certain extent since 1956 from the state feminism[36] of Bourguība and Ben Alī, but whose "liberation," ironically, became part of a Tunisian state master narrative that deploys the discourse of women's rights to brush up the image of these two dictatorial regimes in the West. In August 2016, Youssef declined with a group of other feminist academics like Sanā Ben 'Āchūr (a law professor and former president of the Association of Tunisian Women Democrats) President Essebsī's invitation to be honored on the 60th anniversary of the Tunisian Personal Status Code. This collective feminist act of boycotting this commemoration in Carthage Palace was a protest against President Essebsī's coalition with Islamists which feminist activists saw as a betrayal of the one million Tunisian women who had voted for his party in the hope of thwarting the Islamist threat. The insignificant number of competent women in key positions in the government of Habīb Essīd, the prime minister nominated by President Essebsī himself, was another factor that contributed to Youssef's rejection of that prestigious award. On 13 August 2016, Youssef wrote on her *Facebook* page:

> I thank the Presidency for their invitation, but I cannot accept it given the betrayal of the promises made during the elections, the coalition with the enemies of the Personal Status Code, and corruption that crept into every aspect of life. . . . Today, the hearts of my friends are bigger and more impressive than the Palace of Carthage.
> Waiting for a better tomorrow, *inchallah*!

Like most Tunisian and Arab intellectuals and political activists in general,[37] Youssef dismisses the Arab Spring as the new Sykes Picot engineered by Western governments and their allies in the region to divide the natural resources of the Middle East, using this time not their military forces but Islamists as weapons. Although she is held in high esteem by most Tunisian academics in the humanities, many have criticized her for her political positions such as supporting the death penalty for terrorists and child rapists and murderers, barring those Tunisians with dual citizenship from holding key positions in the Tunisian government,[38] and staunchly defending the legacy of Bourguība,*"le dictateur éclairé"* (enlightened dictator) who built postcolonial Tunisia. To be fair to Youssef, she did critique Bourguība for ill-using the foundations of the republic to create a state dictatorship.[39] Her defense of Bourguibism ought to be understood then as a visceral reaction to the fundamentalists' plan to slowly corrode the political institutions of the republic in preparation for the establishment of an Islamic theocracy. The terrorist attacks against the symbols of the modern nation state of Tunisia founded by Bourguība can be seen in the assassination of Muhammad Brāhmī on Tunisia's Republic Day (25 July 2013), the timing of the threat to kill Youssef herself on the PSC anniversary, and the desecration of Bourguība's mausoleum, not by chance, on the tragic date of 11 September 2012.[40] If despite his many faults, Youssef continues to edify Bourguība as the father of the nation, it is because there are bigger dangers threatening to destroy the model of modernization and social progress that he had built since independence.

One might argue that it is paradoxical that North African feminists like Youssef, Gisèle Halīmī,[41] or even Assia Djebar[42] place themselves at times in the patriarchal and nationalist legacy of the Liberating Father, yet such a reading ignores family dynamics in the Maghreb in which the mother-son connection is often balanced by the father-daughter dyad—an intellectual closeness or complicity that often goes unnoticed because, under Western eyes, the "Muslim woman" can only be the victim of her male relatives. What seems to characterize Maghrebi feminism is both resistance and deliberate self-repatriation in the law-of-the-father, which from this local feminist perspective has not always been repressive. One of the ironies in this respect is that the commemoration of the 60th anniversary of the promulgation of the Personal Status Code on 13 August 2016 was boycotted by the feminist activist lawyer Sanā Ben 'Āchūr (1955–, the very daughter of Sheikh al Fādhel Ben 'Āchūr (1909–1970),[43] the eminent scholar from the Zeytūna Mosque who had written the text of the Personal Status Code that Bourguība passed in 1957. Yet, it is the reformist legacy of the father that the daughter seeks to reclaim through her boycott of the state control of his memory in Tunisia of the post-Revolution.

Youssef's successful career cannot be explained solely as the fruit of her alleged collaboration with former president Ben Alī as many Islamists and some secular centrist critics are keen to argue in the post-Revolution, but through the success of the state-funded public education supported by President Bourguība in the first three decades of independence, which despite some shortcomings gave all Tunisian children, regardless of their social class background, the equal opportunity for an excellent bilingual education that was more or less secular. The ill-thought educational reforms introduced first by the minister of education Muhammad Mzālī in the early 1980s and later by numerous ministers under Ben Alī brought that success story to an end.

The portrait of Youssef challenges the simplistic division in the Anglophone press and even academy that the divide in Tunisia in the post-Revolution is between the Francophone secular educated elite who are admirers of France and the Arabophone poor masses who are attached to their Arabo-Islamic heritage. Born in a middle class family, Youssef had the advantage of being raised by a mother who was not only from the progressive thought of the Zeytūna Mosque, but who was also her Arabic teacher for the entire six years of her elementary education.[44] She had both her undergraduate and graduate education in Tunisia, wrote her dissertation in Islamic Studies. Yet, neither her Arabic education nor expertise in Islamic Studies has prevented her from defending the principle of secularism or the values of a republic. The new dichotomy found in the West between the secular Francophone elite and the Arabophone masses, if it reveals anything, it is the rise of a new school of liberal Orientalism in which neither the Arab language nor the Arab mind, on account of some undiagnosed cultural or genetic incompatibility, is incapable of producing secular thought. This is why "the Islamist," or "moderate Islamist" to use American terminology, appears to be more qualified than the secular Muslim to speak about Islam; Arab secular scholars are seen either as minions of France or Ben Alī. Because Youssef is a Muslim feminist reformer who functions within a Franco-Arabic Islamic secular paradigm that is indebted both to Averroes and Descartes, Monica Marks does not say a word about her work in her article on the Islamic feminism of Tunisia. It is not clear if it is out of oversight or ideological scotoma that she dismisses all "Tunisia's secular feminists" as "urban admirers of French-style secularism" who "see Ennahda women as unwitting agents of their own domination."[45] Marks's erasure of Youssef's scholarly contribution to the history of Islamic feminism seems to lend voice to Fātimah Mernīssī's argument that only the persecuted Muslim Woman is interesting to the West.[46]

If the portrait of Youssef, the urban admirer of both Arabic and French philosophers (Avampace [Ibn Bāja], Rhazes [al Rāzī], Avicenna [Ibn Sīna], Descartes, Lacan, Ibn Arabī, etc.), proves anything, it is the quality of the secular education that existed in Tunisia under Bourguība in both Arabic and French. Youssef has risen from the same meritocracy of the 1970s and 1980s that enabled Tunisian male and female students of her generation to break

social class ceiling, join the competitive Grandes Écoles in France, or participate in USAID transfer of technology program from the mid-1980s until the
early 1990s that even renowned moderate Islamists like Radhwān Masmūdī,
current president of the Center for the Study of Islam and Democracy in
Washington, D.C., benefited from.[47]

Besides being a brilliant scholar who benefited from the Bourguibist educational model of the 1970s and 1980s, Youssef had the advantage of work-
ing in her native country, an unrecognized privilege from the perspective of
North African women academics in the diaspora, who although teaching in
the United States are often offered jobs which require them to serve as native
informants, rather than research positions which would enable them to be
producers of knowledge about Islam and the Middle East. Youssef's success
derives not from her collaboration with Ben Alī as her political enemies are
prone to argue, but from a combination of positive factors: from the fact that
she is a middle class Muslim woman born to educated parents; she is the
product of the Bourguība school system; and she has the advantage of teaching in Tunisia which makes her escape the academic house of "terrorology"[48]
that imprisons the scholarly production of Arab women scholars in Western
academia. Youssef is writing primarily for an Arabic-speaking audience to
whom she does not have to prove that Muslims do not sacrifice/eat/kill their
children before she can use Lacan or Saussure to analyze the Qur'an—an
intellectual freedom that Muslim women academics in the European or North
American diaspora can only dream of. Although she is facing both the religious and secular patriarchy for her religious views and political positions,
neither her race, religion, nor gender identity has been an impediment to her
career as is the case with brown women scholars in North America, who face
institutional sexism and racism of the kind described by Gabriella Gutiérrez
y Muhs et al. in their seminal work *Presumed Incompetent*.[49]

Through this first translation of Youssef's work into English, it is my
hope to break the silence in the Anglophone academia over the critical scholarship of Muslim women who reside in the MENA region in the field of
Islamic Studies. As I argued elsewhere,[50] translation in this particular field of
study is a patriarchal enterprise between Oriental and Occidental men from
which Muslim women are always the object but rarely the subject of discourse. Far from being apolitical, translation is an act of rebellion that dis-
rupts the relations of power in the production of knowledge about the Muslim Middle East. It also places Muslim women as agents of change, instead
of the marketable victim, spoken about, written about, and pitied in the
hom(mo)sexual[51] global capital market of translation.

Through the translation of *The Perplexity of a Muslim Woman*, it is my
hope to continue interrogating the interpretive paradigms through which
Muslim women and the Muslim world are often understood in the West—
such as the dichotomy between Eastern vs. Western thought or Islamic tradi-

tion vs. Western secular modernity—to start a new conversation about Muslim women as legal subjects. Youssef's chapter on inheritance is an invitation to explore the institutionalization of female poverty in the Muslim world through the legalization of gender discrimination in citizen's access to property. The ongoing battle in Tunisia for equity in inheritance cannot be dismissed as a mere bourgeois endeavor with little relevance to other urgent priorities such as redressing social or regional disparities as claimed by some men and women associated with Ennahdha Party[52] and other leftists opposed to this reform. Although she is not the first Tunisian feminist writer to call for gender equity in inheritance—both Tāhar al Haddād[53] in the colonial era and the Association of Tunisian Women Democrats in the postcolonial era addressed this issue—Youssef's book brought this issue to public debate, especially after the passing of the 27 January 2014 new constitution, which guarantees full gender equity for its male and female citizens in Article 46.[54] In spring 2016, independent MP Mahdi Ben Gharbiya introduced a bill for gender equity in inheritance that caused a big controversy. While some MPs from Nidā Tūnis, El Hūrra, and the Popular Front parties welcomed the initiative, it was rejected by Ennahda Party, the Mufti of Tunisia Uthmān Battīkh, and even by some leftists[55] from the Popular Front who claimed that this bill had a hidden Islamist agenda. Ennahdha female MP Yamīna Zoghlāmī, for instance, rejected this initiative under the excuse that it was not the right time to embark on such a social project because it would empower Muslim extremists. To the Mufti's argument that gender inequality in inheritance cannot be changed because the Qur'anic text explicitly allows it, Youssef responded with her usual feminist humor that "slavery itself and the laws regulating it are also explicit in the Qur'anic text."[56]

As I was finishing up the index, news of a mass shooting against a gay club in Orlando broke out on 12 June 2016.[57] The shooter, an American citizen born and raised in the United States to Afghan parents, had killed forty-nine people and wounded fifty-three others before being killed by the police. Without waiting for the investigators' corroboration, various news channels reported that he was a dormant terrorist cell with links to ISIS. Once again, the Allah of Islam, the satanic deity of "the so-called religion of peace" was brought up as the direct cause for his violence. Even liberal voices, which fearing backlash against American Muslims, called for peace between the Muslim and the LGBT communities in America as if these two were binary opposites. Some gay Muslim activists had to come out and explain that they had to cringe twice at hearing the news: first because they are gay and second because they share the faith of the shooter, which makes them guilty by association.[58] Having lived and taught in the Deep South for over ten years, I saw the struggle of my Muslim gay students with the double pain of Islamophobia and homophobia. I also bore witness to the pain of my Christian gay students in their families, schools, and churches during office hours or in their essays. What struck me in the media coverage of this recent event is the construction of homophobia as a foreign virus that legally and illegally entered the land of the free through Muslim immigrants rather than an American problem that derives from a toxic masculinity that finds its raison d'être through violence in all its forms, as seen in the infamous hate crime against Matthew Shepard in 1998 or even in the recent hate speech coming from Christian fundamentalists applauding the Orlando shooting as God's work at the hand of a Muslim man.[59] It was not before long that Pat Robertson came out to ask conservatives to "sit on the sidelines" and watch the liberals "kill themselves" over the inevitable conflict between Islam and gay rights: "We're looking at a favored group by the left, the homosexuals, and that in Islam is punishable by death or imprisonment or some sanction, so what are the left going to do?"[60] When reports came out that the shooter's motive could be self-hatred because he was a closeted-married gay man,[61] the frenzy around his ties to Islam and ISIS slowly died out.

As a student of nineteenth-century Arabic, French, and English literature, I was struck by this recent shift in Western discourses on homosexuality and Islam, from the nineteenth and early twentieth-century Orientalist construction of homosexuality[62] as a sexual deviation and a moral depravity produced by Islam's segregation of the sexes to the new Orientalist fashion in which homophobia is an Eastern malady caused by Islam's violent nature. In *The Second Sex*, for example, Simone de Beauvoir suggests that the separation of the sexes in Islam is the direct cause of the Muslim woman's homosexuality. Secluded in the harem, she "eagerly seeks sexual pleasure" and "finds consolation in creamy sauces, heavy wines, velvets, the caress of water, of sunshine, of a woman friend, of a young lover."[63] What remains constant in these two contradictory discursive productions is the image of Islam as a violent otherness: if it is not the cause of homosexuality because of its oppression of women, it can only be the cause of homophobia because of its inherently oppressive nature. If in the nineteenth century, homosexuality served as a moral trope to colonize the degenerate North Africa and the Middle East, in the twenty-first century, Islam's homophobia functions either as an excuse to justify Islamophobia as seen in the recent Orlando shooting incident, or to justify colonization as illustrated in Israeli pink-washing that uses stereotypes that Palestinian Muslims are violent towards gay people to divert attention from the question of apartheid and illegal settlements.[64]

Youssef's chapter on homosexuality challenges not just Western discursive productions on homosexuality in Islam, but also contemporary Muslim ones. Contrary to many Muslims who condemn today homosexuality as a crime, an illness,[65] or a sin that could be punishable by death in countries like Iran or Saudi Arabia, she maintains in *The Perplexity of a Muslim Woman* that the Qur'an condemns rape not homosexuality. For Youssef, the Qur'anic text does not have any ruling punishing same-sex lovers, male or female, nor does it condemn homosexuality as a sin. Comparing the views of modern Muslim televangelists who call for the death sentence for homosexuals[66] to those of medieval Muslim scholars, Youssef argues that the latter were more liberal in their interpretations towards same-sex relations than twenty-first century Muslim preachers who see it either as an illness that needs treatment or a crime punishable by death as in Iran and Saudi Arabia or by prison as in Tunisia or Morocco. In winter 2015, six Tunisian male students were sent to prison for homosexuality after being forced to take a humiliating anal exam.[67] This incident created a big uproar because Article 230 which criminalizes sodomy has become obsolete under the 2014 new constitution which guarantees freedom of conscience and belief under Article 6. It is noteworthy to mention that Article 230, although modified in 1964, was initially introduced in Tunisia by the French in 1913.[68] Rather than deriving from some Qur'anic essence, the current wave of homophobia we see today in many parts of the Muslim world is a modern phenomenon that is at odds with the long history of accepting and accommodating same-sex relationships in Arab and Muslim societies as seen in the poetry of Abū Nawwās (756–814) for example.[69] In *The Ring of the Dove*, the Andalusian scholar Ibn Hazm (994–1064) casually mentions in his famous treatise on the philosophy of Arab love story about Hippocrates and a man who had fallen in love with him without any indication that same-sex love was even a moral issue from his medieval Muslim perspective.[70] As the case of Tunisia attests, many of the laws criminalizing "sodomy" were introduced during the colonial era only to acquire an Islamic face after independence. Not long ago, the tolerance towards same-sex relations in North Africa has allowed many European and American writers and artists to find there a safe haven such as André Gide, Roland Barthes, Michel Foucault, Paul Bowles, Edith Wharton, and many others. Through this translation, I hope to open a discussion about homophobia, colonialism, and the globalization of a toxic heterosexual masculinity, instead of reading the current production of homophobia in the Middle East only through the narrow prism of Islamic culture.

Another goal of this translation is to find for the young gay Muslims who are struggling with their sexuality in the non-Arabic speaking world a home inside the house of Islam.[71] Although LGBT activism originated in the West, Youssef's new interpretation of homosexuality in the Qur'an has allowed many young gay Tunisians to organize after the 2011 Revolution, and create SHAMS, the first LBGT advocacy group in the country, which is now leading the battle to repeal Article 230 criminalizing homosexuality. Instead of the theory of the *hudūd* or clear-cut frontiers of the sexes which informs Abdelwahāb Bouhdība's reading of sexuality in Islam,[72] Youssef wonders whether the fluidity of sexual identity is not in the Qur'anic text itself, as in His statement: "O mankind! We created you from a male and a female, and made you into nations and tribes, so that you may know one another. The most righteous among you is the noblest in the sight of God. God is all omniscient and knowing" (The Walls 49:13). Avoiding the assertions previously provided by male scholars, she wonders: "And why wouldn't the Qur'an, in asserting that mankind is created from a male and a female, be pointing to sexual, biological, and psychological duality that distinguishes every human being?"[73]

In conclusion, I would like to point out that I have tried in this translation to remain as faithful as possible to the meaning conveyed by the author in the Arabic text. I am aware that every act of reading is an act of reinvention and this English translation is a double feminist reinvention from the Qur'an to Youssef's feminist reading and from Youssef's Arabic text to English. After consulting the canonical translations of the Qur'an (Yusuf Ali, Muhammad Muhsen Khan, Muhammad M. Pikthall, Muhammad Sarwar, and Muhammad Shakir), I opted to use my own translation. There are several reasons behind this choice. First, far from being neutral, translations rest on specific ideologies and my feminist translation is no exception. For example, all aforesaid translators use the Arabic transliteration Allah instead of the English word God, as if God and Allah were different beings or God would perhaps be offended if His name was to be pronounced in a language other than Arabic. The Arabic transliteration Allah is often deployed, either by ignorance or sheer malice by Islamophobes, as an excuse to argue that the Allah of Islam is neither the Christian nor the Jewish God, but Satan. My second reason is that I tried throughout this manuscript to be as faithful as possible to Youssef's poststructuralist and feminist reading of the Qur'an, which constitutes in itself a departure from the canonical male-centered interpretations/translations of the Qur'an in both Arabic and English. For instance, Olfa Youssef's and Khan's views on the necessity of the mahr (dowry) in the marriage contract are at opposite poles. In contrast with Youssef who argues that the dowry is not obligatory because marriage in Islam is not a sales contract as many male Muslim scholars claim, Khan tells his English reader in parentheses that bridal money is one of the prerequisites of marriage in Islam, even when the Qur'an itself remains silent over this particular issue:

> And give to the women (whom you marry) their *Mahr* (obligatory bridal money given by the husband to his wife at the time of marriage) with a good heart, but if they, of their own good pleasure, remit any part of it to you, take it, and enjoy it without fear of any harm (as Allah has made it lawful) (Women 4:4)[74]

In cases where an Arabic expression is vague or has a double meaning, I provided a translator's footnote for additional clarity. For the transliteration of Arabic consonants and vowels, I followed IJMS transliteration of Arabic letters except for the letter ح where I used "h" instead of "ḥ" for editorial purposes. I have provided an index for the sūras and hadiths existing in the original Arabic text. The first index is organized in the English alphabetical order while the second followed the original Arabic alphabet with its English equivalent. To conform to the conventions of English academic writing, the passive voice has been used throughout this translation instead of the "we" in the Arabic text. However, I kept the French spelling of the author's name instead of the English Ulfah Yūsuf, for it is the most common spelling of her name in French as well as in the English articles about her. Instead of chapters, I kept the original book division into three perplexities and their sub-perplexities with the author's introduction and concluding statement in each section as well as the book's general introduction and conclusion. To emphasize the author's work within an Islamic framework and with consultation with the author, I kept the Islamic salutations such as "peace be upon him" or "the Almighty God," for rather than hindering her womanly ability to speak in an Arabic text, these religious expressions enable her on the contrary to tackle sexual taboos some of her Arabic book reviewers thought were not becoming of a woman writer.[75]

Finally, I would like to acknowledge that this English translation would not have been possible without the feedback of my dear friend and colleague in German Dr. Erika Hille Rinker at the Department of Foreign Languages at the University of Alabama at Birmingham. I am very grateful for her editorial skills, suggestions, and encouragement. I also thank the author for her prompt responses to my endless inquiries about the nuances of certain words in her manuscript.

NOTES

1. Invited Panelist, "Writing from the Ghetto: New Trends in North African Exilic Literature," Conference on Critical Theory Concerning Cultural Production of African Literature and Cinema: Comparison across Borders, Michigan State University-The University of Michigan, 29–30 October 2010.

2. "In the Shrink Office of Hannibal-Salambo: Psychoanalysis Psychoanalyzed," Panel Title, New Theoretical Paradigms in North African Literature and Cinema. Session sponsored by the MLA Arabic Literature Division, 2010 Middle Eastern Studies Association Annual Conference, San Diego, 18–21 November 2010.

3. Marie-Cécile Ortigues and Edmond Ortigues, *Oedipe africain* (Paris: Librairie Plon, 1966).

4. See for example Nouri Gana's use of Freud, Lacan, and Derrida in the study of mourning in the work of Elias Khūrī and Tāhar Ben Jelloun in *Signifying Loss: Towards a Poetics of Narrative Mourning* (Lewisburg: Bucknell University Press, 2011).

5. "*Le* Freak, *C'est* Critical and *Chic*: North African Scholars and the Conditions of Cultural Production in Post-9/11 U.S. Academia," in *Rethinking African Cultural Production*, Eds. Kenneth W. Harrow and Frieda Ekotto (Bloomington: Indiana University Press, 2015), 109–126.

6. Ibid., 117.

7. *Le Coran au risque de la psychanalyse* (Paris: Albin Michel, 2007).

Figure 0.1. Photo of Olfa Youssef, by Muhammad Nāsser Shamsī.

8. *Ḥayrat Muslimah: fī al mīrāth wa al zawāj wa al jinsīyah al mithlīyah* (Tunis: Dār sahar li nashr, 2008).

9. The word Jāhiliyyan refers to the pre-Islamic period in the Arabian peninsula.

10. Tais "Islamic Perspectives in Post-revolutionary Tunisia: The Work of Olfa Youssef," *Journal of Religion & Society* 17 (2015), 5.

11. Ibid., 6.

12. Ed. Habīb Qazdaghli, *Nisā wa dhākira: Tūnisiyāt fī al hayāt al 'āma, 1920–1960* (Tunis: CREDIF Publication, 1992).

13. Youssef and Al Adel Khidr, *Buhūth fī khitāb al Sud al Mastrahī* (Tunis: Miskīliyānī lil-Nashr wa-al-Tawzī', 1994).

14. *Nāqisāt 'aql wa dīn: Fusūl fī Ḥadīth al-Rasūl/Muqārabah tahlīlīyah Nafsīyah* (Tunis: Dār sahar li nashr, 1997).

15. *Ta'addud al ma'nā fī al Qur'ān: Bahth fī usus ta'addud al ma'nā fī al lughah min khilal tafāsīr al Qur'ān* (Tunis: Dār sahar li nashr, 2003).

16. *Al Ikhbār 'an al mar'ah fī al Qur'ān wa al sunnah* (Tunis: Dār sahar li nashr, 1997).

17. *Ḥayrat Muslimah: fī al mīrāth wa al zawāj wa al jinsīyah al mithlīyah* (Tunis: Dār sahar li nashr, 2008).

18. *Shawq: Qira'ah fī arkān al Islām* (Tunis: Dār sahar li nashr, 2010).

19. *Wa laysa adhakaru ka al unthā: Fi al huwiyya al jinsiyya* (Bayrut; al-Qāhirah: Dār al-Tanwīr lil-Ṭiba'ah wa-al-Nashr, 2014).

20. *Fī al i'dām* (Tunis: Olfa Youssef, 2012).

21. *Fī al khamr* (Tunis: Olfa Youssef, 2012).

22. *Fī al mithlīyah al-jinsīyah* (Tunis: Olfa Youssef, 2012).

23. *Fī hadd al sariqah* (Tunis: Olfa Youssef, 2012).

24. *Fī ta'addud al-zawjāt* (Tunis: Olfa Youssef, 2012).

25. *Fī zawāj al Muslimah bi-al kitābī* (Tunis: Olfa Youssef, 2012).
26. *Sept Controverses en Islam: Parlons-En* (*7 Controversies in Islam: Let's Speak about Them*), trans. Sihem Bouzgarrou Ben Ghachem (Tunis: Elyzad, 2016) and *Désir: Des dimensions spirituelles et psychiques des pilliers de l'Islam* (*Desire: Spiritual and Psychic Dimensions of the Pillars of Islam*), trans. Mohamed Salah Barbouche (Tunis: Nirvana, 2014).
27. The slain politicians are Chokrī Belaid (from The Democratic Patriots' Movement), shot in front of his house on 6 February 2012, and Mohamed Brāhmī (from The People's Movement), assassinated in the same way on 25 July 2013. See James Legge's article "Tunisia shocked by assassinations: Opposition leaders Mohamed Brahmi and Chokri Belaid killed with the same gun," *The Independent* 23 July 2015, available at http://www.independent.co.uk/news/world/africa/tunisia-shocked-by-assassinations-opposition-leaders-mohamed-brahmi-and-chokri-belaid-killed-with-8733972.html (28 July 2016).
28. Psyco M., "Manipulation New 2010," *Youtube* 13 February 2011, available at https://www.youtube.com/watch?v=_YcT0ykSvHI (24 July 2016).
29. Personal Online Interview, 31 July 2016.
30. Zohra Abid, "Tunisie-Terrorisme: Olfa Youssef menacée d'assassinat le 13 août, journée nationale de la femme," *Kapitalis* 7 August 2013, available at http://www.kapitalis.com/societe/17552-tunisie-terrorisme-olfa-youssef-menacee-d-assassinat-le-13-aout-journee-nationale-de-la-femme.html (26 July 2016)
31. It was dismantled after interim president Marzūkī lost in the 2014 presidential elections to start a new party called Al Irāda (The Will).
32. *The Black Book: The Propaganda Machine under the Rule of Ben Ali* (Tunis: Office of the President of the Republic of Tunisia, 2013), available at http://nawras-univers.blogspot.com/2013/12/telecharger-le-livre-noir-de-marzouki.html (13 July 2016).
33. David Tolbert, "Tunisia's Black Book: Transparency or Witch-Hunt?" *Aljazeera* 9 December 2013, available at http://www.aljazeera.com/indepth/opinion/2013/12/tunisia-black-book-transparency-witch-hunt-2013128517156923.html (14 July 2016).
34. See also "Olfa Youssef persiste et signe: 'Ben Ali est plus cohérent et clair que Marzouki,'" *BusinessNews* 2 December 2013, available at http://www.businessnews.com.tn/Tunisie---Olfa-Youssef-persiste-et-signe--%C3%82%C2%ABBen-Ali-est-plus-coh%C3%83%C2%A9rent-et-clair-que-Marzouki%C3%82%C2%BB-(audio),520,42598,3 (15 July 2016).
35. Ādel Ben Zīd, "Tunisie—Livre noir: Olfa Youssef accuse Marzouki d'être moins courageux que Ben Ali," *DirectInfo* 2 December 2013, available at http://directinfo.webmanagercenter.com/2013/12/02/tunisie-livre-noir-olfa-youssef-accuse-marzouki-de-moins-courageux-que-ben-ali/ (26 July 2016).
36. Although the PSC gave Tunisian women rights unequaled in the Arab world in the 1950s, many of its clauses were still patriarchal. After the 2011 Revolution and the rise of Islamists to power, Tunisian feminist activists were put in the position to defend the rights Tunisian women acquired in the late 1950s rather than mobilize to acquire new ones. For the history of state feminism, see Lamia Ben Youssef Zayzafoon, "Home, Body, and Nation: The Production of the Muslim Woman in the Reformist Thought of Tāhar Haddād and Habīb Bourguība," in *The Production of the Muslim Woman: Negotiating Text, History and Ideology* (*After the Empire: The Francophone World and Postcolonial France*) (Oxford: Lexington Books, 2005), 95–134. For the situation of Tunisian women after the Revolution, see Zayzafoon's article "Is it the End of State Feminism? Tunisian Women during and after the Revolution," in *The Arab Revolution in Context: Civil Society and Democracy in a Changing Middle East/ Islamic Studies Series*, Ed. Benjamin Isakhan, Fethi Mansouri, and Shahram Akbarzadeh, (Melbourne, Victoria: Melbourne University Press, 2012), 43–62.
37. See Wassīm Jday, "The Tunisian Revolution: The Role of Foreign Intervention in Maintaining the Margin in the Margin," *Facebook* 3 July 2013, available at https://www.facebook.com/notes/wassim-jday/the-tunisian-revolution-the-role-of-foreign-intervention-in-maintaining-the-marg/611163738902121 (31 July 2016). See also Muhammad Sālah Omrī's article on the tenth summit of Ennahda Party in "Al mu'tamar al 'āshir li al nahdha: hal tanjah al idāra al amerikiyya fi intāj islām siyāsī'alā maqāsihā," *Facebook* (note) 1 June 2016, available at https://www.facebook.com/notes/mohamed-salah-omri.html (2 July 2016).

38. "Olfa Youssef: Contre l'exercise de la politique par les binationaux," *Kapitalis* 8 February 2016, available at http://kapitalis.com/tunisie/2016/02/08/olfa-youssef-contre-lexercice-de-la-politique-par-les-binationaux/ (29 July 2016).

39. "Olfa Youssef: Ils sont tous pareils," *Business News* 5 February 2015, available at http://www.businessnews.com.tn/olfa-youssef-ils-sont-tous-pareils,520,53362,3 (8 July 2016).

40. "Monastir: Un salafiste saccage le mausolée du leader Bourguiba," *JawharaFM.net* 11 September 2012, available at http://archive.jawharafm.net/tounsia/21284-monastir--un-salafiste-saccage-le-mausolee-du-feu-bourguiba.html (25 July 2016).

41. See Halīmī, *Le Lait de L'oranger* (Paris: Gallimard, 1988).

42. Djebar, *Nulle part dans la maison de mon père* (Paris: Fayard, 2007).

43. Assya al Haj Sālem, "Sanā Ben 'Āchūr," *Fanoos Encyclopedia*, http://www.fanoos.com/society/sana_ben_achour.html (18 August 2016).

44. Olfa Youssef, "Success Story: Olfa Youssef, son parcours, ses combats," *Leaders* 19 July 2011, available at http://www.leaders.com.tn/article/5800-olfa-youssef-son-parcours-ses-combats (18 August 2019).

45. See this new Orientalist dichotomy in Monica Marks's comments dismissing non-Islamist feminists as a tiny Francophile minority in "Can Islamism and Feminism Mix?" *The New York Times* 26 October 2011, available at http://www.nytimes.com/2011/10/27/opinion/can-islamism-and-feminism-mix.html?_r=0 (28 July 2016). See also Graham Usher, "The Nation: Tunisia Is A Lodestar Worth Following," *NPR* 11 November 2011, available at http://www.npr.org/2011/11/11/142238101/the-nation-tunisia-is-a-lodestar-worth-following (30 July 2016). The same bias is found in the French press who misread Tunisian secularism through the lenses of French laïcité in the 2014 elections. For this subject, see Samy Ghorbāl's article "Pourquoi les médias français ne comprennent rien à la Tunisie," *Jeune Afrique* 31 October 2016, available at http://www.jeuneafrique.com/40936/politique/pourquoi-les-m-dias-fran-ais-ne-comprennent-rien-la-tunisie/ (28 July 2016).

46. "Fatema Mernissi: Seules les musulmanes persécutées intéressent l'Occident," *Institut Tunisien des Relation Internationales* 7 August 2013, available at https://tunisitri.wordpress.com/2013/08/07/fatema-mernissi-seules-les-musulmanes-persecutees-interessent-loccident/ (17 August 2016).

47. I see myself neither as a Bourguibist nor as an Islamist, but as a secular independent Tunisian-American scholar. Given Bourguība's torture of leftists in the 1960s, brutal repression of the syndicalist movement in the 1970s that culminated in the bloody events of 26 January 1978, the brutal repression of the Bread Riots of 1984, and the deportation of Islamist and leftist students in the mid-1980s under the guise of military service to Rjīm Ma'tūg labor camp in the Deep South, I cannot claim that Bourguība was "*un dictateur éclairé*" (an enlightened dictator) as renowned Bourguibists like Amdelhamīd Larguèche and Mazrī Haddād often refer to him. See Yves Thréard's article "Mazri Haddad: Le printemps tunisien a détruit plus qu'il n'a construit," in *Afrique Asie.fr* 14 January 2016, available at http://www.afrique-asie.fr/menu/maghreb/9800-mezri-haddad-le-printemps-tunisien-a-detruit-plus-qu-il-n-a-construit (8 July 2016). See also Larguèche, "Bourguiba, despote éclairé," *L'Histoire: D'où viennent les Révolutions Arabes? 150 de combats politiques* no. 52 (July–September 2011), 62, available at http://89.31.148.189/collections/d-ou-viennent-les-revolutions-arabes/bourguiba-despote-eclaire-13-07-2011-10530 (8 July 2016).

48. Word coined by Tunisian scholar Muhammad Sālah Omrī in "A Revolution of Dignity and Poetry," *Boundary 2* (spring 2012), 138.

49. Ed. Gabriella Gutiérrez y Muhs, Yolanda Flores Niemann, Carmen G. González, and Angela P. Harris, *Presumed Incompetent: The Intersections of Race and Class for Women in Academia* (Boulder: University Press of Colorado, 2012).

50. "The Challenge of Translating Arab Women Academics: The Case of Olfa Youssef's *The Perplexity of the Muslim Woman*," in *Translation vs. Globalization Symposium*, 20–21 February 2015, UNC Charlotte Center.

51. By the word "hom(mo)secual," I mean the exchange between men (from the French word *hommes*) as put by French feminist Luce Irigary in *This Sex Which Is Not One*, trans. Catherine Porter with Carolyn Burke (Ithaca, NY: Cornell University Press, 1985), 171.

52. See Rihāb Boukhayatia, "Tunisie: Une initiative du député Mehdi Ben Gharbia prônant l'égalité en héritage ressuscite la polémique," *Al Huffington Post* 4 May 2015, available at http://www.huffpostmaghreb.com/2016/05/04/tunisie-depute-egalite-en_n_9839518.html?ncid=fcbklnkfrhpmg00000005 (31 July 2016).

53. Al Haddād's original Arabic text was published in 1930. See its English translation *Muslim Women in Law and Society: Annotated Translation of al Tahir al-Haddād's Imra'tunā fī 'l-shari'a wa 'l-mujtama,' With an Introduction*, trans. Ronak Husnī and Daniel L. Newman. (London: Routledge, 2007).

54. "Gender equality guaranteed in Tunisia's new constitution," *UNFPA United Nations Population Fund* 7 September 2014, available at http://www.unfpa.org/news/gender-equality-guaranteed-tunisias-new-constitution (28 July 2016).

55. See also "Al Rahwī yad'ū nuwwāb al jabha li sahbi tawqī'ātihim min mubādarati Ben Gharbiyya lil musāwāt fil irth," *Al Shurūq* 4 May 2016, available at http://www.alchourouk.com/175562/151/1/.html (16 July 2016).

56. Youssef's *Facebook* 5 May 2016, available at https://www.facebook.com/OlfaTounes/?fref=ts (25 July 2016).

57. Lizette Alvarez, Richard Pérez-Peňa, and Christine Hausert, *The New York Times* 13 June 2016, available at http://www.nytimes.com/2016/06/14/us/orlando-shooting.html?_r=0 (24 July 2016).

58. David A. Graham, "The Complicated Pain of America's Queer Muslims," *The Atlantic* 16 June 2016, available at http://www.theatlantic.com/politics/archive/2016/06/lgbt-muslims-orlando/486923/ (26 July 2016).

59. Mike McPhate, "Pastors Praise Anti-Gay Massacre in Orlando, Prompting Outrage," *The New York Times* 27 June 2016, available at http://www.nytimes.com/2016/06/28/us/pastors-praise-anti-gay-massacre-in-orlando-prompting-outrage.html (31 July 2016).

60. Bradford Richardson, "Pat Robertson: Let the Left 'Kill Themselves' over Conflict between Islam and Gay Rights," *The Washington Times* 14 June 2016, available at http://www.washingtontimes.com/news/2016/jun/14/pat-robertson-let-left-kill-themselves-over-confli/ (30 July 2016).

61. Louis Nelson, "Orlando Shooter's Alleged Lover: It Was Revenge, Not Terrorism," *Politico* 22 June 2016, available at http://www.politico.com/story/2016/06/orlando-shooter-gay-lover-omar-mateen-224644 (31 July 2016).

62. For this subject see Joseph Boone, *The Homoerotics of Orientalism* (New York: Columbia University Press, 2014).

63. De Beauvoir, *The Second Sex*, trans. H. M. Parshley (New York: Alfred A. Knopf, 1968), 603.

64. Aeyel Gross, "Pinkwashing: Israel's Rainbow Flight to Nowhere," *Haaretz* 20 April 2016, available at http://www.haaretz.com/opinion/.premium-1.715335 (30 July 2016).

65. See for example, Saeed Kamali Dehgan, "Iranian Human Rights Official Describes Homosexuality as an Illness," *The Guardian* 14 March 2013, available at https://www.theguardian.com/world/iran-blog/2013/mar/14/iran-official-homosexuality-illness (31 July 2016).

66. See Maha Smati, "Lapidation, défenestration . . . une émission de la chaîne Zitouna tient des propos ouvertement homophobes (Vidéo)," *HuffPost Tunisie* 15 June 2016, available at http://www.huffpostmaghreb.com/2016/06/15/zitouna-homophobie_n_10475902.html (31 July 2016).

67. "Tunisia: Men Prosecuted for Homosexuality," *Human Rights Watch* 29 March 2016, available at https://www.hrw.org/news/2016/03/29/tunisia-men-prosecuted-homosexuality (10 June 2016).

68. Noah Rayman, "After the Arab Spring, No Bloom for Arab LGBT Rights," *Time* 1 July 2013, available at http://world.time.com/2013/07/01/after-the-arab-spring-no-bloom-for-arab-lgbt-rights/ (22 June 2016).

69. See Shoaib Daniyal, "Orlando Shooting: It's Different Now, But Muslims Have a Long History of Accepting Homosexuality," *Scroll.in* 18 June 2016, available at http://scroll.in/article/810093/orlando-shooting-its-different-now-but-muslims-have-a-long-history-of-accepting-homosexuality (31 July 2016).

70. *The Ring of the Dove: A Treatise on the Art and Practice of Arab Love*, trans. A. J. Arberry and Litt. D. F.B.A. (London: Luzac & Company, Ltd, 1953), 27.

71. Because of homophobia, the vice president of SHEMS, the Tunisian LGBT organization, has attempted twice to commit suicide. He is now in a comatose state. See Yamīna Thābit's article "Ahmed Ben Amor: Derrière le militant, un être humain," *Kapitalis* 17 July 2017, available at http://kapitalis.com/tunisie/2016/07/17/ahmed-ben-amor-derriere-le-militant-un-etre-humain/ (31 July 2016).

72. Abdelwahāb Bouhdība, *Sexuality in Islam*, trans. Alan Sheridan (London: Routledge, 1974), 30–42.

73. *The Perplexity of a Muslim Woman*, chap. 3, 101–102.

74. All canonical Qur'anic translations are available online. See http://corpus.quran.com/translation.jsp?chapter=4verse=4

75. Adnān Mansar, "Fī Maqām al Hayrah," *Tunisiehistoire* 19 June 2009, available at http://tunisiehistoire.blogspot.com/2009/06/blog-spot13_2215.html (30 December 2013).

Introduction

This book is simply an inquisitive reading into some Qur'anic verses most Muslims view as airtight and clear neither posing a challenge nor requiring any thinking. Who does not know that the male has the share of two females in inheritance? Who doubts that what is bequeathed is explicitly defined in the Qur'anic text? Who disagrees that a sexual encounter between men is the same as homosexuality and that it is forbidden in the Qur'an?[1] Who would not recognize the permissibility of polygamy, albeit under specific conditions? And who would contest the meaning of the wife's obedience to her husband in the marital bed?

From the beginning, I uphold that these "truths" have nothing truthful about them. I hold that the Qur'an, even though the word of God, is a linguistic statement subject to diverse interpretations like any other statement and I assert that anyone who claims to possess the true and unique meaning of the Qur'an is speaking in the name of the Almighty, setting himself in the omnipotent position of one who has absolute knowledge, and deceiving people into thinking s/he possesses the truth that only He, the Great and Almighty God, possesses.

I am aware that I am embarking on a dangerous journey questioning that which is established, stirring what is stagnant, and undermining what is consensus in the nation, yet I am driven in this by the profound belief that I am neither proclaiming a final truth nor confirming an unequivocal interpretation when questioning the divine word. How is it possible to confirm any truth when I believe that the knowledge I have been given is little, that only God knows the true meaning of the Qur'an, and concede that only on Resurrection Day the Great and Almighty God will reveal to us that over which we used to differ?

If I do not feel any wrongdoing in questioning verses whose explanations became well-established in Islamic traditional thought, it is because I feel the power of these absolute and well-established explanations of the Qur'an on the Muslim imaginary and jurisprudence in the Muslim world. This impact gave birth to two positions closer to reactions than the discernment of scientific methodology. The first calls for the desertion from a religion which refutes gender equity, calls for the stoning of homosexuals, and forces women to be always sexually available to their husbands even if in labor.[2] However, the proponents of this position forget or pretend to forget that the foundations of culture are unconscious. They may be fascinated by different cultures and civilizations, but being born in Muslim societies—at least in a cultural sense—they cannot erase with one stroke, or through a conscious and rational act, the imprint of the social unconscious.

As for the second position, it calls for the acceptance of the literal interpretations of religious scholars, turning these latter into the official spokesmen of the Great and Almighty God. The supporters of this position forget that in embracing this viewpoint, they are worshiping the scholar in different forms and various manifestations, deluding themselves that they are worshiping God. I am calling neither for reconciliation nor fabrication of facts as some might say. My call is to question and deploy reason out of the desire for a truth I do not claim ownership of as others do.

Even though I have strongly criticized the fundamentalist position which divides human action into unambiguous halal and haram deeds—asserting a monolithic Qur'an and excluding pluralism to thwart division and difference, I perceive this movement to be complicit, in its dangerous babbling, with the narrow-minded and fundamentalist system which proclaims ownership of the one truth. The attacks of those who oppose religion on religion raise disconcert and reveal some confusion between the true meaning of the Qur'an that nobody knows on the one hand and the commentaries and explanations of religious scholars on the other. Thus, the position of those in stark opposition to religion is nothing more than an expression of another fundamentalism and a worse narrow-mindedness.

In this book, I am at the farthest point from fundamentalism in both its religious and modern façade: I do not offer any final or ready-made answers, for I belong to the world of questions before answers and perplexity before certainty. I wish to throw a stone there where thought is stagnant and human readings have been turned into sacred givens which are indisputable and non-debatable. Stagnant thought undoubtedly needs to be dialogued with, shaken, and discoursed with lest it turn into some stinking and putrid water that threatens modern free thought and the acquisitions of human rights.

NOTES

1. For Olfa Youssef, the Arabic word "liwāt" is not homosexuality since homosexuality is not simply a sexual "encounter between two men" (3.68). She believes that the Arabic word means same-sex harassment or rape and this is why it is forbidden in the Qur'an.

2. There are two different explanations for the expression "*wa law ʿala dhahr qutb*" (و لو علی ظهر قتب). Because the word "*qatab*" (قَتَب) means both "*batn*" (stomach) and "*baʿīr*" (camel), this expression was interpreted as "even if in child labor" and "even if she [wife] was traveling/riding a camel." For more information see http://www.almeshkat.net/vb/showthread.php?t=92533 and http://www.islamweb.net/newlibrary/display_book.php?idfrom=6462&idto=6462&bk_no=122&ID=6474 (24 February 2013).

Chapter One

Perplexity in Inheritance

In the Muslim world, the judicial system claims to base its rulings on laws that are explicit in the Qur'an. The Tunisian Personal Status Code (PSC) is no exception. Held to be the most gender-egalitarian in the Muslim world, this code is still following the rule that the "male gets twice the share of a female." [1]

I am less interested in evaluating these laws in themselves or favoring one law over another as I am in probing their jurisprudential foundations. I have not limited myself to what commentators of the Qur'an and religious legal scholars said, but also what modernist jurists said about inheritance. Having gone back to the verses on inheritance in the original text of the Holy Qur'an, I find myself facing various forms of perplexity.

PERPLEXITY ONE: INHERITANCE BETWEEN DIVINE COMPULSION AND HUMAN CHOICE

In Islam, the relation of man with wealth is remitted to the issue of possession. The Muslim man's possession of wealth is based on the concept of divine trust: "And spend of that over which He made you trustees" (The Iron 57:7). A Muslim man is entrusted with God's wealth, and he has to handle it in a way that is defined and secured by legislative regulations that make some ways of earning money, such as usury, a sin and others, such as commerce, legitimate: "God permits trading and forbids usury" (The Heifer 2:275). A Muslim is also required to pay a charity tax (*zakāt*) on his wealth: "And in whose wealth there is a right acknowledged for the beggar and the destitute" (The Heights 70:24–25). This makes spending in the name of God a form of piety, guidance, and success: "That is the Scripture whereof there is no doubt, a guidance for the righteous, who believe in the unseen, observe the prayers, give charity from what We bestowed upon them, believe in what is revealed to you and those before you, and have certitude in the afterlife. Those are guided by the Lord. Those are the successful" (The Heifer 2:1–5). These money-making rules, however, are only general guidelines which do not prevent the Muslim from handling her/his money within the aforesaid limits.

Although obviously people manage their wealth during their lifetime, this fact does not prevent one from looking at this subject from two different perspectives. In the first, the Muslim is alive, manages his wealth, and is witness to how it is amassed and the ways it is spent. In the second, the Muslim manages her/his wealth, and during his lifetime determines how it will be amassed and spent after her/his death. While the first has no bearing on this work, the second is at the heart of this work on inheritance as it encompasses the following question: To what extent is a Muslim permitted, while being alive, to decide what to do with her/his wealth after his death?

In its explicit meaning, the Qur'an explains that man is free to write a will. This is what al Rāzī confirms when he writes: "Know that the explicit meaning of this verse[2] validates the legitimacy of writing a will about all or part of it [my wealth] as I please." This commentator even supports the Qur'an with a statement by Muhammad, peace be upon him: "A hadith told by Nāfi' Ben 'Amr corresponds to this verse: The Prophet Muhammad, peace upon him, said: 'It is the duty of a Muslim who has money to bequeath to not let two nights pass without writing a will about it.' This hadith, too, shows my absolute freedom to write a will."[3]

Despite this explicit recognition, al Rāzī tries to connect this verse with other topics in the Qur'an. He thus considers impermissible a will which includes someone's entire wealth because it requires the abrogation (*naskh*) of God's ordinance: "The men get a share of what the parents and the relatives leave behind. The women too shall get a share of what the parents and relatives leave behind. Whether it is a small or a large inheritance, it is a definite share" (Women 4:7).[4] This hypothetical abrogation can be understood only if the word "share" in the verse indicates the necessity of allocating some of the wealth to the heirs which would nullify wills that outline the inheritance of one's entire wealth. This is one possible reading. Add to it a second one in which this verse asserts women's right to inheritance—of which they used to be deprived—without the absolute necessity of bequeathing the entire wealth or prohibiting wills outlining the inheritance of one's entire wealth. In this case, women and others could still inherit even if the deceased had left no written will, or in case he chose to assign only a portion of her/his wealth in the will or even his entire wealth before his death. However, verse 7 in the sūra of Women could demarcate the laws of inheritance if the Muslim chose to remain silent over his will or a part of it. This verse by no means indicates the existence of an inheritance. What is more important is the fact that it proscribes neither entire nor partial wealth inheritance wills that one may choose to write before one's death.

Paradoxically, those who proscribe the entire wealth inheritance will also rely on a statement by Muhammad, peace be upon him, regarding wills: "The third is much. Leaving your heirs well off is better than leaving them a burden begging people."[5] This hadith was not necessarily cited in a context that is legislative in general, but merely in a consultative context. As such, it is very similar to another hadith cited by Ṭabarī: "They said: When Sa'd became seriously sick in Mecca, he said, the apostle of God came to see him. He said: "O! Apostle of God! I am very wealthy and I have no heirs, just dependents. Should I entrust to them my entire legacy? He said: No."[6] This hadith could be a specific singular case, otherwise, how we can explain its contradiction with the previous hadith allowing man the freedom to write a will in al Rāzī's declaration? While "[it] is the duty of a Muslim who has money to bequeath to not let two nights pass without writing a will about it" is a general hadith, the others are singular isolated hadiths; we do not know how they acquired a general legislative dimension. In addition, the previous hadith, which limits a will to just the third of one's wealth, could be the expression of a commendable deed (*nadb*), but it is not a requirement. Because this commendable deed is attributed to statements by the Prophet, it is at times accepted and at others rejected by commentators.[7]

PERPLEXITY TWO: WHO ARE THEY WHO INHERIT?

Commentators sharply disagree with one another when determining who inherits from whom. The Qur'an explicitly upheld that men and women were equal in their entitlement to inheritance on account of His divine word: "The men get a share of what the parents and the relatives leave behind. The women too shall get a share of what the parents and relatives leave behind. Whether it is a small or a large inheritance, it is a definite share" (Women 4:7). This verse upheld the heirs to be not only the offspring but also relatives. On account of this verse, Abū Bakr al Rāzī went so far as to allow inheritance for blood relatives—paternal aunts, maternal uncles, and the sons of daughters—none of whom was entitled to anything and under any circumstance by other religious scholar.[8] Abū Bakr al Rāzī's position was met with fierce opposition from Fakhr al Dīne al Rāzī under the excuse that God had said in another verse "a required share," that is, an estimated share, and there is no estimated share[9] for blood relatives: "Had these been given a specific share, God would have clarified the amount of that due share as in the cases of inheritance."[10]

It is enough to contemplate this commonplace position to realize its inconsistency in that there is no justification to explain the required share by the estimated share, for His commands are the binding laws as all language dictionaries and Fakhr al Dīne al Rāzī himself admits in a different context when he explains that "the command is that which completely binds people to what God ordained, cutting off all excuses."[11] Furthermore, the Almighty did not give an estimate of all due shares in inheritance but remained silent over many. This silence did not prevent commentators and religious scholars from interpreting laws for those over whom the text was silent. The silence of the Great and Almighty God over some ordinances and the interpretation of a large section of them by commentators are central to the issue of partiality I shall return to later. And what is more important is that the consensus of the *umma* (the Muslim nation) cannot in any case contradict the explicit text of the Qur'an which gave blood kindred relatives a share in inheritance. Is it logical when the text is clear in asserting inheritance on the basis of kinship that some commentators say: "Inheritance for kinsfolk is unheard of as irrefutably demonstrated by the *umma*'s consensus"?[12] From now on, I will, however, hold my surprise and disconcert, for in inheritance the privileging of consensus over the explicit word of God will happen again and again.

When one comes to the following verse, that is, verse 8 of the sūra of Women, one finds out that it opens the door for more heirs: from relatives, orphans, and to the poor if they happen to be present at the time of dividing up the inheritance: "And when relatives, orphans and the needy are present at the time of dividing up the inheritance, you shall give them therefrom and treat them kindly" (Women 4:8). It is no wonder that the religious scholars who felt uncomfortable allocating a portion of inheritance to relatives also felt more uncomfortable including in inheritance the orphans and the needy who are not blood relatives to the deceased. As a consequence, they looked for various stratagems to dismiss those potential heirs. Some of them considered this verse to be abrogated in virtue of the verse on inheritances without relying on any transmitted evidence (*hujja naqliyya* حجة نقلية). The absence of such evidence has pushed others to surmise that even though this verse has not been abrogated, it does signify an action that is commendable (*nadb* الندب) and endeared rather than a requirement. Respectively avoiding the historically and linguistically relative statements on abrogation and associative meanings, others, in order to explain what a division of property inheritance will is, uphold that "the will is what is intended by the division of inheritance."[13] In trying to avoid relativity in its historical and linguistic aspect, these commentators have created a linguistic explanation that does not exist in any dictionary, usurping thus a linguistic concept by turning it from a common usage to a private one, without any logical or precedential evidence. It is no surprise then that Ibn 'Abbas points out to the commentators' disregard of the aforesaid verse and that he counts them among "the three verses from God's book which are left aside and not followed by anyone."[14]

And so, the commentators and religious scholars continue to participate and define with God who the heirs are, suddenly settling that the Almighty's general statement "the male gets twice the share of a female" is specific in four ways: in the first, the free and the slave do not inherit from each other; in the second, a murderer does not inherit from the one he intentionally murdered; in the third, people of two different faiths do not inherit from each other; and in the fourth, prophets, peace be upon them, are not to be inherited from.[15] These commentators do not cite any text that explicitly prohibits inheritance from and to the slave and free man. As for forbidding a murderer inheriting from the one he intentionally murdered, it is undoubtedly founded on a cogent logic in that the murderer could have killed a relative to obtain his inheritance. And thus commentators and religious scholars rely at times on mere cogent insight to uphold divine laws, sanctioning this and forbidding that as they please. Even though the prohibition of inheritance among people of two different faiths rests upon a hadith in which the Prophet, peace be upon him, has said—"People from two different faiths do not inherit from each other"—this prohibition is subject to debate because the aforesaid hadith disallows the Muslim inheriting from the non-Muslim just as it disallows the non-Muslim to inherit from the Muslim. Other commentators, however, object with another hadith transmitted by one person named Mu'ādh and in which the Prophet, peace be upon him, states: "Islam does not decrease, it increases." This hadith is abruptly taken out of a context that we do not know and forced into another that is more beneficial not from a logical but a lucrative standpoint, as it is deployed as an excuse to make the Muslim inherit from the non-Muslim and at the same time prevent the non-Muslim inheriting from the Muslim.[16]

The story of the conflict between Fātimah, the daughter of the Prophet, and Abū Bakr al Saddīq is one of the oddest stories transmitted to us about how the explicit text of the Qur'an was specified then distorted in that Fātimah was denied the inheritance she had asked for under the excuse provided by Abū Bakr that the Prophet, peace be upon him, himself said: "We the Prophets are not a folk to give as inheritance what we left behind as charity." If this hadith is true, it is a statement that has two different meanings because of its interdependent structure. If it is composed of two sentences, then the first is "we the Prophets are not a people to give inheritance" and the second is "what we leave behind is charity." The hadith upholds the interdiction of inheriting from prophets and declares that whatever they leave behind after their death is nothing more than charity. And if the hadith is composed of one sentence on the premise that his statement "what we left behind" is linked to his statement that "we do not give inheritance," then it reads as "what we have left behind as charity is not to be inherited."[17] Thus, the hadith does not mean forbidding the inheritance of Prophets but forbidding inheriting from what they left behind from their wealth as charity, but other than that, they can leave inheritance.[18]

In the end, the explicit text of the Qur'an defines only the gender of the heirs (i.e., males and females), and specifies only their type, that is, their kinship to the deceased in all conditions and the orphans and the needy provided that they are present at the time the inheritance is divided up. Through various forms of interpretation and arbitrariness, the religious scholars wanted to narrow down the all-encompassing divine to the specifically human.

PERPLEXITY THREE: DOES THE MALE GET TWICE THE SHARE OF THE FEMALE?

God says: "God decrees in the provisions regarding your children that the male gets twice the share of the female. If the inheritors are women, and more than two, they get more than the two-thirds of what is bequeathed. If the inheritor is one woman, she gets one-half of what is bequeathed" (Women 4:11). Even though the Qur'an does assert that the male gets twice the share of the female, it does not define what the value of two female shares is. As Ben 'Āchūr ascertained, "The inheritance of the two individual daughters is not laid down in the verse."[19] The absence of this value is a problem recognized by many commentators. Ibn 'Arabī, indeed, saw the Almighty's words "if the inheritors are women, and more than two, they get more than the two-thirds of what is bequeathed" to be "hugely problematic."[20] Commentators went to various directions to explain this issue, none of which, however, is convincing. Some of them have relied on some bizarre linguistic interpretation connecting two with three because two is bigger than one.[21] In this case, it is legitimate to wonder why not four or even five? Are not four and five bigger than one? Hence, they do not only go beyond the rules of the Arabic language which distinguishes between the dual and the plural, they also defy the explicit meaning of the Qur'anic text which not only deploys the plural form *nisā* (women) but goes beyond that to directly affirm that *nisā* are "women beyond two." It is from within this perspective that Ibn 'Abbās ascertained that the two-thirds are the due inheritance for three daughters and up, and as evidence, he used God's statement that "if the inheritors are women, and more than two, they get more than the two-thirds of what is bequeathed." Because in the Arabic language, the word "if" (*en*) expresses condition, this means that the taking of the two-thirds is tied to the fact that they are three and up, denying thus the two-thirds for the two daughters.[22]

In contrast with this logical perspective which derives its authority from the manifest meaning of the text, worried about the Qur'an's silence over the value of the two shares of a female in inheritance, al Rāzī rationalizes the share of the two daughters as that of the two sisters on account of a different verse: "If one dies and leaves no children, and he had a sister, she gets half of what he left behind. If she dies first and has no children, he inherits her estate completely. If there were two sisters, they get two-thirds of what he left behind" (Women 4:176). "Since the share of the two sisters is the two thirds," he says, "the two daughters are more deserving of that portion because they are closer to the deceased than the two sisters."[23] We do not understand why in this discussion al Rāzī did not realize, while insisting that the daughters are closer than the two sisters, that it is legitimate to wonder: why would the share of the two daughters who are the closest to the deceased be equal to that of the two sisters? Why not more?

It is not surprising that both al Tabarī and his *Commentary on the Qur'an* (*Jāmi' al Bayān*) use interpretive models based on precedence to determine what is owed to the two daughters "according to the inherited tradition (*sunnah*) which cannot be doubted"[24] as in the hadith in which the wife of Sa'd Ibn Rabi' went to the Prophet, peace be upon him, and told him that Sa'd had died and left behind two daughters and a brother who set out to take everything he left behind as inheritance, and a woman is married only for her wealth. He did not answer her during that meeting. When she came back, she said: "O Apostle of God! And Sa'd's two daughters?" He replied, peace be upon him, "Call on his brother." When he arrived, the Prophet said: "Pay the two thirds to his daughters, the one eighth to his wife and to you the rest."[25] Even though this hadith has another version with different players (which could be secondary) and number of daughters, it remains quite significant. In this account, Aws Ibn Thābit al Ansāri died and left behind three daughters and a wife. The two men to whom he bequeathed his wealth—known as Suwayd and 'Arjafa on his paternal family side—came and took over everything. So, Aws's wife went to see the Prophet, peace be upon him, and told him the story of the two male trustees who did not pay anything to either her or her daughters. So the Prophet, peace be upon him, said: "Go home until I see what God will decide about your case." This is when this verse was revealed to the Prophet, peace be upon him: "The men get a share of what the parents and the relatives leave behind. The women too shall get a share of what the parents and relatives leave behind. Whether it is a small or a large inheritance, it is a definite share."[26] These two authentic hadiths differ in the number of the daughters who are two for the first narrator and three for the second. Because of this difference, I do not see this passed on and verbally transmitted tradition as a tradition "which cannot be doubted," nor do I see anything settled between this "categorical" tradition that Tabarī upholds and Ben 'Āchūr's assertion that the hadith of Ibn Sa'd's wife is not appropriate to determine the share of two females because in his account there is a disagreement whether the daughters left behind were two or three.[27]

Hence we see how commentators and religious scholars allow themselves to distort the explicit meaning of the text in violation of that which is linguistic and historical. It becomes thus clear that they do not find any wrongdoing in opposing God's choice to remain silent over the share of two females. Isn't it true that anything God does is based on wisdom? Isn't the Qur'an, as the word of the Almighty, one of the manifestations of His wisdom? So why does one not view the silence of the Great and Almighty God over the share of the two females as one of His wisdoms? Why does one not interpret it while being aware that only He knows how to interpret it and convinced that we do not possess the ultimate word but at the same time reassured that the Great and Almighty God cannot haphazardly or arbitrarily remain silent over the share of the two females? Isn't this an invitation for contemplation, thinking, and scrutiny? Didn't Ibn 'Arabī declare that "If the Great and Almighty God had wanted to explain the case of the two daughters as he did with the case of the one and that above the two, he would have conclusively done so, but He presented things in a problematic manner to highlight the place of mankind and elevate the position of those who use independent juristic reasoning"?[28] From this perspective, it is legitimate to wonder: What right allows Ben 'Āchūr to bring himself to ascertain without the shadow of a doubt that "because God's statement that the male gets twice the share of a female makes the share of two females the basis for determining the share of the male (even though no a priori assessment of the share of the two females is available to estimate anything) it is understood that the doubling of the male share over that of the female child is what is intended"?[29] How does he know that the doubling of the male share is what is intended? And why isn't it possible that God's silence over the share of two females is at the same time a silence over the share of the male, implicitly opening up the door for *ijtihād* (independent judicial reasoning) in the question of inheritance which like all legislations and laws is closely tied to its historical context?

What is salient is that Ben 'Āchūr catches an "ironical joke" in that the Qur'an ascertains that "the male gets double the share of the female" without another linguistic possibility such as "to the female half of the share of a male" or "to two females the share of a male." This is in order "to suggest that the share of the female in Islamic jurisprudence has become more important than that of the male. Because she was oppressed in the Jāhiliyya (pre-Islamic societies), Islam called for her share crying aloud initially that the division of inheritance rests upon the number of sons and daughters."[30] Ben 'Āchūr realized the importance of the female share but despite his eminence as a lexicographer, he did not see that the Qur'anic text, whether in its hypothetical meaning (i.e., "to the female half the share of a male") or its explicit one (i.e., "the male gets twice the share of a female") is silent not only over the value of two female shares but also on "the male share," opening up the door for *ijtihād* in the matter of inheritance.

Some commentators have pointed out that the Almighty was silent over the share of the male if the deceased had one son and wondered if he inherited all the wealth as "the consensus of the *umma*" had concluded or the share of two females which that same consensus had determined on the basis of the text. In other words, does the male inherit the two-thirds only? We should not be surprised to find out that the patriarchal society has ascertained the first possibility, that is, the single male child's entitlement to the entire inheritance. We should not be surprised thus to find commentators interpret "God decrees in the provisions regarding your children" as a statement intended for the case of having children of both the male and female gender, not that of a single gender.[31] Like the previous ones, this interpretation is based neither on linguistic nor precedential evidence.

Any *ijtihād* in matters of inheritance has to consider the fact that neither the woman nor the child used to inherit in Jāhiliyyan society and that the early Muslim community used to function according to those same social and historical rules which denied inheritance to those who do not fight wars and confront the enemy in the battlefield.[32] It should not be forgotten that some Muslims were very upset that the Almighty assigned women a share in inheritance. It is those people (i.e., the early Muslims presented to us today in an ideal picture wherein they promptly obey and execute orders without any discussion) who only reluctantly accepted God's decree to give inheritance to women. This is confirmed in the following account by Tabarī: "Only an adult male used to inherit, neither a male child nor a woman could. When the verse on inheritances was revealed in the sūra of Women, it was hard to bear by people who said: 'How come the child and woman alike, who neither make money nor provide, inherit just as any man who works for a living?' And they wished and waited for a revelation to come from above. When nothing happened, they said: 'if this was allowed to happen, it could only be a binding law.'"[33] Perhaps, those who implored God to change His law then reluctantly accepted it, were less disdainful of the divine word than other Muslims who wished that the Prophet either forgot or changed it. In an account mentioned by Tabarī, people said after the descent of the verses on inheritance: "A woman (wife) is given the one-fourth and the one-eighth, the daughter the half, and the child is also provided while none of them fights in battles or takes possession of bounty? Be silent over this statement in the hope the Prophet, peace be upon him, forgets or we ask him to change it."[34] If those perfect and contemporary disciples of the Prophet were hesitant to give inheritance to the daughters, then we should not be surprised that many Muslim countries to this day continue to deprive the daughters of their inheritance rights under the excuse that the wealth she inherits goes to her husband, an in-law who remains an outsider because he is not related to the family by the blood of kinship.

Some modern scholars have attempted to justify giving females half of the share of males in inheritance by the man's duty as a provider for his wife and children and that this obligation to provide necessitates that he has more money so that he can cover all of his various expenses. We do not know if these commentaries are serious or just an excuse, veiled in the garment of equity, to justify clear unfairness towards women. Even though they pointed out that "the woman spent out less because provided by the husband and the man spent out more because providing for the wife, and that he who spent more is more deserving of money,"[35] classical commentators in contrast with the modern ones did not used to feel embarrassed to say that "inequity in inheritance [was] one way of favoring the male over the female."[36] He is superior to women in physical appearance, brains, and religious functions such as jurisprudence and the imamate (religious leadership). Also given that a woman's testimony is half that of a man, his reward should, therefore, be greater. Besides, a woman is deficient in mind and abounding in desires, if given more wealth, greater is her corruption.[37]

While classical commentators like al Rāzī and others admitted that the lesser value in women's share of inheritance compared to that of the male was a favoring of the man, modern ones started looking for a logical explanation for this inequity when they could have learned through the text itself that this lack was created by the consensus, rather than the explicit text. Even if it is hypothetically conceded that doubling the share of the male is linked to his obligations as a provider for the females, it can be deduced then that a woman does not need any inherited money since all of her expenses are covered by the man. Whence, the "logical" justice would be to adopt what was common in Jāhiliyya, which is denying women the right to inherit because she is provided for by a husband, a brother, a father, or a Muslim *umma*. However, when we contemplate today's Muslim societies, we find out that women provide for their families and are in some cases the only providers. There are even some modern laws, as in Tunisia's judicial system, which bind a woman to provide for her family if she has money without granting her equity in inheritance in exchange.[38]

PERPLEXITY FOUR: DO GRANDCHILDREN AND GRANDPARENTS INHERIT?

The Qur'an provides inheritance to children and parents in many verses, but who are the parents and the children? Does the word "parents" include the grandfathers and grandmothers? And does the word "children" include the grandchildren of sons and daughters? Linguistically, there is nothing that would impede the term "parents" from including grandfathers, for in the Qur'an the term "parents" is repeated many times to refer to one's grandparents and is inclusive even of ancestors.[39] It was even reported that Abū Bakr al Saddīq placed the grandfather as a father in agreement with His statement "the religion of your father Abraham."[40] Wondering if the words "father" and "mother" include grandfathers and grandmothers, al Rāzī positively states that they do in that he says: "That is undoubtedly a fact as evidenced by His statement: 'We worship your God and that of your fathers Abraham, Ishmael, and Isaac.'"[41] However, he quickly recants these words when it comes to providing a share to the grandparents in inheritance. "It is not really sure," he says, "for the Sahāba (the disciples) agreed that the grandparent did not have a due share mentioned in the Qur'an."[42] Al Rāzī's statement suggests that the Sahāba's agreement is more important than the Qur'anic text in which the word "fathers" is repeated to refer to the grandfathers—which makes Abraham a father to all Muslims. If this statement by the Sahāba, which legislates without and instead of the Qur'anic text, denies the male grandparent a portion of inheritance, then we should not be surprised that this same statement denies the grandmother any share of inheritance. Take Ibn 'Arabī's statement: "'If the deceased had no son and his parents inherited from him then the mother gets the third,' and the higher mother is the grandmother and by consensus she does not get the one third. So, the removal of the grandmother from this concept of mother is a case settled."[43] It is strange that the same commentators who assert that the word "mother" refers to "every woman who gave birth to you or elevates your lineage by the blood of kinship, whether on the father's, the mother's side, or above you,"[44] ascertain that the mother to whom God assigned a share of inheritance cannot include the grandmother. This strangeness may dissipate in light of the fact that in its original meaning (i.e., in a broader sense) the word "mother" was cited in the context of the list of forbidden or unmarriageable women. Hence it was not possible to use it in its narrow sense because it would prohibit the marriage of the mother to the son and permit the grandson to marry his grandmother. As for the meaning of the word "mother" in its narrow and distorted sense, it is lucrative because it deprives the grandmother from a share of inheritance that the Great and Almighty God assigned her.

The same attitude reoccurs regarding the two words "sons" and "children" applied to one's own offspring and deployed in reference of the progeny of the son as in His divine statement "O son of Adam" or "O sons of Israel"[45] to those present at the time of the Prophet, peace be upon him, who also said that al Hassan and al Hussein were his two sons.[46] Nothing in the Qur'an indicates that the word "children" cannot be simultaneously used in reference to sons and grandsons. Despite this fact, Ibn 'Arabī confirms, with the certainty of someone who does not have a shadow of a doubt, that "God has stated that amongst your children in general there are those who are above and those who are below. Should they be of equal rank, then the latter is to be taken as the distribution criterion. Should they be unequal and some are above others, the ones above overshadow those below because the one above says 'I am the son of the deceased' while the one below says, 'I am the son of the deceased's son'"[47] Looking at this assertion by Ibn 'Arabī, it is legitimate to wonder: Is this statement based on any textual evidence? The answer can only be negative, for this is an assertion that is based on a human construction of what is close and distant that could be in contradiction with His divine statement: "It is God's law that you do not know who among your parents and children is the best and most beneficial to you. God is omniscient and most wise" (Women 4:11).

PERPLEXITY FIVE: AGNATIC INHERITANCE (*AL TA'SĪB*)

If one takes a look at commentaries and other books on Islamic jurisprudence, they shall find the word *ta'sīb* to be commonly used in reference to inheritors. It means that when the Almighty is silent over whom an inheritance goes to, the latter is given to the nearest agnate (male relative). One might think that after handing down the laws, divine silence is little or rare, but upon examining the verses on inheritance, it becomes clear that these explicit laws do not, in most cases, cover the entire inheritance, as indicated in many examples.

Example one: If the deceased is a male widower who left behind three daughters and a father—the mother is long deceased—the two-thirds are cut out for the two daughters and one-sixth to the father according to what is explicitly stipulated in the text: "If the inheritors are women, and more than two, they get more than the two thirds of what is bequeathed" (Women 4:11) and "To each of the parent the one sixth if the deceased left a child" (Women 4:11). If we add the two-thirds to the one-sixth, we will have the five-sixths. In this case the text remains silent over one-sixth.

Example two: In case the two parents survive a daughter or a son who left no children, the mother gets the one-third. In case the two parents survive a daughter or a son who has no children but has siblings, the mother gets the one-sixth as in His divine statement: "If the deceased left children, his parents get one sixth of the inheritance each. If he left no children and his parents are the only inheritors, the mother gets the one third. If he has siblings, then the mother gets the one sixth, and this after fulfilling any will left by the deceased and paying off all debts" (Women 4:11). It is clear that the verse remains silent over the remaining two-thirds in the first case and the five-sixths in the second.

Reading this silence, commentators argued that "if God did not clarify what to be done with the rest of the inheritance once the due shares are distributed, it is because He left things to be taken over by the Pre-Islamic custom of agnatic succession."[48] This statement clearly acknowledges that the Qur'anic text, while identifying those to whom an inheritance is due, remains silent over who inherits besides them. Yet, at the same time, it violates the silence of the Wise and Almighty God by interpreting it in an arbitrary manner that claims it means one thing or rather one truth only, which is the rule of agnatic succession. This position is the ultimate assertion of God's intention, which no one can actually confirm. It is not known if this assertion is based on "the Pre-Islamic custom of agnatic succession" or on a hadith by the Prophet, peace be upon him. If it is based on the pre-Islamic custom of agnatic succession, this implies that the Qur'an is asserting laws. There is no doubt that it did assert some of them, but within a vision that seeks to transform and change them step by step. This means that the acquisition of property within the rules of agnatic succession is compatible with the historical present of the people; believers must rise above it today. [49]

If this form of acquisition is based on some hadith by the Prophet, peace be upon him—such as "give anyone what is due to him and to the closest of males the rest" [50] or "What shares of inheritance are left behind, they go to the male relatives" [51]—then one wonders why this hadith, since it is compatible with the laws of *jāhiliyya*, is not taken as a mere declaration tied to a historical reality? Why is it seen as a final law instead of a historically situated desirable deed (*nadb*)? Since religious scholars and commentators allow themselves to read some of the Prophet's commands as desired deeds on the basis of consensus [52] without providing any categorical textual evidence, why is the aforesaid hadith not taken as such, especially considering that the word *ta'sīb* (agnatic) is absent from the Qur'an, which mentions only "*al 'usba* (i.e., a group of people)? [53] As for *ta'sīb*, it is a word used only by classical and modern commentators whose work became the foundation for legislations in the Muslim world, including those considered the most modern like the Tunisian jurisprudence. [54]

Despite the fact that the law of agnatic succession favoring the nearest male relative in the case that the text is silent over who inherits is absent from the Qur'an and weak in the hadith, the attitude of some commentators explicitly confirms that consensus has been substituted for the text in order to protect male interests in inheritance, as seen in the explanation provided for this verse: "If he left no children and his parents are the only inheritors, the mother gets the one third" (Women 4:11). This verse announces only the mother's share. Should the legitimacy of agnatic succession be hypothetically accepted, the father will then inherit the remaining two-thirds in case the deceased did not leave behind either a husband or wife. In case the deceased left no children and had a husband and two parents and if we were to distribute inheritance shares according to the explicit text of the Qur'an, then the husband would inherit the half—in view of His divine statement: "You have half of what your wives left behind, if they had no children" (Women 4:12)—the mother would inherit the one-third according to the aforesaid verse and the father gets what is left, that is, the one-sixth, according to the law of agnatic succession that is hypothetically accepted. However, the commentators denied that the mother's share was twice the share of the father, that is, they denied—what a surprise!—the clear and explicit application of God's word regarding the share of the husband and the mother and even beaten their own views on agnatic succession. They also went against the statement of Ibn 'Abbās who relied on nothing but the explicit text to assert that in this case: "One half must be bequeathed to the husband, one third to the mother, and the rest to the father." [55]

Most commentators hold that the husband gets the one-third, pays off a third of what is left to the mother, and the rest to the father. [56] It is not known how those transformed the explicit text of the Qur'an which assigns the mother a third of the entire inheritance (without mentioning anyone else to whom inheritance is due) to the third of what is left of inheritance. I am as surprised as Ibn 'Abbās when he says: "I do not find a third of what is left in God's book." [57] One is even more surprised when reading that it is Zeyd Ibn Thābet who transformed the entire one-third to the one-third of what is left. When Ibn 'Abbās sent an inquiry to Zeyd asking him, "Where do you find in God's book the third of what is left?" Zeyd replied, "You are a man who stands by his opinion and I am a man who stands by mine." How can one not be surprised when the explicit text is turned not just into a matter of expressing one's opinion, but also into an individual contest between men of opinions? What is even more surprising is that al Rāzī classifies and assimilates Zeyd's statement (and the statements of those who associated with him) as a "particularization of the general statements in the Qur'an according to the principle of qiyās (analogy)." However, one cannot see the general statements indicated by al Rāzī in His divine and categorical statement: "If he left no children and his parents are the only inheritors, the mother gets the one third" (Women 4:11). [58] What is even more astonishing is that al Rāzī himself acknowledges this explicit command in all cases except when the deceased person leaves behind both parents and a husband pretending that "if we pay off a third to the mother and the sixth to the father, we will have to give the female twice the share of the male which is against His divine statement 'to the male twice the share of a female.'" [59] Of course, al Rāzī forgets his own statement that the rule whereby the male gets twice the share of the female especially when it comes to children or siblings if the deceased has neither parents nor children is in both cases by consensus. [60]

PERPLEXITY SIX: DISINHERITANCE

What is of interest in this verse "If the deceased left children, his parents get one-sixth of the inheritance each. If he left no children and his parents are the only inheritors, the mother gets the one-third. If he has siblings, then the mother gets the one-sixth" (Women 4:11) is the last case where the deceased leaves behind a mother, a father, and siblings. This verse announces that the mother inherits the one-sixth and remains silent over the rest of the inheritance. If the law of agnatic succession is hypothetically accepted and the father is presumed to get a share of inheritance, there is nothing in the text that denies the siblings a share in it. Even though both the father's and the siblings' shares are absent in the explicit text of the Qur'an, most commentators confirm the existence of a share for the father while asserting that the siblings do not inherit anything. They just cut off the mother's inheritance from the one-third to the one-sixth, that is, they just transform the mother's share from the one-third in the absence of siblings to the one-sixth in the presence of siblings. Indeed, "the crowd of commentators" fill in the silence of the text as they please feigning ignorance of the other possibility that Ibn 'Abbās has mentioned which is that "the siblings get the one-sixth they denied the mother."[61] Actually, the siblings could get more or less according to the *ijtihād* that the Qur'an left wide open and which commentators insist on closing down through their assertion of some absolute rulings. Things could have been easier, had they admitted that these rulings as well as these relative judicial explanations were theirs, but things turn serious when human opinion is given the sacredness of the unambiguous and the absolute command that is impervious to either dispute or debate.

The odd thing is that even if it is hypothetically conceded that the commentators were right in denying the siblings inheritance by enhancing the mother's share from the one-sixth to the one-third, once again one finds out that their consensus is based on evidence that repudiates the text to the point of exclusion. Indeed, they disagreed over the meaning of the word "siblings" (*ikhwa*) in respect of numbers. Some viewed that the siblings who are cut off from inheritance are those who are three and above, for three is the smallest plural.[62] Most of them went so far as to say that any two sisters or two brothers cut off the mother's share from the one-third to the one-sixth. When Ibn 'Abbās asked 'Uthmān: "What has enabled the two siblings to cut off the mother's share from the one-third to the one-sixth? God said 'if he has siblings' [*ikhwa*] and in the language of your people *akhawāni* (two siblings) is not *ikhwa* (plural for siblings)." To which 'Uthmān replied: "I cannot change a decree that has been decreed before my time and followed in so many lands."

'Uthmān's discomfort and uneasiness at going against previous rulings seem to be more important than the explicit text of the Qur'an. Similarly, consensus and previous rulings become more authoritative than the word of the Great and Almighty God, and why not, since such disinheritance (*hajb* حجب) improves the chances of decreasing the mother's share from the one-third to the one-sixth, and increases the father's chance of getting an extra third according to the logic of agnatic succession in a patriarchal society which passed on to us its adamant refusal to give inheritance to the female.

PERPLEXITY SEVEN: *AL KALĀLA*[63]

'Umar Ibn al Khattāb has a certain spell on many Muslims. And why not, given that he is the disciple who was in accord with many commands in the Qur'an?[64] And why not given that he was the one who continued, after the Qur'an had been revealed, to interpret it in an absolute way as seen in the prohibition of the marriage of pleasure and in a circumstantial manner as in the cutting off of the thief's hands.

This man who dedicated himself to interpreting the Qur'an into law—the first to give his consent at times and the last to pronounce himself at others—found himself facing an issue known in the Qur'an as *al kalāla* (الكلالة). On his own volition, he paused and said: "There are three things, had the Prophet clearly explained, they would have been dearer to me than the world. These are *al kalāla*, usury and the caliphate."[65] Some accounts explain to us that 'Umar was forced to pause at this issue, for he said about *al kalāla* that "it was not clear to [him]."[66] And he asserted: "I leave nothing behind me that is more important to me than *al kalāla*." And in another story, which is more important to me than ancestors and *al kalāla*, he states, "I did not consult with the Prophet over anything as much as I did in regard of *al kalāla* and he had never spoken to me as rudely as he did over this matter. Pointing his finger at my chest as if stabbing me, he said: 'O Umar! Isn't it enough that you have the summer verse, i.e., the last verse in the sūra of Women?"[67]

Upon examining the Qur'an, one finds out that the word *al kalāla* is mentioned twice in the same sūra; these are verses 12 and 176 in the sūra of Women. The first holds the following: "If the deceased man or woman, having left neither parent nor child, has two siblings, male or female, each of them gets one-sixth of the inheritance. If there are more siblings, then they equally share one-third of the inheritance, and this after fulfilling any will left by the deceased and paying off all debts." As for the second, it holds: "They ask you for a ruling. Say: God imparted to you of His divine ruling regarding the inheritance of distant kindred. If one dies and leaves no children, and he had a sister, she gets half of what he left behind. If she dies first and has no children, he inherits all of her wealth. If there were two sisters, they get two-thirds of what he left behind. If the siblings are men and women, the male gets twice the share of the female."

The problem in these verses is in fact multiple. The first is embodied in the concept of *al kalāla* itself over which religious scholars disagreed in determining its exact referent. In the opinion of the most prominent of scholars, *al kalāla* refers to him who has neither child nor parent or to him who has no child but has either a parent or siblings.[68] The second problem is that the two verses present different rulings for the case of *al kalāla* inheritance and this regardless of the difference in the recipients to whom it should go. Indeed, according to the first verse, the brother and the sister inherit the one-sixth and the brothers and sisters inherit the one-third. According to the second, the sister inherits the one-half, the two sisters the two-thirds, and the siblings (male and female) follow the rule: to the male twice the share of a female.

Because they could not find any solution to the first problem which is the difference in the meaning of *al kalāla*, commentators used as evidence only the arguments of those with authority (*argument par autorité*). Between Ibn 'Abbās, who is reported to have said that *al kalāla* was he who was without a child,[69] and 'Umar, who, to avoid delay of judicial process, had to pronounce the opinion that he who inherited through *al kalāla* was he without a child even if he had a parent, and Abū Bakr al Saddīq decided that it referred to him who was with neither child nor parent, most commentators approved Abū Bakr's choice which might be strange given that 'Umar based his position on the Qur'an and the hadith of the Prophet, peace be upon him, neither of which Abū Bakr relied on. The Prophet, peace be upon him, has in fact pointed only to the last verse in the sūra of Women in which he indubitably defines the word: "They ask you for a ruling. Say: God imparted to you of His divine rules regarding the inheritance of distant kindred. It is when one dies and leaves no children." On the basis of this verse, 'Umar decided that he who was survived through *al kalāla* was he who did not have a child. As for Abū Bakr, in announcing that *al kalāla* referred to him who had neither child nor parent, he had opposed both 'Umar and the explicit text of the Qur'an.[70]

If it is legitimate to wonder why God chose a word over whose meaning people would disagree—especially in determining everyone's dues and inheritance shares which requires accuracy, careful examination, and verification—and if the Prophet, peace be upon him, refused to give an absolute definition for this word, albeit he pointed to a Qur'anic verse, it is also legitimate to wonder why most religious scholars sanctified Abū Bakr's position and dismissed the opinion of Ibn 'Abbās and 'Umar without any legal precedent. Isn't this a violation of the divine word and a distortion of the meaning explicitly mentioned in the Qur'an? Isn't it legitimate among the salafīs to explain the Qur'an by the Qur'an? Isn't Ben 'Āchūr's support of Abū Bakr's viewpoint declaring it to be public opinion a made up argument? Is he not relying on false evidence when he claims that "the context of the verse supports public opinion, because its citation right after the inheritance of the siblings and the two parents immediately dooms it to go against these two cases"?[71]

Regarding the second problem that the issue of *al kalāla* raises, one finds out that the sūra of Women holds two verses with two different rulings on that same topic. This difference might suggest that one of the verses abrogates the other, but to this day, no religious scholar has come to this conclusion despite the fact that abrogation rules are based on the principle that "It is not permissible that some of the commands of the Almighty God that He affirmed in his Book and on the tongue of his Prophet, Peace be upon him, could abrogate or be abrogated by another command, unless the two rulings which made one the abrogating verse and the other the abrogated one, cancel each other, for it is not permissible, under any circumstance, to have two rulings at the same time."[72] To avoid the issue of abrogation, the religious scholars found no better solution to explain the differences between the rulings of these two verses than to state that the intended brother or sister in the first verse was the sister and the brother on the mother's side and that those intended by male and female siblings in the second verse were the male and female siblings on the side of both the mother and the father or on the father's side.[73] There is no doubt that this ruling has no evidence, nor does it have any relation whatsoever to the text. This is what the commentators themselves have acknowledged by legitimating their explanations on the basis of the people and the consensus. While al Rāzī relied on the consensus of the religious scholars, Ben 'Āchūr upheld public opinion.[74] It seems that the linguistic and explicit meaning of the text is not enough to refute those views despite the fact that God's word does not specify that the siblings are on the mother's side, the father's, or on both sides. Is the Qur'an that exists today perhaps missing something or different regarding this same topic?

As if feeling no unease, some religious scholars addressed this issue. Without any quibbling, both al Tabarī and al Rāzī declared that Sa'd Ibn Abī al Waqqās used to misread this Qur'anic verse as: "He has a brother or a sister from the mother's side."[75] It is remarkable that the religious scholars who in search of textual explanations compatible with their patriarchal societies—elevating the share of the siblings on the father's side and decreasing that of the siblings on the mother's side, and in attempting to find an explanation that is well-suited to the consensus and public opinion—were not afraid to include that the distortions to the Qur'an brought harm to the message of Muhammad.

THAT WHICH LIES AFTER PERPLEXITY

Many religious scholars, commentators, jurists who belong to "Islamic" countries, and anyone who refuses the principle of gender equity in inheritance, claim that the Qur'anic text is explicit in the question of inheritance, and that it is impervious to either *ijtihād* or interpretation. In face of this rigid narrow-mindedness, no one is reminded that there are many explicit texts that Muslims have crossed, such as their agreement in the nineteenth-century to abolish slavery that the Qur'an did not abolish, since there are over fifteen verses which pointed to slavery and regulated it. No one will also be reminded of 'Umar Ibn al Khattāb's suspension of two explicit Qur'anic verses which are the cutting off of the thief's hands and the granting of *zakāt* (charity) to those whose hearts have been reconciled.[76] In all aforesaid examples, the suspension of the Qur'anic text is attributed to the historical and social context. No one will be reminded of the possibility of using the historical context of women's entry into the workplace, of their contribution as family providers to the extent that in many families they are single-handedly the bread winners. Nonetheless, we will just point out that if gender justice (i.e., giving women some inheritance) was the main reason the Qur'an addressed inheritance, religious scholars and commentators did not spare in contrast any effort to deploy human (or rather masculine) consensus, monolithic declarations, and bizarre readings for the purpose of denying women their rights at times and depriving of inheritance those on the matrilineal line—and even the orphans and the needy if they happen to be present at the time the inheritance is divided up. They go even further by closing the door to *ijtihād*. At other times, they have even gone against the explicit meaning of the text or entertained the possibility of distorting it to protect their interests. In this regard, "it was reported that when Fātimah, peace be upon her, demanded her inheritance, she was denied it under the excuse that the Prophet, peace be upon him, had said: "We the Prophets are not a folk to give as inheritance that which we left behind as charity." At this, Fātimah, peace be upon her, protested with a general verse: 'To the male twice the share of a female,' as if she were indicating that it was not permissible to take a general statement from the Qur'an and apply it to a specific single case.[77] Both the Qur'an's silence over many rulings and the general statements chosen by the Almighty for a good reason have turned into some bidding contests and individual battlefields that can be explained only through material and worldly interests.

NOTES

1. See book 9, "On Inheritance," in *The Personal Status Code*, collected and edited by Judge Muhammad Habīb Cherīf (Tunis, Sousse: Dār al Mīzān li al Nashr, 2004).

2. In other words, the word of the Great and Almighty God, "after fulfilling any will left by the deceased and paying off all debts" (Women 4:12).

3. Fakhr al Dīnee al Rāzī, *Mafātīh al Ghayb* 5.9 (Beirut: Dār al Fikr, 1985), 231–32.

4. Ibid., 232.

5. Ibid.

6. Abū Ja'far Ben Jarīr al Tabarī, *Jami' al Bayān fi Ta'wīl al Qur'an* 1 (Beirut: Dār al kutub al 'ilmiyya, 1968), 429–30.

7. Abū Bakr Ibn 'Arabī, *Ahkām al Qur'an* 1 (Matba'at al bāb al Halabī, 1986): 429–230.

8. Fakhr al Dīne al Rāzī, *Mafātīh al Ghayb* 5.9:201.

9. Ibid.

10. Ibid., 204.

11. Ibid., 6.11:47.

12. Ibid., 5.9:202.

13. Ibid., 204.

14. Ibid., 12.24:32.

15. Ibid., 5.9:216.

16. Ibid., 216–17.

17. Ibid., 217.

18. Al Rāzī asserts this by declaring that "according to this evaluation (i.e., this second interpretation of the hadith), the Prophet will lose all specificity," in *Mafātīh al Ghayb* 5.9:218.

19. Muhammad Tāhar Ben 'Āchūr, *Al Tahrīr wa al Tanwīr* 4 (Tunis: Al dār al tūnisiya li al nashr, 1984), 258.

20. Abū Bakr Ibn 'Arabī, *Ahkām al Qur'an*, 1:336.

21. Ben 'Āchūr, *Al Tahrīr wa al Tanwīr*, 4:258.

22. Fakhr al Dīnee al Rāzī, *Mafātīh al Ghayb,* 5.9:212.

23. Ibid., 213.

24. Al Tabarī, *Jāmi' al Bayān*, 3:618.

25. Ben 'Āchūr, *Al Tahrīr wa al Tanwīr*, 4:256.

26. Fakhr al Dīne al Rāzī, *Mafātīh al Ghayb,* 9:201.

27. Ben 'Āchūr, *Al Tahrīr wa al Tanwīr*, 4:258.

28. Abū Bakr Ibn 'Arabī, *Ahkām al Qu'ran*, 1:336.

29. Ben 'Āchūr, *Al Tahrīr wa al Tanwīr*, 4:257.

30. Ibid.

31. Fakhr al Dīne al Rāzī, *Mafātīh al Ghayb*, 5.9:213.

32. Al Tabarī, *Jāmi' al Bayān*, 3:616.

33. Ibid., 4:298.

34. Ibid., 3:617.

35. Fakhr al Dīne al Rāzī, *Mafātīh al Ghayb*, 5.9:214.

36. Ibn 'Arabī's *Ahkām al Qur'an*, 1: 253 and Fakhr al Dīne al Rāzī's *Mafātīh al Ghayb*, 3.6:102.

37. Fakhr al Dīne al Rāzī, *Mafātīth al Ghayb*, 5.9:214.

38. *The Personal Status Code*, article 23.

39. For example, see The Heifer 2:17; The Banquet 5:104; The Purgatory 7:28; and Jonah 10:78.

40. Abū Bakr Ibn 'Arabī, *Ahkām al Qur'an*, 1:337.

41. Fakhr al Dīne al Rāzī, *Mafātīh al Ghayb*, 5.9:216.

42. Ibid.

43. Abū Bakr Ibn 'Arabī, *Ahkām al Qur'an*, 1:337.

44. Ibid., 372.

45. Ibid., 215.

46. Bukhara, *Sahīh*, 3.7: 14.

47. Abū Bakr Ibn 'Arabī, *Ahkām al Qur'an*, 1:335.

48. Ben 'Āchūr, *Al Tahrīr wa al Tanwīr*, 4:256.

49. Olfa Youssef, *Al Ikhbaar 'an al Mar'a fi al Qur'an wa al Sunnah* (Tunis: Sahar, 1997), 81–83.

50. Ben 'Āchūr, *Al Tahrīr wa al Tanwīr*, 4: 256.

51. Fakhr al Dīne al Rāzī, *Mafātīh al Ghayb*, 5.9:213.

52. See for example, Abū Bakr Ibn 'Arabī, *Ahkām al Qur'an*, 1:429–30.

53. Ibid.

54. The Personal Status Code, Vol 5: "Succession on Agnatic Lines" (*Fī al irth bi al ta'asub*).

55. Fakhr al Dīne al Rāzī, *Mafātīh al Ghayb*, 5.9:221.

56. Ibid.

57. Ibid.

58. The Qur'anic citation is provided by translator. Only the verse is mentioned in the Arabic text.

59. Fakhr al Dīne al Rāzī, *Mafātīh al Ghayb*, 5.9:221.

60. Ibid., 213.

61. Ibid., 223.

62. Because Arabic language has a dual system, three is the smallest plural.

63. This word refers to a person who dies leaving behind neither a child nor a parent. S/he is survived by relatives.

64. Jalāl al Dīne al Suyūtī, *Al Itqān fī'Ulūm al Qur'an* 1 (Beirut: Dār al Ma'rifa, n. p.): 46.

65. Ben 'Āchūr, *Al Tahrīr wa al Tanwīr*, 4:264.

66. Abū Bakr Ibn 'Arabī, *Ahkām al Qur'an*, 1:519.

67. Ibid., 348.

68. Ibid., 435.

69. Ben 'Āchūr, *Al Tahrīr wa al Tanwīr*, 4:264.

70. Fakhr al Dīne al Rāzī, *Mafātīh al Ghayb*, 5.9:229.

71. Ben 'Āchūr, *Al Tahrīr wa al Tanwīr*, 4:26.

72. Al Tabarī, *Jāmi' al Bayān*, 3:607.

73. Fakhr al Dīne al Rāzī, *Mafātīh al Ghayb*, 5.9: 231.

74. Ibid., and Ben 'Āchūr, *Al Tahrīr wa al Tanwīr* 4:265.

75. Al Tabarī, *Jāmi' al Bayān*, 3:629; *Mafātīh al Ghayb*, 5.9:231.

76. The expression *Al mu'allafa qulūbuhum* (المؤلفة قلوبهم or those whose hearts have not been reconciled) refers to those people who entered Islam without conviction and they had a strong impact on early Muslim society because of their high social standing. The most famous of them was Abū Sufyān Sakhr Ibn Harb, the father of Mu'āwiya who founded the Umayyad Dynasty.

77. Fakhr al Dīne al Rāzī, *Mafātīh al Ghayb*, 5.9:217.

Chapter Two

Perplexity over Marriage

Even though researchers have different opinions about marriage, none of them denied that it was the most prevalent form of human gathering, the goal of which is the regulation of sexual life or family and social relations in different ways and myriad styles throughout the ages. The common belief that marriage is between a male and a female is being challenged today by gay people who demand the right to marry. While Part III focuses on homosexuality, by unveiling the commentators and religious scholars' readings of marriage provisions and inter-spousal relationships, this part discloses some of the incidental and historical worldview which may at times be opposed to the meanings of the shari'a law. Indeed, this section's purpose is only to raise questions and a spiritual perplexity which fall under the intersectional point between the often close-ended readings of commentators on the one hand and the openness of the Sunnah and the Qur'an to a multiplicity of independent readings on the other.

PERPLEXITY ONE: IS THE DOWRY A MARRIAGE REQUISITE?

Islam did not invent the dowry as it seems to have been a widespread practice in the Arabian Peninsula since the Jāhiliyya period. It consists of having some men give money to the women they wished to marry.[1] Bearing witness to that are the Jāhiliyya historical records and the Qur'an which commands relatives and husbands not to prevent wives from remarrying[2] for the purpose of confiscating their dowries: "Unless they are proven guilty of abomination, you shall not put constraint upon them to take away a part of what you have given them" (Women 4:19). These "words are directed at those husbands, who because in dispute with their wives, prevent them from having another loving companion until they take what they had given them."[3]

Thus, the Qur'an mentions the existence of some money that a husband would pay to the wife, but it is called *sidāq* or *ajr*,[4] not *mahr*.[5] Nowhere is it asserted in any single verse of the Qur'an that the dowry is one of the requisites or conditions of marriage. As to the verse which states, "And to the women give *sidāq* as gift" (Women 4:4), it is not a command to give them *sidāq*. Rather it asserts that *sidāq* is a donation (i.e., without expecting anything in return). This is why it is surprising to have Ben 'Āchūr state: "This verse proclaimed the paying off of a dowry and legalized it. It became thus one of the fundamental requisites of marriage in Islam."[6] Grammatically, the word *nihla* (نحلة) (gift or donation) in this verse functions as a *tamyīz* (an accusative of specification) which sets up the type of donation, rather than the principle of donation itself. It is as if the verse stated that if gifts were given to women, they must be bestowed as donations without expecting anything in return. What proves that the verse does not command the obligation of giving dowries is the disagreement among commentators over the addressee of this verse. The command was believed to be addressed to the husbands who had given dowries—if they ever did—out of their own free will. The parents are also believed to be the addressee and this to rescind the Jāhiliyyan practice of taking away the daughter's dowry. They used to say: "Congratulations on the rise in wealth for he who gave birth to a daughter. By this they meant, you take her dowry to enlarge your own money, i.e., to increase it."[7]

The commentators resorted to a second verse to ascertain that the dowry was a necessary condition in marriage and one of its requisites. After enumerating the women one is forbidden to marry[8] He states: "And lawful to you are all others beyond these. So, seek them with your money in wedlock, not in prostitution" (Women 4:24).[9] In Ibn 'Arabī's view, the reference to money here is a proof of the "obligation of *sidāq* in marriage."[10] In contrast with Ibn 'Arabī, I do not see anything in this verse that decrees *sidāq* in marriage, for God's words only give men permission to marry those women other than those forbidden by the Great and Almighty God. The verse allows man to use his wealth in marriage, but it is not known if this is the *sidāq money* (also mentioned in other verses) which the husband has to give the wife without expecting anything in return, or if it is just the money a husband would need to provide for his wife and children.[11] If we theoretically postulate that the money the man would use for marriage was nothing but *sidāq*, the verse's explicit text does not mention it as a "prerequisite," but as a possibility. The difference between the two is obvious as asserted in al Rāzī's statement: "The verse signifies that seeking marriage with money is possible. *Nothing in it signifies that seeking marriage other than with money is not possible.*"[12] If prerequisites and possibilities become equal, the Great and Almighty God's statement, "During fasting, permitted to you is sex with your wife at night" (The Heifer 2:187), would mean that the husband is required to have sex with his wife on the night of fasting. According to the same logic, the statement of the Great and Almighty God, "Permitted to you is the meat of the female donkey in your livestock" (The Banquet 5:10), would require of every Muslim to consume the meat of female donkeys. And woe to he who happens to be a vegetarian then!

Ibn 'Arabī uses another verse to prove the dowry was a prerequisite in marriage which is the Almighty's statement: "Those among you, who cannot afford to wed free believing women, may wed the believing slave women your right hands possess. God knows best the faith of each and every one of you. You shall obtain permission from their guardians before you wed them and give them in fairness what is due to them in wedlock, not as prostitutes or secret lovers" (Women 4:25). Ibn 'Arabī is either forgetting or feigning to forget that the context of this verse is unrelated to free women in that the command to pay dues does not refer to anyone but the slave women. It is not known how Ibn 'Arabī used it to generalize that the dowry was a prerequisite of marriage. One is even more astonished to learn that the word *al ujūr* does not necessarily mean dowry. This is what al Rāzī indicates when he states that "commentators had two views of this verse. In the first, what the word *al ujūr* refers to is the dowry. From this perspective, this verse proves that the dowry is a prerequisite of marriage. In the second, a judge stated that what was intended by *al ujūr* was financial support for the wife. This reporter stated the latter was a more plausible explanation, for given the fact that the dowry amount was already defined; it would be meaningless to require fairness as its condition. It is as if the Almighty was explaining that the needs and financial support of a slave woman must not be less significant than those provided for a free woman."[13]

Granted that the Qur'an uses twice the word "*ujūrihinna*" (their wages), does this mean that married women must be paid wages "*ujūr*" (wages)? The first context was His divine statement, "Permitted to you this day are all things good. The food of those who received the Scriptures is permitted to you and permitted to them is your food. Also permitted to you is marriage with believing married women and the married women who received the Scriptures[14] revealed before, provided that you pay them what is due to them in wedlock, not as prostitutes or secret lovers" (The Banquet 5:5). This verse was revealed in the context of allowing marriage with married women from the People of the Book. This is a specific context that does not call for any generalization. In addition this permissibility did not earn the consensus of commentators for the son of 'Umar, for example, believed that it was not lawful to marry a Woman of the Book because she was a non-believer.[15]

The second time the *ujūr* expression is mentioned in the Qur'an is in the context of marriage as in the Great and Almighty's statement:

O you who believe, when immigrant women who are believers seek asylum
with you, you shall test them. God knows their faith best. Once you establish
that they are believers, you shall not return them to the disbelievers. They are
neither lawful for the disbelievers, nor are the disbelievers lawful for them.
Give back to the disbelievers what they have spent on them and it is no sin for
you to wed them provided that you pay them what is due to them. (The Test
60:10)

This verse, which makes it lawful for believers to wed immigrant believing
women on the condition they be given what is due to them, was exclusively
cited in the specific case of such marital unions. Therefore, it is not right to
generalize that giving a woman her due is a prerequisite in the sense of
dowry. Transmitting the specific historical and contextual circumstances
Tabarī asserted from Qutāda that when those believing women, "[U]sed to
run away from the disbelievers who had a pact with the Prophet of God,
peace be upon him, to the disciples of the Prophet, peace be upon him, the
latter would marry them and send their dowries to their disbelieving husbands, with whom the Prophet of God, peace be upon him, had a pact."[16]
    From this statement by Tabarī, it seems that the dues being paid in this
verse, besides being contextually specific to the immigrant women who con-
verted to Islam, are compensations for the unbelieving men who were divorced from their wives. Therefore, these *ujūr* cannot be gifts because these
are to be given to the wives as donations or bestowment, and under no
circumstance are they compensations. Even though Ben ʿĀchūr presents a
different reading of this verse—in that the purpose of giving the *ujūr* "is to
avoid the assumption that, by paying off the dowry to the previous husband,
a man earns the right to marry the woman he desires"[17]—this reading does
not refute that the whole verse is linked to a specific context, with neither
precedential nor rational incentive to generalize it.[18]
    Clearly, nowhere is it indicated in the entire Qur'an that a man must give
money to the woman he intends to marry.[19] If *sidāq* (dowry, money) had
been a requirement, how can one explain the fact that the Prophet, peace be
upon him, had in a famous hadith made a Muslim man marry with what he
possessed from the Qur'an. Is learning the Qur'an money? It is strange that
Abū Hanīfa, ignoring this authentic hadith, argues that a man's marriage to a
woman with a sūra did not constitute a dowry and that he still owed her
one.[20] Is it possible that the issue of dowry is merely a social custom that the
Qur'an has at the same time neither prohibited nor imposed? Has not the
Great Almighty God left things for human *ijtihad* and historical contexts,
changing in view of them and transforming themselves accordingly? Had the
dowry been a prerequisite, then how come the Prophet, peace be upon him,
has helped a man get married without any dowry (even if symbolic such as
learning a Qur'anic verse)? And this according to ʿUqba Ibn ʿĀmer who
reported that "the Prophet, peace be upon him, said: The best marriage is the

easiest. And he told a man: Do you consent that I marry you to this particular woman? When she said yes, the man married her and consummated the marriage without giving her a dowry or anything else."[21] How does even the Prophet of God himself, peace be upon him, get married without a dowry?"[22] Does it suffice to say that the Prophet, peace be upon him, is an exceptional case? If the Prophet is an example and a role model for Muslims, then how come he let go of the dowry which religious scholars asserted as a prerequisite to the point of turning it into the demarcating point between marriage and fornication?[23] Is it not significant that there is a disagreement among eminent scholars over the marriage of the Prophet, peace be upon him, as explicitly put in their statement: "They disagreed over his marriage (the Prophet's) without a dowry?"[24]

Through the above, I declare that the Qur'an did not assert that the dowry was a prerequisite of marriage, or one of its cornerstones. Nonetheless, given that it was a prevalent practice among many communities during the Jāhiliyya, the Qur'an neither repudiated nor advised against this practice. Thus, one can say that the dowry is optional rather than a prerequisite in the Qur'an as declared by contemporary laws which pretend drawing their authority from religious texts while relying in fact on the commentaries and interpretations of religious scholars.

PERPLEXITY TWO: IS THE DOWRY A PAYMENT FOR A WOMAN'S SEX?

Given that the dowry is not required in the Qur'an, one wonders why commentators and religious scholars were so adamant upon making it a prerequisite of marriage. Most commentators saw the marriage contract like any other sale contract. For some, it is not different from the latter, given that there are goods for sale (woman), or more accurately, given the availability on the one hand of women's goods and buyer or recipient on the other hand who is the husband who pays sum of money to transform the goods to the property of the buyer. In this regard, Mālek writes that "marriage is a lot like a sale contract."[25] If what is sold in marriage is a vagina, then the husband buys it not only by providing for his wife, but also by paying her a dowry. Without any equivocation, Ibn 'Arabī states: "The High and Almighty God forbade access to this organ—i.e., the goods—except when there is something substituted for them in return. This is to be determined in a way that would be commensurate with its importance and honor."[26] Al Rāzī also asserts that "If the Almighty God had added the giving of a dowry to them, it is because it is the price for their goods."[27] In an assertive statement, he repeats that "the dowry is the payment for the goods."[28] Replacing the word "price" with "reward," Al Zamakhsharī states that "the dowry is a reward for the goods."[29] There is not much difference in meaning for the reward is a recompense, which makes the dowry a reward for the woman in return for giving away her goods.

If one is to take a look at the Qur'an, he/she will find out, that in addition to what was previously said about the absence of the dowry as a prerequisite, the Qur'an is devoid of anything that would indicate that the dowry, when possible, is the price for the woman's goods. Many pieces of evidence attest to that, the first of which is the Almighty's statement, "If you divorce them before touching them, but after you had set the dowry for them, give them half of what you had set for them, unless they forfeit their rights, or the rights of the party in whose hand the marriage tie is forfeited" (The Heifer 2:237). Indeed, the dowry is related to a possible or non-possible obligation among all parties involved in the marriage[30] (i.e., through agreement, due consideration, and possible or non-possible titles[31]). If that agreement is carried out, the dowry or part of it must be paid, regardless of the occurrence or absence of touching between the spouses. If one is to presume that touching was sexual intercourse—although this is a disputed issue[32]—and if one is to presume that the dowry was the price for a woman's goods, it becomes illogical that the Qur'an would force the husband to pay a sum of money to the wife while the spouses have not touched each other and the husband did not collect "his goods." It is true that the dues agreed upon by the two sides or all sides involved in the contract must be entirely paid in case there is touching and just the half if none occurred. This means that the clauses of the contract which are based on consent and agreement make the sexual relation between the two spouses the very condition for the completion of the contract. Thus the terms of the contract can be fulfilled only with sexual consummation. The Prophet's statement to Muslims, "The obligation to fulfill that which gave you lawful access to a vagina is the highest of obligations,"[33] asserts that consummation and agreement are the only things required in a contract. Neither in the aforesaid verse nor in the Prophet's hadith, is there any indication, implicit or explicit, that a correlation exists between the payment of a dowry as a price and the perception of a woman's vagina as goods. The verse does nothing other than regulate marriage contracts *if both partners (or partners) involved in the marriage have chosen to have a marriage founded on sidāq (dowry)*[34] or any other possible provision. In light of the above, it is not understood where in the Qur'an al Rāzī found out the following: "She who divorces after signing the marriage contract and before touching, deserves the dowry not as compensation for granting lawful access to the goods, but because she was denied pleasure. And she who divorces after the consummation of marriage deserves the dowry as compensation for granting lawful access to the goods."[35] Al Rāzī's words can be understood only as projections of historical perceptions and social imaginary onto a Qur'anic text which deems women's vaginas far above any goods for sale. Because this issue is tied to a historical context, Ben 'Āchūr, who belongs to a different time and who is bound by a different social imaginary, is embarrassed to say that the dowry is a form of exchange, in that he states:

> The dowry is not an exchange for the consummation of women's sexual goods. Marriage is a contract between a man and a woman for companionship, close bonding and recognition of each other's rights. These are more precious than any monetary compensation. Were there one, like all compensations, it would be plentiful and renewable, given that remunerations are renewed and extend over centuries. But God required that the husband gives it as a gift in honor of the wife. [36]

Embarrassed by the word "*ujūr*" (wages), in another passage, this same commentator states: "*Al ujūr*: The dowries are called here wages on a metaphorical and plain figurative level, in the sense of compensations for the benefits accumulated through the marriage contract. Had the dowries been real wages, the value and duration of those benefits would have been determined. This is what the marriage tie rises above." [37]

PERPLEXITY THREE: THE OBEDIENCE TO THE HUSBAND IN BED

In the Qur'an as well as among commentators and religious scholars, marriage rests on the principle of "*al ihçān*" (الاحصان) in that the Almighty God mentions "*al muhaçanīn*" (married men المحصنين) and "*al muhaçanāt*" (married women المحصنات) in contrast with the "*musāfihīn*" (debauched men المسافحين) and "*al musāfihat*" (debauched women المسافحات). [38] One of the many meanings of "*al ihçān*" is protection and one of its faces is the protection from *zinā*. [39] Therefore, he who has protected himself with marriage has protected himself from *zinā*. This presupposes in principle that there is sexual relationship between the two spouses. In case it is missing, there is something wrong with the marriage. Through the following table, it is possible to illustrate this concern as it is in the eyes of religious scholars.

It is not by chance that I started with the wife's desire in case no sexual intercourse takes place, nor is it arbitrarily that I placed it before the husband's. This is because this possibility is rarely raised among commentators and religious scholars in comparison with their prolixity over the case when the husband's desire is denied by the wife. What is odd is that they point most often, not to the husband's rejection or denial of the wife's desire, but to his impotence. Basically, the husband always desires the wife. If despite the wife's desire, there is no sexual intercourse between the two spouses, the only explanation for this lack is the husband's sexual impotence, which

Table 2.1.

The Wife	The Husband	The Prevalent Law
"desiring"	impotent/not able	allows the wife to get a divorce
"desiring"	denying her sex	difference of opinion, not a serious issue though*
The Husband	**The Wife**	**The Prevalent Law**
desiring	denying him sex without providing a good reason (*nāshiz* from the point of view of religious scholars)	punishment for the wife
desiring	denying him sex for a good reason	husbandly consideration for the wife's condition

*To see the opinions of religious scholars regarding this subject, refer to Amāl Grāmī, *Al Ikhtilāf fī al thaqāfa al 'arabiyya al islāmiyya* (Beirut: Al Madār al Islāmī, 2007), 665.

religious scholars refer to as *al 'unna* (sexual incapacity or weakness). The explanations commentators provide for the husband's impotence are limited to the incapacity of penetration. This is why they do not consider the castrated man, who can still perform penetration with what is left of his penis, to be impotent. Commentators did not raise the issue of the man's ability to sexually satisfy the woman. For them, penetration is enough to qualify as sexual intercourse. Despite the preponderance of Arabic sexual manuals which direct the man on how to synchronize his pleasure with the woman's, and despite the allusion in a hadith that a kiss was a "messenger" between the two spouses, and recommendation for the man who has reached his climax not to precipitate the wife until she reaches hers,[40] religious scholars do not view the absence of sexual pleasure as one of the reasons to ask for divorce. Given the religious scholars' quantitative conception of sexual relationship, how can they care about women's sexual pleasure? To them, conjugal equity between wives has more to do with the number of nights a husband would sleep with each wife than the "quality"[41] of the sexual relationship or ways of establishing a sexual relationship between the two spouses.

What is peculiar is that in contrast with the silence of religious scholars over women's sexual pleasure, there is a hadith by the Prophet, peace be upon him, which asserts a woman's right to sexual pleasure. A woman is said to have visited the Prophet, peace be upon him, and told him that she was married to Rifā'a, but he divorced her three times. After him, she got married to 'Abdul Rahmān Ibn al Zubeyr. And pulling a piece of cloth from her *djellaba*, she said to the Prophet of God that he had nothing but a similar piece of cloth. This was said, according to the person who transmitted the hadith, in the presence of Abū Bakr who was sitting with the Prophet, peace be upon him, and Ibn Sa'd Ibn al 'Āç, who was at the door waiting to be let in. Then, Khāled started shouting at Abū Bakr asking him to restrain this woman for what she dared to say in front of the Prophet, peace be upon him. The Prophet could not stop laughing. Then he said to her that perhaps she wished to return to Rifā'a so that they could taste each other's honey.[42]

It is true that the Prophet would not allow the woman to return to her husband before she was to have a sexual relationship with the new husband, but this refusal was not grounded on some disrespect for women's sexual pleasure, but on the Shari'a law which has proclaimed that a woman can return to a husband who has divorced her three times only if she has a sexual relationship with a new husband.[43] It is not the Prophet who resented the wife's declaration that her current husband was incapable of satisfying her sexually. The one who resented it was that man who was present [at the meeting] and who condemned her for speaking out about her sexual "grievances" in front of the Prophet. This man's feeling of repugnance is nothing but the echo of a male-centered society which resents all reference to a woman's sexual pleasure as previously seen among religious scholars and commentators. From a historical perspective, it is not strange to have such a feeling of repugnance in a society that does not see woman as a full human being, but a sexual object for man; he has vaginal intercourse with her at any time he wishes, from the front and the back. He may also have sex with her while she is standing, lying, or on her knees.[44]

From a scholarly viewpoint, it would be prejudicial to explain the repugnance to speak about a woman's sexual pleasure only by the historical context, for there is a psychological dimension to this repugnance that is attached to the masculine fear of a sexual pleasure that is neither perceptible nor concrete. If a man's sexual pleasure materially manifests itself in ejaculation, a woman's sexual pleasure, which is not manifest through some outright material evidence, is still the subject of disagreement among doctors and psychoanalysts.[45] This "mysterious" sexual pleasure is perplexing, given that it could be faked and from thence capable of making men doubt their "virility." Nothing is better than erasure when dealing with the mysterious and the perplexing, eliminating it from the unconscious and keeping it veiled from that which is visible.

And since woman is merely a sexual object, her desire to have a sexual relationship and its denial by a man is nearly inconceivable except in two cases. In the first, the man's sexual rejection of the woman is caused by some imperfection in her such as her advanced age or lack of beauty, etc. In the second, the man intentionally chooses to turn her away because desertion in bed was the punishment for a disobedient woman according to the commentators' interpretations of His statement: "As for those women from whom you fear *nushūz*, first admonish them, then desert them in bed and beat[46] them" (Women 4:34).

In the first case, the husband's sexual rejection of the wife on the ground of a physical imperfection is in fact constrained by His statement: "For if you dislike them, it may happen that you dislike a thing in which God placed much good" (Women 4:19). If religious scholars maintain the possibility of replacing one spouse with another on the basis of the next verse, "if you want to replace one spouse with another" (Women 4:20), they are oblivious of the fact that the wife, too, can replace her husband with another as attested in the visit of Thābit Ibn Qays's wife to the Prophet, peace be upon him. She told him: "O Prophet of God. I am not accusing Thābit of lack of religion or morals, but I cannot stand him. He said: Return to him his garden. She said: Yes."[47] Another hadith version ascribed to this same woman indicates that while she is not accusing him of lack of religion or morals, she "disliked his ugliness."[48] Given that marriage is a contract based on the consent of both sides, it may break even at the wish of one partner. Because the Qur'an and the Prophet allowed the wife to get a divorce from her husband without a reasonable cause and because religious scholars, following this same path, saw that divorce was not restricted to those cases when there is a crack in the marriage, it is strange to see more conservative views on divorce among modernist "religious scholars" than their predecessors.[49] Even the judicial systems which claim to derive their authority from the shari'a law, such as the Egyptian judicial system, recognized divorce only after endless delays and debates. I believe that clause 31 in the Tunisian PSC allowing a woman to divorce her husband is only an autonomous reading of the original legal texts about the legitimacy of having a woman divorce her husband.

In the second case, the husband's sexual rejection of the wife is for the purpose of punishing her for being a *nāshiz* woman. The most peculiar thing about *nushūz* (noun form of the female adjective *nāshiz*) is that no commentator was able to ascertain in an absolute manner the meaning of this figurative expression. While the original meaning of the word *nushūz* is to stand up and leave a place, in dictionaries, the usage of the figurative meaning is restricted to the spouses' relationship with each other: the wife *tanshuz* (she becomes *nāshiz*) in case she despises the husband and becomes difficult to live with, and the husband *yanshuz* (he becomes *nāshiz*) in case he harms the wife by his disaffection. Commentators and readers of the Qur'an differed from one another in interpreting and delimiting the meaning of general words like despise and disaffection, which makes the husband's desertion of the wife's bed foregrounded on a foggy and mysterious condition. It is not clear why many commentators and religious scholars commonly define *nushūz* as the refusal to share the husband's bed to the point of not only restricting it to the *nushūz* of a woman who refuses to share her husband's bed[50] but also of limiting the concept of obedience (*tā'a*) to a woman's resumption of sexual intercourse with her husband.[51] Even though not supported by any linguistic evidence, this explanation has become predominant, all the more perplexing, because how can a husband punish his wife who refuses to have sex with him by not having any sexual relationship with her? In doing so, does he not fulfill her wish? Where is therefore the punishment in this? It seems that Tabarī has realized this discrepancy when he states: "If God has really commanded the husband of the woman whose *nushūz* is feared to admonish her so that she reverts to being obedient when he calls her to his bed, it is not right to have the husband admonish the wife so that she returns to God and obeys her husband while he is commanded to desert her in bed, which is the very thing against which he was sermonizing."[52]

What is most important from the above is that in the Islamic social imaginary, sexual impotence is perceived to be the primary cause for the husband's sexual rejection of the wife, which allows for the wife to demand divorce according to provisions and historical conjectures which vary from one school of religious jurisprudence to another. Also legitimate to them is the husband's choice of sexually rejecting the wife for a physical imperfection or for a moral flaw that requires discipline. This sexual rejection is absolutely legitimate for al Shāfi'ī, for whom sexual intercourse with the wife is one of those things which "is not an obligation because it is his right. It is therefore not an obligation as with all of his other rights."[53] Nowhere in this is it required of man to sexually satisfy his wife when he comes unto her as clear in Ibn' Arabī's statement,

> The argument that the two spouses sexually enjoy each other and that they are equal in the marriage contract is erroneous, for the dowry requirement gives the husband authority over the woman. *And because of what he paid to her in return, when he comes down unto her, he does it as a master would unto a slave.* Therefore, only he finds enjoyment in her: she fasts, goes on a pilgrimage, and leaves her house only with his permission. And if his command extends to all her wealth except for the third, what is one to say then about her body?"[54]

What is peculiar is that when the Great and Almighty God mentions *al ihçān*, He imputes it to both men and women[55] contrary to the commentators who view that *zinā* prevention is just for the husband. As for the wife, the husband is less to prevent her from *zinā* than to prevent her from doing anything without his permission. In this regard, al Rāzī states: "The husband prevents the wife from doing many things and the wife prevents him from falling in *zinā*."[56] In contrast with al Rāzī who provides an indiscriminate list of the many things a husband may prevent his wife from doing, other commentators give more details. They mention not just prevention from pilgrimage and going out without his permission, but also the specific case of *nawāfil*:[57] "In *nawāfil* the obedience to the husband is prior to the obedience of God. She (wife) fasts only with his permission."[58] Significant in al Rāzī's statement is the implication that the husband does not prevent the wife from committing *zinā*. This viewpoint is perplexing because if *al ihçān* is deemed to be there to prevent both the man and the woman from committing *zinā*, one can wonder: How can a woman count as *muhaçana* (protected), if her husband is permitted to desert her in bed and substitute for her another woman, not to mention those slave women whom his right hand possesses? How can a woman count as *muhaçana* if her husband can fast and go on a pilgrimage without her? Is it not legitimate for a woman to desire her husband while he is fasting without her permission? And if he rejects her sexually, may she not fall in the sin of *zinā*? In general, how can marriage protect the woman if her sexual pleasure is completely erased and if she is merely goods purchased to protect the husband alone? Do not these readings of commentators and religious scholars constitute a slighting to the concept of *al ihçān* which comprises women in the Qur'an? Do not these readings count as a slighting of the Prophet's assertion of the existence of a female sexual pleasure in the aforesaid hadith?

What counters this slighting is the warm welcome given to the sexual pleasure of the male spouse. Commentators and religious scholars have all agreed that a woman who refuses to sleep with her husband is at a great fault. None of them, however, mentions any "impotence" in the wife, but rather *nushūz*, rejection, and refusal. A "sexual object" cannot be impotent, for impotence marks only those who can be active, not those who are incapacitated. As for woman, she has no role to play during copulation.[59] All that she is required to do is to answer her husband's call whenever and however he wants to have sex with her. Commentators draw their authority from His statement: "Your women are a tilth for you, so go to your tilth as you please" (The Heifer 2:223). The revelation of this verse was not related to the wife's sexual rejection of the husband, but rather to sexual positions, a subject I shall return to in a different context. In any case, grammatical books show that the preposition *anná* (أنَّى) could refer to the expression "how." This is what concords with the cause of this verse's revelation which revolves around sexual positions. In addition, *anná* (أنَّى) could also express time which would suggest the legitimacy of having sexual intercourse at any time. Looking at the general usage of this preposition in the Qur'an, one finds out that it is most often used in the meaning of "how," which would make the meaning of "how" most likely in this verse and thus legitimize the use of different positions in sexual intercourse.[60] Even in case one does not lean toward this possible meaning and considers *anná* (أنَّى) as a preposition of time, the verse only legitimates a man's right to have a sexual relationship with his wife without any time restrictions. In fact, the verse makes no mention at all of whether the women desire or not to have this relationship. This absence can be read in two ways: While the first prioritizes the commentators who view woman as a sexual object, rather than the participant in the sexual act, the second draws its authority from the fact that women's absence, that is, non-existence as interlocutors in the Qur'an, is not limited to the sexual act but goes beyond it. If one was to see it as total absence, then the previous verse would lose its pertinence and would not necessarily mean that the husband has the right to establish a sexual relationship with his wife even if against her will. The verse, however, may denote that a sexual relation that is legitimate at any time and circumstance concerns only the man and the woman (i.e., both spouses) even though the speech, as usual, is addressed only to a group of men. From hence, the verse would also permit the wife to have sexual intercourse with her husband at any time she wants. Why would one negate such a reading given His statement: "And if you are ill, or on a journey, or one of you has finished answering nature's call, or you have touched women, and you find no water, then seek clean earth and wipe your faces and hands therewith" (Women 4:43). In this verse, the Great and Almighty God addresses only men. If one is to stop only at what is explicitly stated, the text then allows men to have ablutions in case there is no water after having touched women[61] and remains totally silent over the case when women touch men. Yet, despite this silence, there are commentators who have indicated that "this command has equally included men and women as did His statement, 'And if you were impure (*junuban*),' for obviously, meaning and not a person's name is what is taken into consideration."[62] And Glory Be to God for having commentators swing between "consideration of the name" and "consideration of the meaning," according to their interpretive whims and intellectual motives. And Glory Be to God who made them purposefully overlook or disregard other Qur'anic verses in which woman was not mentioned as a sexual object, but rather as a sexual "partner" and this on the basis of the verb *tamāssa* (تماسّا), a quadrilateral verb on the meter of *tafā'ala* which signifies participation, as in His statement about the expiation for "*al Zhihār*,"(الظّهار)[63] "And those who say to their wives, 'Be as my mother's back,' and then take back what they have said, they shall set free a slave, before the two of them touch one another" (The Dispute 85:3).

Even though I pointed out that the Qur'an does not necessarily count woman as a sexual object and that it is the interpretations of commentators which made her mere goods that can be owned, and even though I asserted that the verse "Your women are a tilth for you, so go to your tilth as you please" (The Heifer 2:223) does not imply that a woman must be obedient to her husband in bed, I do not deny the existence of texts which assert this obedience. These texts to which commentators cling are from the Sunnah, not the Qur'an, as exemplified by these hadiths by the Prophet, peace be upon him: "If a man calls his wife, she must answer him even if in labor" and "If a man calls his wife to bed and she refused to answer him, the angels will curse her till the morn."[64] It is clear that while the first hadith is just imposing a duty on the woman, the second goes beyond that duty to describe a symbolic punishment for the woman who sexually rejects her husband. Needless to comment on the time frame which extends the curse till the morning, implying that sexual relationship must be at night, or perhaps, that she who rejects her husband in the morning calls upon herself more cursing, especially given that it would last a whole day, from morning until the next one. But what I would like to look into is the relation of these two hadiths with the Qur'an as well as other hadiths by the Prophet and ask: How is one to reconcile the Qur'anic command of amicable companionship with the Holy Book's requirement of affection and mercy in a marriage?[65] How is one to reconcile Muhammad's call to show women affection[66] on the one hand and forcing them to engage in sexual relations they do not desire for whatever reason on the other hand? It is true that in the various accounts of the aforesaid hadiths, there are differences between those which compel the wife to show absolute obedience to the husband in bed and those which permit her to sexually reject the husband if with a good reason. Regardless of the elasticity of the "good reason" and its ability to extend and also include the absence of sexual desire at the moment of the call, what is important, in my opinion, is that the insistence of commentators and religious scholars on the wife's obedience in bed derives from a prevalent medieval worldview in which it was possible for one being to own the body of another human being. Slavery, which neither the Qur'an nor the hadith have abolished with an explicit text, are only the most obvious pieces of this possession as well as of its acceptance in the social imaginary, given that it was held as an ordinary matter then, and especially that some religious scholars used to believe that: "If a slave woman is to be sold and she has a spouse, her master (i.e.) is most deserving of her vagina."[67]

In one statement, the Prophet, peace be upon him, speaks to men about women: "These middle-aged women in your trust are of the same station as a slave or prisoner of war."[68] Despite the ideas of intentional and practical measures one could infer from this hadith, whose purpose is to urge men to treat women with kindness and care, that same hadith does certainly reflect a prevalent social imaginary that is tied to a specific time and place. Does not the Prophet, peace be upon him, make a correlation between the slave and the wife: "Your wife says, 'spend on me or divorce me' and your slave says, 'spend on me or sell me.'"[69] Does not Ibn Taymiyyah assert that "possessing someone through a marriage contract is one type of slavery and having right hand possessions is absolute slavery"?[70] Does not al Ghazālī unequivocally declare that marriage was a form of slavery for woman?[71] I do not understand how all the "Islamic" judicial systems which have agreed to abolish slavery because incompatible with the essence of the Islamic tradition, which is based on the respect and dignity of every human being, yet, have at the same time ascertained the wife's obligation to be obedient to her husband in bed. This would denote not just that a human being would possess another but also an acceptance of the idea of slavery in the context of marriage. All "Islamic" judicial systems have refused to recognize marital rape as a crime. Is this not one of the many faces of enslaving to have sex with his wife against free women? Is not the court's protection of the husband's right to coerce his wife into having sex with him one of the most blatant forms of this enslavement?

PERPLEXITY FOUR: THE MARRIAGE OF PLEASURE

The term "marriage of pleasure" has no existence in the Qur'an, however, the three-root "*m/t/'*" (م/ت/ع) has been mentioned in various verses and different contexts. From those related to marriage, one mentions his command to men, "You are not to blame, if you divorce women while as yet you have not touched them nor determined what is owed to them. Yet give them generous gifts, the affluent man and the needy man each according to his needs—an obligation on the righteous" (The Heifer 2:236) and "O you who believe! If you wed believing women and divorce them before you have touched them, then the *'iddah*[72] (عدّة) period shall not be required of them. But indulge them and handsomely set them free" (The Parties 33:49). The two verses indicate that a woman with whom the marriage has not been consummated, and whose dowry has not been agreed upon, either could or must receive gifts from the man.[73] Here, the word *mut'a* (متعة) means that a man would give the woman some money:

> [A]nd the origin of pleasure (*mut'a* متعة) and belongings (*matā'* متاع) is that which could be fully-benefited from, yet non-everlasting and about to come to an end. It is called pleasure (*taladhudh* تلذّذ) because it does not last and quickly ends.[74] The word *mut'a* is also cited in the context of marriage after consummation, in particular, in relation to the Prophet, peace be upon him, as in His statement: "O Prophet! Tell your wives: 'If you want this worldly life and its glitter, then come. I shall allow you to enjoy it and handsomely set you free.'"[75] (The Parties 33:28)

In another Qur'anic verse, the root "*m/t/'*" is also used in the context of marriage. Rather than giving the divorced woman some pleasure, the command is about the obligation to give her wages in exchange for enjoying her as in His statement: "Such wives you have enjoyed thereby, you must give them their wages" (Women 4:24). If this verse itself means anything, it is the existence of a correlation between men's enjoyment of women and the necessity of paying them their wages in return for that enjoyment. Reflecting this same meaning, some commentators held that in His statement, "God wanted for marriage to be enjoyed to the full. A group of people maintained this including al Hassan, Mujāhid, and one of the two accounts by al ʿAbbās."[76] Al Rāzī has also declared that a man has to give a woman her full dowry if he consummated the marriage and half of it if he only enjoyed the marriage contract.[77] This interpretation is surely in accord with what I previously asserted about the dowry being an option rather than a requirement. However, it is in perfect accord with the religious scholars and commentators' conception of marriage as a sale contract in which the husband pays wages to the woman in exchange for enjoying her.

Commentators, however, have a second reading of this aforesaid verse which derives its legitimacy from elements originating in the historical context. It suggests that there is a type of marriage, labeled "the marriage of pleasure," whereby a man hires a woman against a specific amount of money to have sexual intercourse with her during a determined time period.[78] All commentators agree that this form of marriage was made lawful during the lifetime of the Prophet, peace be upon him. They also agree that it was a marriage type practiced during the Prophet's time. In this respect, al Rāzī states, "The umma is in agreement that Islam sanctioned the marriage of pleasure. In the umma, no one has ever contested this."[79] Ibn ʿArabī also states that the marriage of pleasure was sanctioned in early Islam.[80] Not one commentator, not even a modernist, would veer from the consensus on the lawfulness of the marriage of pleasure. Ben ʿĀchūr, for example, states: "The marriage of pleasure is that in which the two spouses determine the duration or circumstance of the marriage contract. If that deadline is passed, the contract is non-binding. Islam has definitely sanctioned this marriage contract."[81]

While no disagreement occurred among commentators about the lawfulness of the marriage of pleasure, there was one about the abrogation of the marriage of pleasure. This is because this presupposed abrogation was not from the explicit text of the Qur'an, but rather derived its authority, to use Ben ʿĀchūr's words, from "some pretty shaky stories" about the Prophet, peace be upon him. The facets of this shakiness are different. The first is linked to the reiteration of prohibition and sanction more than once. According to Ibn ʿArabī, "As for the enjoyment of women, it is one of the mysteries of the shariʿa law because it was allowed in early Islam, then forbidden at the Battle of Khaybar, allowed again at the Battle of Awṭās, and forbidden again afterwards. It has since been settled now that it is forbidden."[82] This shakiness is linked to some disagreement over the times it was either forbidden or allowed as well as over their contexts. Al Rāzī, for instance, states:

> In most accounts, the Prophet, peace be upon him, forbade the marriage of pleasure and the eating of domestic donkeys on the Battle of Khaybar. In most accounts, he sanctioned the marriage of pleasure during his Farwell Pilgrimage and the Battle of Victory. These two days, which happened long after Khay-

bar, indicate that the story of the Prophet's abrogation of the marriage pleasure on the Battle of Khaybar is erroneous, because that which abrogates cannot precede that which is abrogated."[83]

Ben 'Āchūr also transmits other stories which are different, not to say, contradictory. If al Rāzī mentioned accounts indicating that the Prophet sanctioned the marriage of pleasure in his Farewell Pilgrimage, Ben 'Āchūr draws upon the authority of other accounts to indicate that the marriage of pleasure was forbidden by the Prophet during that same pilgrimage,

> Certainly allowed in Islam, it was forbidden on the Battle of Khaybar or most likely on the Battle of Hanīn. And those who maintained it was forbidden at the Battle of Khaybar stated are the ones who said it had been allowed at the Battle of Victory, and then forbidden on the third day of that battle. It is also said to have been forbidden on the Farwell Pilgrimage. Thus, said Abū Dāwūd who is mostly likely to be right. What is to be concluded is that the accounts regarding it are pretty shaky."[84]

Besides the shakiness of the "so-called" abrogation of the marriage of pleasure, accounts, strangely enough, are in accord that this kind of marriage continued to be practiced during the reign of Abū Bakr as Saddīq and 'Umar Ibn al Khattāb.[85] It is hard to believe that during the rule of these two caliphs the acting of seeking pleasure used to be against the shari'a law or a secret pleasure. If the supposed marriage of pleasure had occurred, it is hard to believe that Abū Bakr and 'Umar who were so close to the Prophet, peace be upon him, did not know anything about it. All of this leads to the conclusion that while certainly the marriage of pleasure is a controversial issue that draws its authority, not from an authoritative precedent, but rather on human *ijtihād*. Accounts almost all agree that it was 'Umar who first forbade the marriage of pleasure at the end of his reign.[86] On the authority of 'Alī Ibn Abī Tālib, al Tabrasī asserts that if it had not been for 'Umar who forbade the marriage of pleasure, only a wretch would have committed fornication.[87] If some refute this authoritative statement because al Tabrasī is a Shi'ī and the Shi'īs allow the marriage of pleasure, I shall point out that this story is reiterated in several other commentaries such *Jāmi'al Bayān* by Tabarī, *Mafātīh al Ghayb* by al Rāzī, and more recently the example of Ben 'Āchūr.[88] Commentaries relay 'Umar Ibn al Khattāb's declaration that it was he who had forbidden the marriage of pleasure, in that he said: "I forbid two types of pleasure which were allowed in the time of the Prophet, peace be upon him: the pleasure of al Hajj and the marriage of pleasure." Perplexed by 'Umar's explicit declaration, al Rāzī resorted to interpreting 'Umar's words stating: "What he meant ('Umar) was that the marriage of pleasure was allowed in the time of the Prophet, peace be upon him, and I forbid it when it was proven to me that he abrogated it, peace be upon him."[89] It is obvious that this interpretation is contrived for 'Umar's words assert that he was the one who abrogated these two pleasures, otherwise how will one explain that even though 'Umar forbade it, the pleasure of pilgrimage has not been abrogated, for one kind of pilgrimage that continues to be practiced today is the one branded the pilgrimage of pleasure? How is one to explain the practice of the marriage of pleasure during the reign of Abū Bakr on the one hand and 'Umar's silence over this explicit abrogation supposedly decreed by the Prophet on the other? Did 'Umar remain silent over that which had been confirmed about the Prophet, or did he remember this confirmed abrogation only after the death of the Prophet, peace be upon him, that is, after he had become caliph to all Muslims? Also, why did the disciples but 'Umar miss this obvious abrogation? The fact of the matter is simply that a man expressed his own opinion about the marriage of pleasure.[90] Let one not forget that 'Umar had prevented the application of two explicit Qur'anic decrees which are the cutting of hands and the giving of charity to those whose hearts have been reconciled. If the man dared to challenge the original text of the Qur'an, which the Great and Almighty God protected from any flaw or corruption, why is it surprising to see 'Umar forbidding the marriage of pleasure that the Prophet allowed?

What is agreed upon is that the accounts surrounding the marriage of pleasure are so shaky that some found only two ways out of this uncertainty. The first relies on quantity as a substitute for the absence of consensus. Al Rāzī, for example, strikes a comparison between the majority and the greatest majority of Muslims in that he says: "The greatest majority of the umma is of the opinion that it had become abrogated and the majority that it remained permissible as it had been."[91] It is not known what "statistical criteria" al Rāzī deployed to draw such distinctions. To bypass the shakiness of those accounts surrounding the marriage of pleasure, the second method asserted that it was allowed but only out of necessity such as eating the flesh of dead animals, blood, and swine. This is summarized in Ben 'Achūr's statement: "What is to be concluded from these various accounts is that the Prophet, peace be upon him, allowed the marriage of pleasure twice and forbade it twice. What is to be understood from that it was so, not by repeated abrogation, but through the authorization of its permissibility when necessitated. This is what made some people mistake this circumstantial license for an abrogation."[92] In the absence of an explicit text about the marriage of pleasure, it is peculiar to find Ibn al 'Abbās provide a different reading of the Qur'anic verse on pleasure, and one which would authorize the marriage of pleasure. In response to a question about the marriage of pleasure, Ibn al 'Abbās is said to have explained: "Such wives as you enjoy thereby for a limited period of time." That was how God revealed it, Ibn al 'Abbās swore. According to Habīb Ibn Thābit, "Ibn al 'Abbās gave me the Qur'an and said: 'This is my father's reading. In it you shall find what was previously stated.'"[93] A similar story exists in the commentary of al Tabrasī who states: "In his commentary on Habīb Ibn Abī Thābit, al Tha'labī mentions that he said: Ibn al 'Abbās gave me a Qur'anic book and said: This is according to my father's reading. In the Qur'anic book, I saw "such wives as you enjoy thereby for a limited period of time." Citing the authority of Abū Nadra, he said, I asked Ibn al 'Abbās about the marriage of pleasure, he said, Do not you read the sūra of Women? He said, do you not read "Such wives as you enjoy thereby for a limited period of time"? I said: "No, I do not read it that way." Ibn al 'Abbās said: "By God, this is how He the Great Almighty God revealed it three times."[94]

One may disregard the fact that this story is reminding of another one which as I demonstrated was tied to *al kalāla* and the disagreement over it. It is as if whenever the text was missing, the opinions different and the umma divided, a need was born for a story that had better be from the Qur'an that Ibn al 'Abbās cites, preferably one that is a verse comprising supplementary linguistic elements which explain what has been concealed and give the final verdict. Despite their importance, these stories are not the focus of my study. What is essential to me are these questions: What causes most commentators to feel embarrassed asserting the existence of the marriage of pleasure even though no text explicitly forbids it, and even if as I have shown, they themselves acknowledge the differences of opinions and the shakiness of the stories about it? In other words, is it possible to ask: What embarrassed the commentators and bothered them to the point of not allowing the marriage of pleasure?

What is sure is that the marriage of pleasure is not fornication because not based on debauchery. This is asserted in al Rāzī's statement: "Fornication is called debauchery because the only thing one intends is the spilling of water. This is not the case in the marriage of pleasure whereby the intent to spill water has been sanctified by God."[95] If the marriage of pleasure is "for a man to hire a woman for the purpose of sexual intercourse within a limited time period,"[96] it is then different from an "ordinary" marriage only in the type of contract that religious scholars view in both cases as a commercial transaction; a sale in the regular marriage contract and a lease in the marriage of pleasure. From this perspective, it is not possible to assume that the marriage of pleasure bothered commentators because it besmirched women's dignity as one often hears from modernist commentators. This is because selling and leasing are just the same in debasing women. The repugnance in the opinions of some people towards the marriage of pleasure is not because it is a marriage that does not allow the creation of a family. Indeed, the prevalent meaning of the family is a modern concept. In the lifetime of the Prophet and his disciples, even ordinary "marriage" did not used to be for the purpose of creating a "family." This was to come much later. The common practice of bedding slave women, polygamy, the easy way of getting a divorce, and the persistence of tribal ideas, did not give any weight to concepts unconceivable at the time, such as the family concept. The human gathering of Muslims used to give weight to another essential concept which is that of lineage (*nasab* نسب) as in "the child belongs to the marriage bed, and the adulterer gets the stone (i.e., nothing)."[97] The marriage of pleasure did not used to affect lineage because the status of children follows that of the enjoying father.[98]

It seems that the marriage of pleasure does not affect the social foundations of the old Muslim society as it upsets neither lineage nor does it transgress social fabric. What is perplexing, however, is the reservation against this marriage, which besides being mentioned in the explicit text of the Qur'an, is confirmed that it occurred during the time of Muhammad. Is not the reason for the embarrassment toward the marriage of pleasure that it is a form of marriage which allows woman to have some freedom contrary to the ordinary marriage contract which compares her not only to a sale contract, but also to those related to slavery and servitude? Does the one who leases have not more freedom than he who purchases? Does not the marriage of pleasure allow the woman to determine the duration of marriage then the annulment of the marriage contract, which to this day, is very difficult for her to do in many Muslim countries, even when the shari'a law allows it? Amāl Grāmī is of this opinion:

> If one is to contemplate the marriage of pleasure, it seems it would enable the woman to limit the duration of marriage, choose her husband, and go about her life away from male domination. Indeed, the motive behind the Shi'ī view of this type of marriage was less about the protection of women's rights than it was a denominational and political conflict.[99]

While I agree with her that the disagreement over the marriage of pleasure has a denominational and ideological dimension, I believe that the Qur'an's validation of the marriage of pleasure is one way of facilitating sexual life which Islam did not spurn contrary to its historical practices in modern societies, which under the conscious or unconscious influence of Christian views on sex started to view the temporary marriage of pleasure, not just as debauchery but even as a type of fornication. With this attitude, they forget or pretend to forget that the purpose of marriage from an Islamic perspective is the regulation of sexual life. Through this viewpoint, I become closer to 'Alī's position when he observed that if had not been for 'Umar who forbade the marriage of pleasure only a few people would have committed fornication. To this, one adds that if it had not been for 'Umar, there would not have been in Muslim societies today such a huge number of young men and women who are suffering from emotional deprivation and sexual frustration. I prefer for a child to be born at least within the context of a marriage of pleasure and be related to his/her father legitimately and legally, rather than see in many societies this increasing number of illegitimate children who find neither support, a caring guardian, nor any social recognition.

PERPLEXITY FIVE: ANAL INTERCOURSE

"Although the ulemas disagreed over the permissibility of having anal intercourse with women, many of them allowed it."[100] Those who did drew upon the Almighty's statement: "Your women are a tilth for you, so go to your tilth as you please" (The Heifer 2:223). Because the manifest meaning of the general verse does not specify the place of penetration, Ibn Nāfi' has reported that Ibn 'Umar used to say: "The verse is intended to allow anal intercourse with women." Those who sided with this statement were Mālek Ibn Anas and the Shi'i Sayyid al Murtadh. Other commentators refuted this reading of the verse holding that what is intended is that man has the choice of having vaginal sex with her either from the front or the back. This is implied in His statement "as you please."[101]

If those who allowed anal intercourse relied on the manifest meaning of a general verse, those who rejected it cited a number of arguments compiled by al Rāzī, which I will cite for the question marks they raise. In the first argument, al Rāzī proclaims that God forbade sexual intercourse with women during menses because harmful.[102] "Harm has no meaning other than what harms a human being." For al Rāzī, "it is in the foul smell of the menstrual blood that resides the harm to man. The existence of this same cause in the contentious location (i.e., anal intercourse) seems more obvious. Therefore, if that cause subsists here, it must not be allowed."[103] Deploying that same analogical reasoning, Al Tūsī states, "It is not allowed to penetrate a woman anally in any case because for reasons of temporary impurity God forbade her vagina during menstruation. Similarly, her anus must be forbidden because of its permanent impurity.[104] It is on the principle of analogy that this argument is based. In fact, al Rāzī and al Tūsī are comparing the prohibition of anal intercourse to the prohibition against having sex with a menstruating woman. The analogy requires the existence of a common cause for the prohibition, which is harm, impurity, and foul smells, in the opinion of the two commentators. If one is to look at the explicit text of the Qur'an, one finds that the Almighty God forbade going unto women during menstrual cycle on the proclamation that it is "harm." It is not known from where al Rāzī established that the harm meant the foul smell of menstrual blood, nor is it known from where al Tūsī established that impurity was what was intended by harm. The cause for forbidding sexual intercourse with women during their menstruations is general and imprecise, for harm, according to the explicit text of the Qur'an, has various and different sources, and does not necessarily refer to impurity and foul smells.[105]

The second argument of those who forbade anal intercourse draws authority from the Almighty's statement: "When they have purified themselves, then come unto them from wherever God has commanded you" (The Heifer 2:222). If the imperative tense may signify in this context the existence of two possibilities—the command to go in unto them on the one hand and the command to go in unto them in a particular place on the other—al Rāzī rejects the first possibility in that he says, "Since the command's manifest meaning is obligation, one cannot say that what is meant is the obligation to go in unto them, because that is not compulsory."[106] It is odd that al Rāzī would categorically affirm that having sex with the wife is not an obligation while some religious scholars hold that a husband who does not have sex with his wife for a while causes her harm, which could be a ground for separating the two spouses.[107] Let's hypothetically suppose that the command was to go in unto the woman in the place God has ordained. In this case, who determines this place? Al Rāzī just states: "This (place) is not understood as the anus because by consensus that is not a requirement." Do these words by al Rāzī mean that "from wherever God commanded you" can indicate only one place while the verse, because of the ambiguity in the adverbial expression of place "haythu" (حيث), defines neither one place nor one sexual practice at the exclusion of another. For al Rāzī, consensus is more significant than the general and explicit meaning of the text.

The third argument of those who forbade anal intercourse is that the Almighty God counts women as a tilth for men and only from this perspective allows the coming in unto them: "Your women are a tilth for you, so go to your tilth as you please" (The Heifer 2:223). For al Rāzī, this verse is about the act of tilling. He also considers that the place of this tilth denotes the coming in unto women vaginally for the purpose of having children.[108] In his viewpoint, al Rāzī explains the metaphor of tilling by the resemblance between sowing seeds into earth and women. Since anal intercourse does not lead to procreation, it is forbidden for it does not count as tilling. However, this argument is perplexing because in stylistics, the referent in a metaphor is absent while resemblance is possible but not absolute. For example, to say that this woman is a flower may indicate that she is beautiful, but it may also mean that she has a nice smell. The same applies to the above cited verse. On the one hand, what indicates that the metaphor of tilling does not refer to amazing sex in addition to the male organ's penetration of the vagina? Also, why is the sowing of seeds the only point of resemblance between woman and earth? Why cannot the point of resemblance be the possibility of tilling in the active sense? On the other hand, all commentators and religious scholars allow men to have sex with women in ways other than vaginal sex or anything similar, whereby penetration is not restricted to those places where procreation occurs. [109] If one is to refute that, then a second look is to be given at those transmitted accounts in which the Prophet, peace be upon him, used to have sex with Aysha while she had her period. If he did not approach her as one would a tilth, in the sense asserted by al Rāzī, then how did he do it, he who is a Prophet and a model for all Muslims? Al Rāzī's argument denies all sexual practices except for vaginal penetration and this for the sake of procreation. Yet, "consensus" goes beyond that to include other practices delineated by the religious scholars themselves.

The three aforesaid arguments all rely on an interpretation of the Qur'an that I tried to show was monolithic and contrived or at least open to discussion and refutation. As for the fourth argument, it relies on the Sunnah as in the following statement by al Rāzī: "Khuzayma Ibn Thābit reported that a man had asked the Prophet, peace be upon him, about coming in unto women in the anus. The messenger said it is halal. When the man came back, he called him and said to him how he put it, in what two orifices, openings, or slits. If it is from front to front, it is yes. If it is from back to front, it is yes, but from back to anus, it is no. God shies not away from what is righteous, 'Do not come in unto women in the anus.'" [110] It is difficult not to raise questions regarding the authenticity of this hadith. Indeed, proving it would make us perplexed regarding the assertion of Mālek and of other religious scholars that of the permissibility of having anal sex with women, especially given, that this religious scholar is well-known for accepting only the Prophet's authenticated hadiths. Has Mālek heard of this hadith, or is this hadith itself fabricated? And if there is consensus about the authenticity of this hadith, what makes a commentator like al Rāzī interpret the Qur'an, use analogy, and look for hidden resemblances in order to forbid anal intercourse while the hadith was enough to confirm that it is forbidden? Take for example, Ben 'Achūr. Despite his uneasiness to raise this question and declaration that it was worth looking into given its frequency on people's tongues and pens did not cite the aforesaid hadith, but even asserted "some dispute over the content of this verse in the opinions of commentators and religious scholars." [111] As for Tabarī, despite his verbosity on the subject of anal intercourse and the long section he devoted to present the opinions of those who allowed and forbade it, he makes no reference at all to the aforesaid hadith and concludes his extensive exposition, which is always the case with the readings he favors (i.e., those which forbid). What is important is that Tabarī, who has most relied on precedence in his commentaries, does not favor forbidding on the basis of a hadith, but on a figurative interpretation of the word tilth in that he states: "Obvious is the error of he who claimed that His statement 'so go to your tilth as you please' is proof that it is allowed to have anal intercourse with women, for nothing could be tilled from an anus." [112]

On the other hand, it is difficult not to raise questions about the form of the hadith itself, which although based on segments and elaborate details, does not mention any place (i.e., any "specific locale") when the Prophet enumerates the various ways of coming in unto women. The hadith acknowledges that he, peace be upon him, mentioned and allowed vaginal intercourse from the front and the back while forbidding anal intercourse from the back. However, he did not say anything about anal intercourse from the front. Why not? Does that mean that this sexual practice was not common then or simply that the hadith was fabricated in support of the view that anal intercourse was forbidden?

The Prophet's hadith sends one back to the cause of revelation some claimed for the verse, "Your women are a tilth for you," was revealed in connection with opposing the Jews who said if the man had sex with his woman from the back, her child would be cross-eyed.[113] In another account, "Some people, who were friends to the Prophet, peace be upon him, sat together one day with a Jewish man. So, some of them said: I come in unto my wife when she is lying. The other said: I come in unto her when she is standing. Another said: I come in unto her when she is lying on her side. The Jewish man said, 'You are like donkeys. We come in unto women only in one way.' So, God revealed his statement, 'Your women are a tilth for you.'"[114] What is important is that this account in its two versions locates the verse in the context of opposing the Jews and it is an opposition that is echoed in several verses and hadiths which call for dissimilarity from all disbelievers, Christians and Jews, whether in the *qibla*[115] one follows or on the level appearance.[116]

Interestingly enough, Tabarī, who is known for collecting and accumulating the hadith, mentions another cause for the revelation of the verse on "tilling" which would make anal intercourse allowed in that he says: "Zayd Ibn Aslam reported that Ibn 'Umar said: A man had anal intercourse with his wife. Then his conscience troubled him. So, God revealed his verse, 'Your women are a tilth for you.'"[117] Because of their contradictions and differences, these accounts show that the issue has not been resolved yet. If they prove anything, the conditional statements found among some commentators such as "He who comes in unto a woman in the anus is cursed," it is that these hadiths were fabricated to confirm a prohibition, which had an absolute text asserted, would have been the subject of dispute among Muslim ulema and religious scholars.

The condemnation of most Muslims today of anal intercourse is perhaps due to the sexual relations between two men which are seen as repulsive and horrible as it shall be seen. This condemnation which is based on some unconscious comparison finds echo in ancient texts. Indeed, Ibn al Kathīr mentions a hadith which not only establishes a relation of contiguity and connectedness between sexual intercourse between homosexual men and men's sexual intercourse with women in the anus, but also makes punishment for those who do it. This hadith, which is attributed to the Prophet, says,

"God does not look at a man who comes in into a man or a woman in the anus." Even though Ibn al Kathīr stressed the strangeness[118] of this hadith, the association of these cited sexual practices became so common that some recent commentators described anal intercourse with women as "minor liwāt." Yet, the early commentaries are devoid of this fabricated concept. It is interesting that the comparison between "minor liwāt" and "major liwāt" did not only generate condemnation, but a reading which allowed penetration in the anus among some groups who did not see anything wrong with it, given their interpretation of the statement of the High and Almighty God: "What! Of all creatures do you come unto the males, leaving your wives that your Lord created for you? Nay! You are but a transgressing people" (The Poets 26:165–166). In their opinion, why would you leave behind what you could get from your wives implies that if God had not allowed that (i.e., sexual intercourse with spouses in the anus), His statement would not have made any sense.[119]

What is important is not to analyze if a husband's anal intercourse with his wife is allowed or forbidden, because this is a personal issue that concerns only the two spouses. It only depends on their approval and on their reading of the previous verse in light of the various meaning of the word tilling and coming in unto the spouse, either in the place ordained by God or elsewhere. What is important in these accounts is the sharp conflict or rather contradictions which commentators not only did not accept, but also attempted as usual to do violence to the Qur'an's general nature and openness to interpretation, and this by trying to refute the opinions of "a good number of disciples and followers"[120] to ascertain one viewpoint on the basis of hadiths which are either weak or fabricated.[121]

PERPLEXITY SIX: CHILD MARRIAGE

Child marriage is a relative issue that differs from one society and one century to another. Yet, some "Islamic" laws set a minimum legal age for marriage to the man and woman, which vary from one Islamic law to another. There is a big difference, indeed, between the Tunisian law which holds eighteen to be the minimum legal age for the marriage of girls and other cultures where girls still get married at ten. Very often, those who study this question rely on the established historical account of the Prophet's marriage to Aysha, peace be upon him, in that he signed the marriage contract when she was six and consummated the marriage when she was nine.[122] This story became widespread and became the subject of controversy between those who saw this marriage as "strange" and unbecoming of a Prophet and those who saw it as an ordinary matter in specific historical time periods and particular societies. Many of us, undoubtedly, remember that at the beginning of the last century child marriage was a common practice in Tunisia. Those of us who did not have a grandmother or great grandmother who got married very young are very few. On the one hand, I will not defend the Prophet because he does not need it after he has himself proven many times that he is only a human being and after God asserted this in the Qur'an by reproving his messenger and blaming him at times.[123] On the other hand, I will not wear out the story of the Prophet's marriage to Aysha and count it as a simple ordinary issue that all people accepted at the time of the Prophet. This marriage has caused the bewilderment of Abū Bakr who was astonished by the Prophet's request to marry Aysha. If the cause of this astonishment was not necessarily Aysha's age and her father's worries about her, it was at least the age difference between the bride and bridegroom. Indeed, "'Abdullah Ibn Yūsuf narrates from Layth, who narrates from Yazīd Ibn 'Irāk, who narrates from 'Arwa that when the Prophet asked for Aysha's hand from Abū Bakr, Abū Bakr said to him: I am your brother. He said: You are my brother in God's religion and Book and I am allowed to marry her."[124] In another account, Abū Bakr said to the Prophet when he asked for Aysha's hand, "Can a man marry the daughter of his brother?"[125]

I will not seek justification for an incident in the Prophet's personal life, for he has never requested that his personal lifestyle be taken as a model. The amalgamation between the Prophet's personal and intimate life and what he transmitted from the Almighty God is the biggest illusion religious scholars have ever believed and passed on to the Muslim masses. If the Prophet has certainly presented himself as a role model for Muslims through the sacred statements and actions mentioned in the mission he preached, what is also undoubtedly true is that the Prophet used to act like any human being sometimes. His behavior is not one to be necessarily followed, given the fact that it is question of personal taste and historical context. Is the love of the Prophet, peace upon him, for porridge good enough reason for Muslims to like it? Is his reluctance to eat lizards or drink almond milk a good enough reason for them to be repulsed by lizards and avoid almond milk?[126] Is his marriage to nine women a good enough reason for Muslims to marry nine wives like him, which many commentators allowed in their readings of the verse about marrying two, three, and four women?[127] Or is his marriage to a woman older and richer than him a call for the necessity of young Muslim men to marry women who are older and richer than they are? Or are the accounts in which he is said to have in one single night[128] sexual intercourse with all of his wives a good enough reason to count any Muslim who is incapable of matching that performance as a dissident from Islamic tradition? The vacillation between on the one hand the assertion that only certain matters apply to the Prophet—such as his betrothal to a woman who asked him for marriage, the women who gave themselves to him as a gift, or his own marriage without a dowry—and the assertion on the other that it was part of the Sunnah to follow in his footsteps shows a big contradiction, for what marks the human character from the divine message conveyed through Muhammad's tongue and behavior? It is true that the High and Almighty God urges one to follow that which was given by the Prophet and abstain from that he forbade,[129] but what is meant by this verse is that *one follows what God commanded his Prophet to reveal to us and that one abstains from what God commanded his Prophet to forbid to us.*[130] As we emphasize the historical context behind Muhammad's message, we do emphasize at the same time the private context of the Prophet's personal life, for nothing in the marriage of this fifty-year-old man to a nine-year-old girl indicates explicitly or implicitly that Muslims should follow in his footsteps. While this is a personal issue that is tied to a historical context, the words of the Almighty are general and valid in any time and place. This leads me to look at the Qur'an's position toward child marriage.

It is ascertained that the Qur'an did not set any minimum age for marriage for either men or women. However, one of the Qur'anic verses allows, as the occasion may require, the possibility of marrying a woman who has not menstruated yet. This is based on His statement: "As for your women who have despaired of further menstruating, if you are in doubt, their *'iddah* waiting period shall be three months; and those who have not menstruated as yet" (Divorce 65:4). Transforming this possible linguistic possibility into an explicit text, Ibn 'Arabī asserted that "His statement, 'And those who have not menstruated as yet" refers to young girls whose *'iddah* is to be counted by month, given the absence of the possibility of verifying it by other means usually." God's statement is *"proof that it was possible to give one's young children in marriage*[131] because in His statement, the Almighty God made three months the waiting period of that woman who has not menstruated yet. And unless the marriage has been consummated, she is not bound by the *'iddah*. So marvelous is He in his wonders!"[132] Under no circumstances can this occasional necessity, which is conveyed through language and endorsed by the following cause of revelation, be refuted. A man is said to have stood and said, O Prophet of God! What is the *'iddah* of a young one who has not menstruated yet? And so came the revelation, "and those who have not menstruated as yet."[133] The fact that the High and Almighty God allows the marriage of those women who have not menstruated yet is not a negation of the marriage of those men who have not reached puberty yet. In another context, the Qur'an makes reference to those who reached the age of marriage, male or female, and distinguishes them from those who reached maturity, stating: "Test well the orphans, until they reach the age of marrying; then, if you perceive in them right judgment, deliver over unto them their property" (Women 4:6). Thus, reaching the age of marriage does not necessarily mean one has reached maturity in the diverse opinions of commentators who restricted it to a number of time frames. For them, a marriageable age usually necessitates wet dreams in the case of the male and menstruations in the female, which contradicts Ben 'Achūr's assertion "that people may marry their daughters before puberty and also their sons in some special cases" which he sees as circumstantial cases. [134]

Marriage has two dimensions, a sexual and a social one. For the sexual dimension, it rests on the existence of a sexual relationship between the two spouses in marriage. If it is possible to marry one who did not reach puberty yet, male or female, to a male or female who also did not reach puberty, there might be no sexual relationships, at least in the commonly held sense. If it happens in one way or another, it would not raise an important issue as it would be taken as "children's play." As for the marriage of one who reached maturity (i.e., an adult or an old man to one who did not), it does raise a problem because it falls within what is called in modern laws as a "child sexual abuse." While aware that the concept of the "child" as an independent self is a modern concept and that the rights of the child are perhaps even more modern, the modernity of these concepts must not preclude one from reading the position of the Qur'an, which is valid in any place and time, regarding the marriage of an adult male to the young girl who did not menstruate yet. If the Qur'an allowed this type of marriage, it is most likely not to set a rule or as a goal in itself, but to accommodate a historical reality that was common. It is remarkable that the only Qur'anic verse, which would sexualize little girls by allowing on occasional necessity the marriage of those who have not menstruated yet, coincides with another verse which removes anyone who did not reach puberty from the sexual realm. Indeed, a woman is permitted to reveal her non-outward adornments to those children who know naught of women's private parts. [135] And here there was a dispute over the meaning of the word "male child," which is an all-inclusive label that applies to all male children until they have wet dreams. Here, it has two meanings: In the first, "it is those male children who neither pictured women's private parts, nor knew anything about it since their tender age." In the second, "it is those male children who have not grown enough to be capable of coming in unto women." [136] And although al Rāzī has incidentally pointed out that a grown-up woman may lust after a male child, it is most likely that in Jāhiliyyan and early Muslim society it was acceptable to view a prepubescent male child as a sex object. This may explain why on the legal level no text explicitly forbade marriage to under-aged female children and on the cultural level the poetry about the fully-ripe *ghilmān* [137] as well as the emphasis on their prepubescent young age. This is what transpires from the following story: "A pimp brought a lūtī client a male prostitute who just grew a beard. The lūtī asked: How much is he? He said, 'Last year, he was a 100 dirhams.' He said, 'I asked you about this year, not last year. My grandmother's dowry used to be 10,000 dirhams and when she died and was taken to the cemetery, it was 20 dirhams. This one's death is the growth of his beard.'"[138] The Qur'an's accommodation of the practice of child marriage, given that it was a historical reality then, has become to some an anachronistic law. This anachronistic ahistorical reading explains why some Muslim countries to this day continue to allow the marriage of under-aged girls which may lead to disastrous consequences on both the physical and psychological level.[139] Some people's argument that some girls mature faster than others is of no consequence because medicine proves that if penetration is to occur between a grown-up male and a prepubescent girl, it could cause a young a girl physical pain, not to mention psychological troubles. This is echoed in the following account by Aysha who attended the Prophet's explanation, peace be upon him, of the following two verses, "We have created them anew and virgins we made them" (The Event 56:35–36). He said, peace upon him: "The word "*atrāban*" means people who are of similar or equal in age. Every time a husband comes in unto his spouse, he finds her a virgin. When Aysha, peace be upon her, heard that from the Prophet, peace be upon him, she said, 'Oh! It is so painful!' And he said, peace be upon him, there is no pain."[140] As previously stated, marriage has two dimensions, a sexual and a psychological one. While the first has been covered, the psychological dimension, which is tied to the foundation of a family and which I held to be a modern concept since my discussion of the marriage of pleasure, is yet to be seen. The non-existence of this dimension in the past is perhaps what explains why child marriage was not an embarrassing practice. This is because concepts such as family responsibility and intellectual and emotional maturity which would allow a girl to be a mother were not conceivable concepts in the context of a society founded on the steadiness of tribal lifestyle. No wonder that in such cases, a girl could give birth at the age of thirteen or fourteen.

I shall go beyond that and argue that viewing puberty as the starting point of legal responsibility was only a relative and historically situated perspective, for nothing in the Qur'an indicates that puberty is the crucial starting point of legal responsibility. Can one imagine a law which would hold a fourteen-year-old child accountable to the same degree as a forty-year adult, who reached full strength in the explicit words of the Qur'an?[141] What is meant here is not to accustom the child to praying or fasting or any other religious duty. Rather, what one has to be conscious of is that the child's view of the world is different from that of a young person or a grown-up. In drawing such an explicit distinction between attaining the age of marriage and maturity (Women 4:6) (i.e., between biological and intellectual maturity), the Almighty is opening for us the door to *ijtihād* in this field. If some commentators have asserted that it is not possible to give an orphan any of their money until they turn eighteen or twenty-five,[142] or until one is sure about the righteousness of their beliefs and present life, or their ability to handle money for others, it would be more appropriate and more becoming that a Muslim gets married only when she or he understands the responsibility of marriage and of having children, unless one considers handling money is more difficult than bearing the responsibility to build a family and rear children (i.e., if one is to understand material capital more important than the human one). One has to reconsider the concept of biological maturity as the beginning of total responsibility and this by starting with the Qur'an's distinction between biological and intellectual maturity. One has also to reconsider the view in which biological maturity alone. is the condition for the possibility of marriage. This is what the Tunisian law reflects for example. And even if the primary issue, that is, responsibility is a pure intellectual matter—because each person's responsibility is to the Great and Almighty God—the second issue is a legal and social issue which affects equilibrium in society at large and invites one to legalize the minimal age for marriage in a way that is commensurate with societies' natures and the differences in the way they construct their own values and beliefs throughout time.

PERPLEXITY SEVEN: POLYANDRY AND POLYGAMY

In the pre-Islamic Arabian Peninsula, taking multiple spouses was not exclusive to men, for it seems it was as common for men to take more than one wife as it was possible for women to take more than one spouse in one type of marriage known in Jāhiliyya as the marriage of *al dhimād* (الضّماد).[143] There was also another type of marriage called the marriage of *Istibdhā'* (الاستبضاع). It consists of having the husband tell his woman after she had purified herself from menstruation, "Send for so and so and get pregnant from him." The husband would then avoid his wife and not touch her until her pregnancy from that man she had sexual intercourse with shows. If the pregnancy is confirmed, the husband lies with her. It was for the purpose of giving birth to a son, that he would do that. It was also possible for a group of men, who are less than ten, to share one woman. If she gets pregnant and gives birth, she sends out for all of them—and none of them can decline—and tells them, "You know now the consequence of what you did. I gave birth. Here is your son, o, so and so," and she would designate whoever she likes by name, so that he (the son) be affiliated with him.[144] Islam has apparently annulled all of these types of marriages according to the accounts transmitted by Aysha who asserts: "When Muhammad was sent out to preach righteousness, he destroyed all the marriages of al Jāhiliyya."[145] In the Qur'an the only wedding or marriage that is allowed is the one based on *Ihçān* or protection, which requires, according to religious commentators, the existence of a dowry, vows and consent, two witnesses, and a legal guardian for the woman. As I explained the dowry is possible but not required in marriage. As for the witnesses, who are at least two, they are required because with them one distinguishes between marriage and "*mukhādana*" (المخادنة) cited in the Qur'an and which consists of taking a secret lover. As for vows and consent, these delineate the required approval of both sides. As for the guardian, there is a dispute over it among religious scholars, which denies it the quality of an absolute prerequisite.[146]

Nothing in the Qur'an prohibits the marriage of a woman with more than one man. Despite that, commentators, to justify their invalidation of the practice of having two male spouses share a woman, rely on the two verses in which the Almighty enumerates the women one is prohibited to marry and among them are married women.[147] What is problematic in the explicit statements of all commentators is their reliance on the one word "*muhaçana*" (محصنة). This word, indeed, denotes several meanings. According to commentators, the *muhaçana* refers to free and chaste women, polytheist women who have spouses, Muslim women who have spouses, and women in general. The context of the verse cannot denote the meaning of chastity because, for it is unimaginable that the Great and Almighty God would forbid marriage to chaste women. As for the meaning of *ihçān* in the sense of freedom, it is possible if the verse is read as, "We forbade you among women those who are free and allowed you those your right hands possess."[148] In this sense, the verse allows sexual intercourse with slave women and prohibits *zinā*, which would concord with the rest of the Qur'anic context. Yet, this explanation would not prohibit the marriage of a Muslim woman to more than one man. If one was to hold that the word "*muhaçanāt*" refers to all women, the verse would mean then, "And we forcefully forbade to you those women previously cited and forbade to you all women, save those your right hand possesses or those you shall buy, and all of them are what your right hands possess."[149] This prevalent interpretation does not prohibit in turn the marriage of a Muslim woman to more than one man.

As for reading the word "*muhaçanāt*" as those women who have spouses, it continues to be allowed and it is this meaning which prohibits the marriage of a Muslim woman to more than one spouse. However, even if on the one hand this meaning resolves the problem of the absence of any explicit Qur'an prohibition of polyandry, it places on the other hand commentators and Muslims in front of another embarrassment which is even greater. If the Great and Almighty God's prohibition of marrying women who are protected (i.e., married), is common and logical, but excluding from them those who are slaves is embarrassing. Does the Qur'anic statement mean that slave women are not forbidden to have more than one spouse? Or does it mean that a Muslim man can snatch a woman from her husband just because she is a slave? Many commentators are of this opinion and hold that it is permissible for the kidnapper to marry a woman he kidnapped during a slave raid even if she had a spouse and that it was allowed to sell a slave woman even if this would separate her from her husband. This made Mālek Ibn Anas state:

"Save those your right hands possess, it is forbidden to marry those women whose spouses are free men. And he does not see anything wrong in the fact that a man would snatch his slave woman from his slave man."[150] Slave-raiding in itself is an embarrassment from the modern point of view of human rights, let alone snatching a kidnapped woman from her husband during a slave raid. This is what brought a commentator like Ben 'Āchūr to say: "God made in slave-raiding the destruction of marriage, in accord with was customary among previous nations in times of war and in order to scare them from standing against Islam. Had slave-raiding been lifted, they would have rushed to fight Muslims like rabid dogs, for nothing terrifies Arabs in times of war more than the kidnapping of their women."[151] Regardless of the fact that Muslims did not fight only Arabs during their futūhāt conquests, in his attempt to explain why slave raiding still existed and how it destroyed marriage, the modernist commentator Ben 'Āchūr reflects an attitude that is clearly defensive and self-justifying.

In fact, Ibn 'Abbas and Mujāhid were perplexed by the verse which proclaimed that except for those who were slaves, marriage with married women was forbidden. It was Mujāhid who said: "If I knew anyone knowing its meaning, I would slaughter a camel and serve him its liver."[152] But this perplexity was not a stumbling stone for commentators, who despite the fact that they agreed that the previous verse absolutely prohibited the marriage of a Muslim woman to more than one husband, have all asserted this prohibition on the ground that it was an evident issue, even though not asserted in any existing text. It is superfluous to state that one's goal behind this observation is not to assert the possibility that a woman could be married to more than one spouse, but to demonstrate that what allows this assertion is not an absolute text, but a prevalent custom in patrilineal societies which continues to be used in those societies branded as modern. Indeed, the Tunisian law for example prohibits only polygamy, not polyandry, and on the basis of custom, undoubtedly.

If one takes a look at what used to be allowed with a Qur'anic text such as having sex with slave women, one finds that the Qur'an did not restrict sexual relations with slaves to men, but rather refers to those whom your right hand possesses in a general manner just as it does in reference to spouses in general. It is the commentators who restricted those whom your right hand possesses to men at the exclusion of women. This is most evident in their reading of the Almighty's statement: "Successful indeed are the believers, who are humble in their prayers, who turn away from idle talk, who give charity, and who guard their private parts save for their spouses or those their right hands possess, for no blame is to be laid on them" (The Believers 23:1–6). Even though the believers' characteristics are general and for men and women, commentators were of a different opinion. Ibn 'Arabī, indeed, stated:

One of the Qur'anic wonders is that the words regarding men and women are general like all other words in the Qur'an which involve them except for His statement, "who guard their private parts," which is addressed only to men at the exclusion of women, as demonstrated in His statement, "save for their spouses or those their right hands possess." And in sexual intercourse women are not allowed to have sex with those whom their right hands possess. Indeed, it is known through other evidence that a woman has to guard her private parts generally through verses such as those particularly on *ihçān* and other evidences.[153]

Ibn 'Arabī's reading is remarkable in that it illustrates how commentators project their own social or tribal concepts on the general and text of the Qur'an and its multiplicity of meanings, which although one may not fully grasp, it is sufficient to proclaim their probability. One of these multiple meanings is what brought a free Muslim woman to have sex with her slave boy. Indeed, Ibn al 'Athīr has reported the following story,

> Ibn al Jarīr said: Muhammad Ibn Bashār reported on behalf of 'Abd al 'A'lā, on behalf of Sa'īd, on behalf of Qutāda, that a woman came unto her slave man and said, I have interpreted a verse from God's book, "or what your right hands possess." He said she was brought to 'Umar Ibn al Khatāb. Some people from the disciples of the Prophet, peace upon him, told him, "She interpreted a verse from God's book in an improper way." He said: He struck the slave with his sword cracking his head. And said [to the woman]: You are forbidden for Muslim men after him.

Even though Ibn al Athīr acknowledges the strangeness of this account,[154] it is repeated in a similar story by al Qurtubī. Whether this story is a true event or a fabrication, in both cases it reveals two essential matters: The first is tied to the fact that the woman interpreted the verse. This proves that the woman's reading is permissible, at least on the linguistic level. Indeed, al Qurtubī explicitly asserts this permissibility by emphasizing that consensus is what restricts having sex with slaves to men and the Qur'anic text has nothing to do with it.[155]

The second issue the account reveals is closely tied to 'Umar's severe punishment, for he kills the slave and deprives the woman of sexual relations for the rest of her life. Even though this severity matches 'Umar's rough personality especially towards women, it has a broader significance in that it shows that the idea that a free woman could have sex with a slave, which means she can have sex with two men (a husband and a slave that her right hand possesses), was such a strange idea considering the symbolic representations of social relations in Muslim society.

It follows that polyandry does not seem to be an issue that can be seriously raised among Muslims, for it is only an odd or rather comic possibility, given the fact that it is not conceivable at all in the real world. As for polygamy, it is a serious issue which existed in Jāhiliyyan period and continued after Islam, albeit with a quantitative delimitation making any number of wives above four akin to *zinā*. Only in two verses does the Qur'an refer to polygamy. The first is in the Almighty's statement, "If you fear that you will not act justly towards the orphans, marry such women as seem good to you, two, three, four; but if you fear you will not be equitable, then only one, or what your right hand owns; so it is likelier you will not do injustice." The second is the statement of the Great and Almighty God, "And you will not be able to be equitable between your wives, however much you see to it" (Women 4:129). Needless it is to go another time over the commonplace view that the first verse requires equity between the women as a condition for having multiple wives and that the second verse asserts the impossibility of that equity which would negate the permissibility of having multiple wives according to some. It is also needless to indicate that other commentators solved this problematic on the level of consistency by considering that the equity that is possible is that which pertains to financial support and the number of nights with each wife and the equity which is impossible is that which pertains to emotions and feelings because hearts rest with the Great and Almighty God. This way, having multiple wives is allowed because one has achieved material equity even if not that impossible equity on the emotional level.[156]

What is central is neither the comparison of the two verses, nor the debate over the meaning of equity. Rather, what I seek to reexamine is the first verse frequently seen as the one verse which allows polygamy. This is in order to elucidate the confusion behind this widespread position. It is my argument that this verse was not cited in the context of allowing multiple wives, for it is asserted in Sahīh that

> 'Urwa asked Aysha about this verse and she has said "This verse is about the orphan girl who lives with her guardian and shares his wealth. Her wealth and beauty may tempt him to marry her without giving her an adequate *mahr* (dowry) which might have been given by another suitor. So, such guardians were forbidden to marry such orphan girls unless they treated them justly and gave them the most suitable *mahr*; otherwise they were ordered to marry any other woman."[157]

In another story, Aysha mentions what the Qur'an said in regard of those orphans who are girls: "This is about the orphan girl who lives with her guardian and shares his wealth. Because he has no desire to marry her and hates that another suitor marries her and has a stake in what has been so far his wealth, the guardian would imprison her. So God forbade them to do that."[158] The permissibility of polygamy, before even one comes to the disputed condition of equity, is subject to the fear of the guardian's injustice to the orphan girl in the two meanings mentioned by Aysha. In the first sense, a man was not allowed to marry more than one woman unless he was intending to do injustice to an ophan girl in his care by marrying her. In the second sense, a man is not allowed to refuse marrying an orphan girl he raised with her money while preventing her from getting married out of fear another man may share the wealth. In the absence of these two circumstances, the Qur'an did not allow polygamy even if it did not forbid it. It is however the commentators who pretended not to know all of this without really being unaware. While they were not oblivious of the Qur'an's condition for polygamy which the Sunnah also endorses, they negated it by relying as usual on consensus as an argument to substitute human concepts for the meanings in the divine text. For example, Ibn 'Arabī asserts that the indication in this discourse is obsolete by consensus, for it is permitted to anyone who knows he is fair to the orphan girl to marry someone else. Should he fear being unfair, he is likewise allowed to marry her."[159]

It is a fact that religious scholars and commentators view polygamy as a given. They not only ignore the Qur'an and what has been transmitted through Aysha, but also go beyond that to ignore an authentic hadith attributed to the Prophet, peace be upon him, according to which he forbids 'Alī Ibn Abī Tālib to take more than one wife. From his pulpit, the Prophet, peace upon him, said: "Benī Hishām Ibn al Mughīra requested my permission to marry their daughter to 'Alī Ibn Abī Tālib. And I won't allow it, and I won't allow it and I won't allow unless Ibn Abī Tālib wants to divorce my daughter and marry theirs. She is a piece of me. What upsets her upsets me and what harms her harms me."[160] This account confirms in an explicit text by the Prophet that polygamy causes harm to the first wife (i.e., to Fātimah, the daughter of the Prophet). The harm is not so much specific to her as it is tied to the principle of the second marriage itself, for the Prophet, peace be upon him, did not mention anything wrong in the desired second wife. Al Bukhārī himself classifies this statement by the Prophet as a matter of "protecting the daughter, out of concern and justice." One person cannot protect another unless some harm may befall them. Does not the word *adhdhabbu* (الذبّ) mean defense, prevention, and advocacy? The Prophet's declaration that polygamy causes harm can be interpreted in two ways. The first is in accord with my previous statement that the Qur'an neither allowed nor prohibited polygamy. And from here, the Sunnah would be endorsing the Qur'an in that it shows how polygamy is harmful and seeks its prohibition according to the principle of an abrogation which extends over many centuries to gradually fight one of the evils of Jāhiliyya.[161] This is not anomalous for slavery, which the Qur'an neither supported nor forbade, has been forbidden by Muslims in the same way as polygamy from the viewpoint of law. As for the second interpretation for the Prophet's declaration that polygamy was harmful, it rests on the assumption that the "I" who speaks in the previous account was not the Prophet, but the father. This means that the human side of the Prophet could, for personal reasons, forbid that which the Almighty allowed in that he allows polygamy to all Muslim men except the husband of his daughter. I will not stop at this position as this could undermine the universality of the Mission and its holiness. Is this transmitted account about the Prophet as Fatimah's father really different from that supposed statement that has been transmitted through Ummu Salmah? "She, who dies and her husband is pleased with her, shall enter paradise."[162] Is not Fātimah counted among those women whose husbands are pleased with? Is it not important that 'Alī Ibn Abī Tālib marries the woman he wanted to marry so that he dies pleased with his wife Fātimah so that she may enter paradise?

If one is to posit that polygamy is allowed in Islam despite the Qur'anic provisions and the Prophet's worries, it is then important to investigate the reasons for its permissibility as in the eyes of religious scholars and commentators. Only three reasons keep reoccurring:

1. The number of women who are righteous enough for marriage is higher than that of the men who are righteous enough for marriage This is because "in every nation there are more women than men, especially given that females outnumber the males among the newly-born infants."[163]

2. "The fertility period in man extends up to the age of seventy and above while it stops at fifty in woman." Since the primary goal of marriage is procreation, one "must benefit from the extra period of fertility in man." And because some men are inclined and naturally disposed to have several women, "the shari'a law," therefore, broadens his options with the possibility of having more than one wife instead of resorting to *zinā* which is a sin.[164]

If the first reason is the farthest from scientific inquiry because no statistics have ever asserted that the number of women was greater than that of men in any society and at any time period, the commentators' second and third reasons for allowing polygamy are perplexing. The second reason posits that the primary goal of marriage is to have as many children as possible. What wrong is there in marrying a man in his sixties to a girl in her twenties if this marriage could allow one "to benefit from the fertility rate in men"? We might even reconsider all the current laws. Why limit oneself to just the laws on polygamy? How can the law permit the marriage of "those women who are disabled" while they are incapable of increasing the number of men and women in the umma?

The matter requires neither extensive research nor an in-depth look to find out that the primary anxiety of commentators is the justification or rather the defense of polygamy as if they did not take into consideration scientific advancements and social transformations which allow spouses to control the act of reproduction, especially given that it is a cultural, not a natural practice.

When one comes to the third reason posited to justify polygamy, that is, the inclination of some men to have several women and their constant need for more and more women, to the point that one woman does not protect him from *zinā*, he or she finds out the problem here is more difficult and dangerous. What solution is there for a man who tired of his four women still desires others for some God-given natural disposition? How is one to protect him from *zinā*? This man may divorce his wives and marry four other women. Is not the number of women in the worldview of commentators greater than that of men? What harm is there if children were shattered and lost all emotional ties? Protecting man from *zinā* is more important and dangerous. Perhaps, the easiest way to solve this profound sexual problem is to have sex with slave women. Only then, man is saved from the danger of boredom and the perils of getting used to one wife who may not protect him from *zinā*. However, this idealistic and easy solution cannot be carried through in modern societies which abolished slavery, making polygamy alone incapable of solving the problem of "he who was inclined and naturally disposed to have several women."[165] Besides, how does one distinguish between he who is and he who is not naturally disposed to have several women? Should one think of clinical psychological tests or practical sexual tests? What should one do if faced with a woman who is naturally disposed to have several men, or at least has desire for it?

Raising the question of polygamy generally raises many comic discrepancies. The commentators' readings of this question in the past and the clinging of some sheikhs to them in the present reveal a clear confusion between marriage as a social institution that regulates sexual and social life on the one hand and sexual fantasies which no law can delimit except that of desire. Those people are oblivious of the fact that man, from the beginning, is part of culture, not nature in that he accepts the prohibition against marrying the *muharramāt* (certain women he is related to by kinship) as well as the regulations of his sexual desires within frameworks which narrow down and broaden depending on societies and their symbolic representations.

PERPLEXITY EIGHT: THE *'IDDAH*

The *'iddah* (عدّة) is the time period during which a Muslim woman is not allowed to get married and waits by herself after the husband has either divorced her or passed away. The Qur'an sets it to three cycles or *qurū'* (قروء) for a divorced woman who is not pregnant ("Divorced women shall wait by themselves for three cycles" [The Heifer 2:228]) and three months for she who has not menstruated as yet or despaired of further menstruating

("As for your women who have despaired of further menstruating, if you are in doubt, their *'iddah* waiting period shall be three months; and those who have not menstruated as yet . . . " (Divorce 65:4) and four months and ten days for she who lost a husband ("And those of you who die leaving behind wives, they [the wives] shall wait by themselves for four months and ten nights" (The Heifer 2:234).

Differing over the significance of the word "menstrual cycle" or *qur'* (قرء), commentators gave two opposite meanings: purification and menstruation, which religious scholars and linguists, past and present, tried hard to give one precedence over the other.[166] Despite the importance of this issue from the orderly standpoint of Islamic jurisprudence, I will skip it because the difference between the two readings cannot in any way go beyond one month and because what is interesting in the *'iddah* subject are two issues exposing two scholarly perplexities in connection with the commentators' readings of the leitmotiv for the *'iddah* (i.e., the rationale behind legislating it).

Commentators hold that the primary purpose of the *'iddah* is to clear out the innocence of the womb from a potential pregnancy to the point that some commentators have attributed to the *'iddah* the nickname of the innocence of the womb.[167] From this perspective, the *'iddah* is a necessary time period which asserts that the woman's womb is devoid of any fetus, for the latter has to be affiliated with the divorcing or the deceased father to avoid all mingling of lineage. The Qur'an, however, did not restrict the imposition of the *'iddah* solely on those women who are of a child-bearing age, but also enacted one on those young girls who have not menstruated yet and on those women who despaired of further menstruating. An exhaustive examination of God's words reveals a difference in the way the *'iddah* obligation has been imposed in these two different cases. If the woman who is being divorced has her menses, the menstrual cycle will be the absolute method to find out the necessary period to determine the womb's innocence. If the woman does not have her menses, either because of her young or old age, her *'iddah* is constrained by the condition of being in doubt as illustrated in the Almighty's statement: "As for your women who have despaired of further menstruating, if you are in doubt, their *'iddah* waiting period shall be three months; and those who have not menstruated as yet" (Divorce 65:4). On the basis of this reading, Dāwūd al Dhāhirī held that the *'iddah* was void when one was sure about a woman's despair of further menstruation.[168] This interpretation was fiercely opposed by commentators. It could not have been otherwise for it was a reading that somehow provided a sort of alleviation for women. In their opinions, the condition of being in doubt was not tied to the *'iddah*, but with the general context of the verse's revelation which came after some Muslims wondered about the *'iddah* of women who despaired of further menstruating and those who are very young. If that was the matter, then why does not one find the expression "if in doubt" or "in want of" or even "if you wonder" on other contexts in the Qur'an while many other commands for Muslims are preceded by questions or rather their uncertainties and doubts? It is most remarkable that in seeking to make things harder for women, commentators do not shy away from redirecting the explicit text of the Qur'an into the direction that pleases them, making not only the preposition if (*en* or اِنْ) mean "in that" (*ith* or اِذْ), but also the doubt in the *'iddah* command occur before the revelation of the verse.[169] One sees how prepositions change their meanings and are substituted for one another without any grammatical rule or linguistic basis; all of them lose their worth before the noble cause of confining the woman as long as possible. If the ends justify the means, one is not surprised by the other forms of contest commentators put forth such as "the *'iddah* was decreed for the innocence of the womb before being joined by the desert of the womb, i.e., the woman who is very young and the one who despaired of further menstruating."[170] And this without determining the legitimacy for this connection or indicating its contravention of what is indicated in the Almighty's divine words.

The intent to show severity toward women reaches its apex perhaps with 'Umar Ibn al Khattāb who distinguished himself by making the woman whose despair of menstruating is in doubt wait nine months (i.e., the duration of a normal pregnancy).[171] If no signs of pregnancy show on her, she starts the three month *'iddah*, completing thus a full year. It is not possible for the wise reader not to notice the huge difference between the Qur'an's explicit assertion that the *'iddah* of a woman who despaired of menstruating was three months if in doubt and the transformation of this *'iddah*, which is only a possibility (or an option?), into a compulsory one on the other hand and the extension of its duration with the addition of full nine months on the other. This difference is the difference between the openness of the Qur'an and the possibilities for *ijtihād* on the one hand and the closure and severity provided in human interpretations on the other hand.

This closure is further illustrated in the second purpose of the *'iddah* in the opinion of commentators, which is to allow the divorcing husband a period during which he may take back his wife and cancel the divorce. From this perspective, the *'iddah* is a period of contemplation that concerns exclusively the husband. Meanwhile, the wife only waits for her husband's final decision. The husband may take this granted right as an opportunity to cause some harm to his wife by taking her back then divorcing her for the second time, which was quite prevalent in Jāhiliyya. This is why the Qur'an limited divorce to three times: "Divorce must be twice: Either a woman is kept in honor or released in kindness (The Heifer 2:229). Despite the fact that the Qur'an through this delimitation calls for lifting harm over the woman, and even goes beyond that to the explicit declaration of not harming her, "and do not keep them, intending harm, to transgress against them" (The Heifer

2:231). The commentators could not miss "the opportunity" of the '*iddah*'s continuance under Islam without exploiting it to remind of the husband's authority over the wife and asserting his ownership of her even after divorcing her. To reach this goal of theirs, most commentators and religious scholars ignored the '*iddah*'s length and conditions set by the Qur'an and even made light of them at times.

Whether or not they considered purification or menses in the cycle, the reason why they made light of the '*iddah*'s duration is that they do not entrust the wife with her womb while the Great and Almighty God entrusted her with it and warned them if they concealed their menses or pregnancy, in that He says: "Divorced women shall wait by themselves for three cycles. It is not lawful for them to hide what God has created in their wombs; if they believe in God and the Last Day" (The Heifer 2:228). It is true that it is permissible for a woman to lie about her '*iddah*, but God made her bear an immense responsibility. So why would commentators take it away from her and hold her incapable of assuming it as if they knew more about this issue than God? This human intervention is clear, for Ibn 'Arabī states: "There are two opinions about the woman who says her '*iddah* period has ended, and this is rare. 'The first proclaims to believe the woman because some women menstruate more than once per month.'" As for the second, it ignores the menstrual cycle that the Almighty God asserted to rely on a general circumstance, as in "[A] judge and generally our women said once per month. *If religions hardly trust any men, then, what about the women?*[172] I do not see that a divorced woman could remarry before three months since her divorce and this without having to inquire if the divorce occurred at the beginning or end of purification."[173] Is it not odd that a judge would use his own statement "three months" instead of the Almighty's "three cycles"? Is not granting the husband the possibility of taking back his wife whenever he wanted the goal of extending the '*iddah*'s duration? Is it not odd that women are considered outright as less religious than men? Is not Mary, peace be upon her, and the Mothers of the Believers, among women or does symbolic violence against women allow to overlook those and ignore the divine words of the Almighty?

This carelessness continues and appears in a second purview which makes light of the Almighty's divine words. After making light of the '*iddah*'s explicit duration in the Qur'an and in women as God's trustees, commentators, there they are, making light of the explicit conditions of taking back a wife in the Qur'an, for the Almighty states: "And their husbands have better rights to take them back if they desire to set things right" (The Heifer 2:228). Without equivocation, the verse indicates that the right of taking back the wife is tied to the intent of setting things right, cancelling out what used to be practiced in Jāhiliyya in that the wife was taken back and forth without any limit and to the point of harm. This is what al Rāzī asserts when he says:

"The cause for revealing this verse is that during Jāhiliyya, men used to take back the women they had divorced with the intent to harm them, and divorce them after reconciliation until the woman becomes accustomed to a damaging *'iddah* period. This is why they proscribed that and made the intent setting things right the condition for taking back the wife as in His statement, 'if they desire to set things right.'"[174] This proclamation did not prevent al Rāzī from following the path of most commentators who viewed this condition as a formality owing to the impossibility of knowing the intent of taking back the wife, whether to set things right or not. This is why they made a distinction between what is hidden inside a husband's heart and for which he is accountable in front of God and the law that grants him total right to get back his wife. This is what Tabarī's response clarifies in response to a logical question:

> Does a husband, who divorced one or two of his wives after informing her or them that she will be taken back to him after three cycles, intend to set things right or is it the command to take her back that is to be set right? It was said: As far as what is between him and God is concerned, it is not permitted if he wants to take her back with the intention of harming her by ordering her return instead of setting things right. *And if he wants to cause her harm by taking her back, he has the right to do it,* even if he is at fault because of his duplicitous action in being about to commit that which God has not permitted him. And only God shall be the judge of what he otherwise did. As for people, they are not permitted to intervene between him and his wife that he took back through divine command. [175]

Of the same opinion is al Rāzī:

> To those who say that the word "if" ("*en*") is to express condition, that the condition requires the absence of a command when it becomes non-existent, and requires in case there is no intent to set things right that the right to take back the wife be not asserted, the response is that intent is an internal characteristic one cannot perceive. Indeed, it is not law that has made the legitimacy of taking back the wife contingent on intent. Rather, it is its permissibility between him and God that depends on intent, even if, in taking her back for the purpose of harming her, he is guilty of wrongdoing. [176]

It is legitimate then to ask a simple and logical question: If one is to exclude the time frame, what is the difference then from the point of view of religious scholars between taking back a wife during Jāhiliyya and under Islam, given that in both cases the husband is not required not to cause harm to the wife and she becomes an absolute right? Is the condition that the Great and Almighty God has set mere decorum? What gives Ben ʿĀchūr the right to proclaim that "His statement (if they desire to set things right) is a condition meant to encourage one to set things right and that *it is not to put chains on anyone?*"[177] Is it so hard for ancient and modern commentators to acknowl-edge those chains which the Qur'an has declared? Is giving the husband free license to take back the wife more precious to their hearts than the words of God?

If one is to theoretically agree with them that a husband's intent to set things right with his wife is one of those private matters that no one should know, is it not possible that behind God's wisdom in choosing this condition lies a deep meaning that opens up the door to *ijtihād*, one that does not rest on the husband's absolute right to take back his wife whether the intent was to set things right or harm, but rather on the ground that even when mere doubt in the intent to set things right would be a cause for negating the right to take back the wife unless she so desired. Desire is enough to tell us if both sides have the intent of setting things right and deem if the marital relation-ship is far above any rift. Going further than that, one wonders, "how did commentators know that the Great and Almighty God referred to husbands alone when He says, "'if they wish to set things right'?" The rules of Arabic grammar allow one to count that the personal pronoun that performs the intention combines husbands and wives together. This reading is closer to logic because the intent to set things right is meaningful and free from harm only if shared between both spouses.

Everything preceding has shown how commentators' perception of the husband's ownership and authority over the wife has drawn their attention away from the possible deep meanings of the Qur'an. The important thing for a commentator like al Rāzī is that the *'iddah* is there to assert that "the husband is like the Emir and the shepherd and the wife is like the ruled and the flock. And because he is an Emir and a shepherd, the husband has to provide her with her needs and what is due to her and in exchange, she has to show submission and obedience towards the husband."[178]

If commentators have ignored the words of the Almighty God, one should not be surprised that they scoffed at the explicit prophetic tradition whether it comes to extending the *'iddah* period or preventing the wife from getting back her freedom, for one is not to forget that marriage is a type of slavery as Ibn Taymiyya and al Ghazālī stated. This latent attitude is perhaps what made opinions differ over a matter already settled in the Qur'an starting with His statement, "And for those with child, their term shall be when they bring forth their burden" (Divorce 65:4). This statement entails that childbirth is what ends the pregnant woman's *'iddah*, but some commentators were of the opinion that it was a particular statement about pregnant women who are divorced at the exclusion of those who are widows who have to observe at least a fourteenth month *'iddah* period or more until they give birth. In doing this, they overlooked the Sunnah which supports the general Qur'anic mean-ing in that Sabi'a al Aslamiyya gave birth a few nights after her husband passed way. So the Prophet, peace be upon him, said to her: "You have been made free, marry whomever you want."[179] This case has embarrassed commentators for a woman can give birth a few hours after her husband's death and it is difficult for them to accept that she could become so rapidly free. As such, does she not resemble those men who can legally marry even one hour after the wife's death? Does not the *'iddah* lose then the embodiment of the male authority and power that many have imposed on women? What one has grasped after reading what commentators said about the *'iddah* is that the wisdom in the words of the Almighty sees deeper than their perspectives. Indeed, the Qur'an is valid at any time and place. Its readers are affected by their historical context, the schools of religious thought they belong to, and even by personal desires. And this is what makes the door to *ijtihād* always flung wide open on the one hand and what counters the final one opinion on the other one.

PERPLEXITY 9: SEX WITH ONE'S HAND

It is legitimate to wonder about the reason for including masturbation or sex with one's hand in a section dedicated to marriage. The answer is that masturbation from the point of view of religious scholars and commentators is a necessity one resorts to in the absence of marriage and slaves. Indeed, sex with one's hand is a type of sexual practice that was debated in relation to the possibility of marriage. It has also generated two positions that shall be presented and discussed while explaining the perplexity and interrogation marks they raise.

The first position disproves of masturbation and views it as a sin. Those who support this position—and among them is Imam al Shāfi'ī, peace upon him, and those who agree with him on forbidding hand masturbation—rely on this noble verse, "And those who guard their private parts save from their wives or what that their right hands possess."[180] He said, "This is a deed that falls outside these two categories." He also said, "Those who want other than that are the ones who are blameworthy."[181] On this ground, those two categories forbid all sexual relations except between spouses or with slaves. It seems that the discussion about saving one's private parts is related as far as saving goes to a possible human sexual subject. Is having sex with one's hand or using "another instrument" which brings about sexual pleasure the equivalent of a normal sexual subject? In other words, is it possible to ask someone to save his private parts from all women except his wives and slaves and that this request includes saving his private parts from his own hand and from any instrument that gives him sexual pleasure? Kishk mocking this reading goes so far as to say, "if one is allowed to have sex with what one's right hand possesses, then why not have sex with the right hand itself?"[182]

Should we go beyond this type of hasty positions and consider that saving one's private parts is with one's spouses and slaves, and consider then that the cited verse proclaims that believers must have sex only with their spouses or slaves; this verse becomes non-forbidding of sexual relations between gay people given the possibility that those may be spouses. It is also possible for a man to have sex with his female slaves and *ghilman* (young male slaves), which did occur in the history of Muslims. If one is to argue that homosexuality is forbidden by other verses, I will answer that the expression "saving one's private parts" raises a second problem because in contrast with the word *nikāh*, it is too general. The statement "do not have sex with anyone other than your wives or slaves" is relatively clear.[183] As for the statement "save your private parts from everyone save your wives and female slaves" it is quite perplexing because of the diverse meanings of the word "save." Is "saving one's private parts" restricted on the level of meaning to saving it from normal sexual relations (i.e., from the encounter between two genitals), or does it go beyond that to protect it from touching or even from someone's gaze? This second possible meaning suggests that doctors may neither look at the genitals of believers who are sick, nor touch them, be they men or women. This is because gazing or touching violates the law about saving one's private parts. Drawing on the authority of those necessities which permit that which is forbidden does not resolve the issue, for the delimitations of what is a necessity differs from one commentator to another. Some may even go so far as to claim that repressed sexual desire is a necessity under which masturbation, which is forbidden, is permissible (i.e., it is a necessity that may invite one not to save his private parts from what his right hand possesses), and this is the opinion of those religious scholars who authorized sex with one's hand.

What is important at this level is to clarify that the cited verse is not a strong enough proof to forbid masturbation. Commentators themselves view the prohibition of masturbation on the basis of this verse as mere deduction. This is the case for al Zarakshī (1344–1392) that many Qur'anic laws are formulated through deductions like "al Shāfi'ī's prohibition of masturbation with one's hand from God's statement 'save for their spouses or those their right hands possess' to his statement that "those who want other than that are the ones who are blameworthy."[184] Some of those who prohibited masturbation on the basis of the Prophetic tradition also relied on that same deductive methodology. It was reported about the Prophet, peace be upon him, that he said, "O' Young People! Whoever among you is able to afford marriage let him be married. And whoever is not able to get married, he should fast, for fasting curbs sexual desire."[185] Some from the Mālikī school used this hadith to forbid masturbation because he (the Prophet) recommended that in case of the inability to get married, one has to fast because it kills sexual appetite.

•

Had masturbation been permitted, recommending it would have been easier."[186]

As for me, I see that the aforesaid hadith was mentioned in the specific context of advising young Muslims and I do not believe that it provides all possible solutions to those who cannot afford to get married. One does not even imagine the Prophet, with his shyness, present masturbation as a solution, given that it is a private issue that all youths undoubtedly know and that there is no need for the Prophet to mention it. In addition, had this hadith been taken as a binding law, anyone who could afford to get married and did not would have been at fault because in violation of the Prophet's statutory commands. My position is confirmed by a second hadith in which Abū Hurayra addresses the Prophet, "I said, O Prophet of God, that I was a young man who fears the sin of fornication, yet I could not find any woman to marry. He remained silent. Then I said something similar and he remained silent. Then I repeated my question a third time and he remained silent. In the fourth, he said, O Abū Hurayra! The pen has run dry after writing about what you are going through. Either castrate yourself, or sow your seeds."[187] Can one imagine that this hadith is the source of an absolute law? Would then any youth who can't afford marriage have to stop thinking about sex and castrate himself if he can't do it? Has not the Prophet handed that command? How can one not obey him? In addition how can one reconcile this authentic hadith commanding castration and another authentic hadith in which the Prophet's disciples say: "We were fighting with the Prophet, peace be upon him, and we did not have women? So we told him, O Prophet of God! Should we get ourselves castrated? And he prohibited it."[188] Such superficial readings which seek to transform daily events and individual news into legal grounds are dangerous because it makes one fall into slippery contradictions, discrepancies, and sophistry. Investigating the intentions and great values of the Islamic Shari'a, on the opposite pole, would give resolution to many impasses in jurisprudence.

One example of these impasses is the attempt of those who forbade masturbation to find absolute textual justifications even if they do not exist. Using as pretexts hadiths which are strange, to say the least, such as this statement attributed to the Prophet,

> Seven kinds of people God shall avert his eyes from on Resurrection Day. He will deny them His grace and they shall not be with those who are saved. They will be the first to enter Hell unless they repent, for God gives repentance to those who seek it. These are: He who has sex with his hand; he who initiates fornication; he who is seduced into fornication; he who is addicted to alcohol; he who beats his parents until they cry for help; he who harms his neighbors until they curse him; and he who has sex with the lawful sexual partner of his neighbor.

From the point of view of precedence, this hadith is not acceptable because of its "strangeness." In addition, its transmitter is unknown because of his ignorance, to quote the expert testimony of Ibn al Kathīr.[189] It is a hadith that the mind cannot accept for how is it conceivable that sex with one's hand even if prohibited is a sin similar in weight and punishment as that of he who beats his parents until they cry for help, especially given that the Qur'an indicates nothing about masturbation but is bursting with verses which preach kindness and tenderness towards one's parents.

A big number of ancient religious scholars permitted masturbation for a preliminary simple reason which is the absence of any text forbidding it. This is the position of Ahl al Dhāhiriyya[190] who claim that the Almighty God set forth in details that he had forbidden them, "And He has set forth in details that he had forbidden you . . . "(The Livestock 6:119). Those who permitted masturbation did not rely on any of the weak hadiths by the Prophet reinforcing thus their weakness, for had they been categorical, Ibn Hazm and Ibn Hanbal, for example, would not have overlooked them. Despite his devoutness, Ibn Hanbal authorized masturbation arguing that it was lawful because a bodily secretion, thus permissible when the need is felt. Further, its foundational basis is to be found in grooming and the extraction of extra body substances. Other commentators allowed masturbation in case of necessity, out of fear of falling into fornication, considering the lesser of the two evils. Perhaps it comes in three-way comparisons at times, for "it was reported on behalf of Ibn 'Abbās that "having sex with slaves was better but it [masturbation] is better than fornication."[191]

As often is my inclination in this book, I do not wish to favor one viewpoint over another. However, what draws one's attention is the great number of commentators who seek to give such severe interpretations of the Qur'an and the Sunnah, narrowing down the configurations of human sexuality and feeling embarrassed by it. Some "modern religious scholars" feel perhaps even some sadistic pleasure in exaggerating the prohibition of masturbation, transforming it into a huge sin, disavowing even the resort to it out of necessity, overlooking the fact that most youths in Muslim countries today get relatively married late (i.e., ten years or more after the manifestation of sexual desire).

What is more bewildering is that the sheikhs who are forbidding masturbation do not mention those religious scholars and commentators who authorized it. Rather, they do not cite the opinion of those who allowed it out of necessity, that is, those for whom it was lawful to have slaves and who also had the possibility of getting married early—let alone today's youths! Is not the masturbation that many Muslim youths practice today a necessity imposed by the poverty of one's sexual life in Muslim societies today, theoretically and in practice?

The new religious scholars sometimes rely on some chopped religious evidence and some laughable medical information at other times. An example of the false medical information that the sheikhs cite today on the internet is what 'Abdullah Ibn 'Abd al 'Aziz al Bāz, the president of the Administration for Scientific Research and Legal Rulings says:

> Science has demonstrated that masturbation causes many hereditary diseases. It weakens one's eyesight by reducing to a great extent its usual sharpness. It also devitalizes the sexual organ and causes it to sag partially or totally in such a way that the one who practices masturbation comes to resemble a woman because he lost the most important mark of his manliness, i.e., that with which God favored man over woman. As a result, he can no longer get married and even if he is forced to get married, he can no longer accomplish his marital duties as required of him. As a result, his wife is bound to look at someone else since he was incapable of making her chaste. There are many ills to that which cannot remain concealed. To mention a few of them, the masturbator will pass on a weakness in the nerves due to the effort spent during that action. He will also pass on trouble in the digestive system by weakening and deregulating it. This deed stunts organ growth especially the penis and testes preventing them from reaching the full scope of their normal growth. It also causes an inflammation in the testes making the man who has this condition quick to ejaculate to the degree that he discharges if the slightest object rubs against his penis. Further, he passes on pain in the bone marrow, which constitutes the loins from which the semen is discharged, causing the back to bow and bend as a result of this pain. Further because of this practice, his water gets diluted. After being strong and thick as one is accustomed to see a man's sperm, it becomes weak and void of sperm worms.[192] Perhaps a small number of sperm worms will remain incapable of fertilization. The result will be a weak fetus. This is why the son of the masturbator—if he has one—is weak and prone to diseases unlike other children who are born from a normal sperm. Among the diseases he inherits is some shakiness on the level of limbs such as the legs some weakness in the cerebral glands which affects his perceptive powers. An intelligent man's comprehension diminishes after practicing masturbation. The cerebral glands may grow so weak that they may cause lunacy. Hence, the prohibition of masturbation becomes undoubtedly clear for anyone who asks because of the aforesaid evidence and harms. Likewise is the extraction of semen with cotton swabs and other similar things. And God knows better.

If the reader of these words is to compare them to the opinions for example of Ibn Hanbal and Ibn Hazm and juxtaposes next to the reality of the Arab youths' sexual life, she or he cannot not wonder: does the reliance of religious scholars on some chopped religious evidence and false medical results on the one hand and exaggerated scare tactics threats, scolding, and menaces on the other hand, resolve the problem of spending one's sexual energy?

THAT WHICH LIES AFTER PERPLEXITY

The most important thing that describes the commentators' and religious scholars' perception of marriage is their view that it is a sales contract with which a man buys a woman's goods. In exchange for them, he pays her an instantaneous monetary dowry and pledges to provide for his wife in time. While nothing in the Qur'an confirms this perception, the Qur'an does however confirm that the dowry has been a prevalent custom since the Jāhiliyya. Although it did not forbid, it did not encourage it either let alone command it. As for what the husband provides, it is tied to the meaning of *qiwāma* (the state of being in charge of someone especially women), especially given that men are in charge only if they fulfill the condition of being providers.[193] In case the two spouses jointly provide, then the task of being in charge, in the sense of responsibility, becomes a joint charge.[194]

It is odd that despite their violence to the text, it is the position of the religious scholars and commentators which will prevail in the social imaginary of Muslim societies today including even its laws and this despite the fact that women left the home to work and provide for many families. If one is to take the country of Tunisia as an example, it is clear that to this day language carries connotations related to the world of sales in that the expression "he gave away his daughter" to refer to the daughter who is about to get married confirms first the continuity of the principle of marriage through a guardian and second that marriage is just an "object" to be delivered to the husband, not to say "goods." As for Tunisian laws, despite the progressive milestones towards equality between the spouses, they still implicitly require that "the husband buys the woman's goods," for the husband cannot force his wife to consummate the marriage unless he pays her a dowry.[195]

Without a shadow of a doubt, the inclusion of marriage within the category of the sales contracts has a strong bearing on who shall have authority inside the family. While the buyer makes decisions, the merchandise, given that she is only an object, has for only duty obedience. The previously discussed association between the wife and the slave woman in the opinion of the jurists is not arbitrary, for both relationships are based on the duty to provide and the duty to obey in return. The endeavor of commentators and religious scholars to assert the husband's authority is perhaps what swayed many of them to forbid the marriage of pleasure which was forbidden by 'Umar Ibn al Khattāb alone, not the Qur'an. Indeed, the marriage of pleasure grants the woman some free choice and a quick separation not allowed by the judicial apparatus whose complexity goes so far as to contradict the previously cited clear hadiths of the Prophet which allow a wife to divorce her husband even if neither his religion nor behavior is at fault. There are even some hadiths which allow her to get a divorce for a reason as simple as being repulsed by the husband's ugliness. Extending the woman's enslavement beyond marriage, religious scholars attempted to stretch and complicate the *'iddah* period even if in contradiction with the Qur'an and the Sunnah or distortion of the significance of their otherwise clear language.

Among the myriad facets of husbandly dominance which commentators and religious scholars have sought to assert, sexual dominance is undoubtedly one of the most prominent. Despite the fact that the Qur'anic concept of *Ihçān* includes both men and women, most religious scholars overlooked it and sought to discard a woman's sexual pleasure, given that she is just a sexual object who has to respond to the sexual needs of the husband. The dismissal of female sexual pleasure timewise coincides with the celebration of male sexual pleasure which is basically a celebration on a quantitative level, calling for sexual diversification and polygamy which neither the Qur'an allows nor does the Prophet allow for his daughter, as a given, or rather as some quintessential cornerstone of Islam.

If one is able to understand why ancient commentators accepted polygamy because it was a social reality, the position of the modern ones who support it in some countries and call for it in others is worth looking at in that polygamy is presented as an ideal or magical solution to the problems of adultery, celibacy, and many others. The modern commentators clearly confuse two perspectives: the first is marriage as an institution which regulates human sexuality which is so different from natural sexual behavior encountered in the world of animals. I have already explained that human sexuality is a cultural behavior that starts with the avoidance of *mahārem* or non-marriageable relatives. If one is to open up the door of sexual diversification as an excuse for polygamy, it is possible that this same door turns into an excuse for both men and women to have multiple spouses, which while being acceptable in the shari'a's literal interpretation is contested by its noble intents that seek to regulate and cultivate societies. This cultivation is the essence of the second perspective on marriage, for it is a social institution that seeks to build family relations which are founded on a minimum of psychological and emotional equilibrium and which polygamy cannot in most cases, which leads to the breakup of family relations and dislocation of the social and family core values.

The awareness of both perspectives does not prevent one from taking a second look at the way Muslim societies apprehend marriage today between legal obstacles and social reality. Indeed, the delayed age of marriage in opposition to early Islamic societies on the one hand and the tightening of legal impediments against sexual practice on the other presents for the youth the challenge of spending their sexual energy between sexual repression and its devastating psychological and physical consequences and unhappy sexual practices accompanied most often by a feeling of guilt deepened and anchored with mastery by modern religious institutions.

NOTES

1. Jawād 'Ali, *Al Mufassal fī tārīkh al 'arab qabl al Islām* 5 (Beirut/Baghdād: Dār al 'ilm lilmalāyīn/maktabat al nahdha, 1970), 530.

2. Trans. Given the Arabic reader's acquaintance with the cultural context, the author uses the verb "to marry" to refer to the possibility of a second marriage. For the purpose of clarification, the translator is using the verb "to remarry."

3. Abū Bakr Ibn 'Arabī, *Ahkām al Qur'an*, 1:361.

4. For example, Women 4:4, Women 4:25, The Banquet 5:25 and The Test 60:10.

5. Trans. With the author's approval, for the sake of clarity, I am using the English word "dowry" to refer to both *mahr* and *sidāq* even though Arabic linguists see some differences between these two terms for the reasons explained in this chapter.

6. Ben 'Āchūr, *Al Tahrīr wa al Tanwīr*, 4:230.

7. Abū al Qāsim Jār Allāh al Zamakhsharī, *Al Kashāf 'an Haqāeq Attartīl wa 'Uyūn al Aqāwīl aqāwīl wa fī wujūh atta'wīl* 1 (Beirut: Dār al Ma'rifa), 245–46.

8. "Forbidden to you are your mothers, daughters, sisters, the sisters of your fathers, the sisters of your mothers, the daughters of your brother, the daughters of your sister, your nursing mothers, the girls who nursed from the same woman as you, the mothers of your wives, and the step-daughters on your lap from the wives with whom you have consummated the marriage. If the marriage has not been consummated, it is not sin to wed them (the step-daughters). Also forbidden to you are the women who were married to the sons of your own blood. Also, you shall not be married to two sisters at the same time, except for what has already occurred in the past. God is most forgiving and merciful. And forbidden to you are all married women save those slave women whom your right hands possess. These are God's commandments to you" (Women 4:23–24).

9. In Arabic, *sufh* means incest, adultery, and fornication.

10. Abū Bakr Ibn 'Arabī, *Ahkām al Qur'an*, 1:387.

11. One is not to forget that women did not use to work at the time the Qur'an was revealed.

12. Fakhr al Dīne al Rāzī, *Mafātīh al Ghayb*, 5.10:48. Original emphasis.

13. Ibid., 64.

14. Trans. The reference here is to the free Women of the Book. *Ihçān* has multiple meanings in Arabic such as freedom, marriage, and protection.

15. Fakhr al Dīne al Rāzī, *Mafātīh al Ghayb*, 6.11:150.

16. Al Tabarī, *Jāmi' al Bayān*, 12:67.

17. Ben 'Āchūr, *Al Tahrīr wa al Tanwīr*, 28:159.

18. Fortunately, the *ujūr* expression was mentioned another time in the Qur'an in the specific context of the marriages of the Prophet, peace be upon him.

19. "A woman visited the Prophet, peace be upon him, and told him, I came to give you myself as a gift. He looked at her peace be upon him. Then he looked at her more closely, then he, peace be upon him, lowered his head. When the woman saw that he did not decide anything about her case, one of his disciples rose and said: O Prophet of God, if you do not need her, marry her to me. He said: "Do you have anything?" He said: no, I swear to God. He said: Go to your family and see if you find anything. He went then said: I swear to God, I found nothing. The Prophet, peace be upon him, said: Look for even an iron ring. He went, came back, and said: "No, O Prophet of God, not even an iron ring, I have nothing but this lower half cloth. He said: Easy, if he has a piece of clothing she has its half. And the Prophet, peace be upon him, said: What will she make with your lower half cloth? If you wear it, she does not own any part of it. If she wears it, you do not own any part of it. The man took a seat and stayed there for a long time. The Prophet, peace be upon him, saw him and when he saw him leaving, called him and said: What do you have from the Qur'an? He said: I have this verse and that verse and he enumerated them. So he (the Prophet) said to him: Learn them by heart. He said: I will. He said: you can go. You have married her with what you have learned from the Qur'an," in *Sahīh al Bukhārī* 3.9 (Dār Matābi' Asha'b): 5. *Sahīh Muslim* 2 (Cairo: Dār Ihyāa al kutub al 'arabiyya, 1955), 1040–41.

20. Fakhr al Dīne al Rāzī, *Mafātīh al Ghayb*, 5.10:48. The strangest thing is that contemporary Tunisian law, in its own turn, ignores this hadith by the Prophet, by making "anything

lawful and of a monetary value" labeled as a dowry" (The Personal Status Code, Section 12). Qur'anic recitation is not seen as having any monetary value.

21. Abū Bakr Ibn 'Arabī, *Ahkām al Qur'an*, 1:365.

22. Ibid., 388. This is a controversial issue, for Ibn Hanbal it was possible to view the manumission of a slave woman as *sidāq*. He asserts that the Prophet, peace be upon him, made it his *sidāq* in his marriage to Safiyya Bent Huwayy, whom he has emancipated by through marriage, and used *açīdā* [Trans. pudding] for her manumission. This is reported by Anas in his *Sahīh*. As for Abū Bakr Ibn 'Arabī, he denies the possibility of manumission through *sidāq*. He considers that the Prophet, peace be upon him, was a specific case when it comes to marriage and other matters, among these specificities is that he used to get married without either guardian or *sidāq*.

23. "Marriage without a Dowry is Fornication," Abū Bakr Ibn 'Arabī, *Ahkām al Qur'an* 1:397. *Trans. Sifāh* means in Arabic, fornication, adultery, prostitution, and debauchery. In this particular context, it is debauchery, not prostitution. Hence, the translator's choice of "fornication" in this particular case.

24. Abū Bakr Ibn 'Arabī, *Ahkām al Qur'an* 1:388 and 3:1551.

25. Ibid., 1:389. It is significant that the Prophet, peace be upon him, brings together in one hadith *bey'* (marriage/selling) and *khutba* (engagement) in that he cautioned against marrying the spouse of one's brother and getting engaged to the fiancé of one's brother, in *Sahīh al Bukhārī*, 3.7:24.

26. Abū Bakr Ibn 'Arabī, *Ahkām al Qur'an*, 1:387.

27. Fakhr al Dīne al Rāzī, *Mafātīh al Ghayb*, 5.10:64.

28. Ibid., 15.29:306.

29. Abū al Qāsim Jār Allāh al Zamakhsharī, *Al Kashāf 'an Haqāeq Attartīl wa 'Uyūn al Aqāwīl Aqāwīl wa fī Wujūh atta'wīl* 1 (Beirut: Dār al Ma'rifa, n.p.), 262.

30. Those entering a marriage contract are at least two. They are the two spouses. Other parties can be implicated if it is believed that a guardian's consent is needed to marry a woman.

31. Abū Bakr Ibn 'Arabī, *Ahkām al Qur'an* 1:218 and *Mafātīh al Ghayb*, 3.6:149.

32. Fakhr al Dīne al Rāzī, *Mafātīh al Ghayb*, 3.6:152.

33. *Sahīh al Bukhārī*, 3.7:26.

34. Words in italics are the original emphasis.

35. Abū Bakr Ibn 'Arabī, *Mafātīh al Ghayb*, 3.6:149.

36. Ben 'Āchūr, *Al Tahrīr wa al Tanwīr*, 4:230–31.

37. Ibid., 6:124.

38. Women 4:24–25 and The Banquet 5:5.

39. Fakhr al Dīne al Rāzī, *Mafātīh al Ghayb*, 5.10:49.

40. Ibid., 662. I may agree with Grāmī that the commentators' readings of these hadiths suggest that "foreplay with women" is one of the means of arousing male lust. However, I seek to make a distinction between the Qur'anic text and the hadiths that are open to multiple possible interpretations on the one hand, and the readings of religious scholars which impoverish these possibilities on the other.

41. *Sahīh al Bukhārī*, 3.7:4 and *Sahīh Moslem* 2 (*Dār Ihyā al kutub al 'arabiyya*, 1955), 1084.

42. Ibid., 3.8:27–28.

43. The Heifer 2:230.

44. Fakhr al Dīne al Rāzī, *Mafātīh al Ghayb*, 3.6:78. Grāmī fully addresses this sexual issue in *Al Ikhtilāf fī al thaqāfa al 'arabiyya al islāmiyya*, 661–706.

45. Vladimir Granoff et François Perrier, *Le Désir et le féminin* (Paris: Flammarion, 1979), 27–43.

46. Trans. The verb *dharaba* means to beat, to go on a strike, to avoid, etc. Commentators and religious scholars chose this meaning.

47. *Sahīh al Bukhārī*, 3.7:60.

48. Al Tabarī, *Jami' al Bayān*, 2:475.

49. Muhammad Ben Sālih al Munjid, *Muharramāt Istahāna bihā kathīrun mina ennās* (Saudi Arabia, 1993): 33.

50. Al Tabarī, *Jāmi' al Bayān*, 4:65.

51. Ibid., 66.
52. Ibid., 68.
53. Grāmī, *Al Ikhtilāf fī athaqāfa al 'arabiyya al islāmiyya*, 665.
54. Abū Bakr Ibn 'Arabī, *Ahkām al Qur'an*, 1:317. Trans. Words in italics are Youssef's original emphasis.
55. Qur'an, Women 4:25.
56. Fakhr al Dīne al Rāzī, *Mafātīh al Ghayb*, 5.10:40.
57. These are extra supererogatory acts of devotion in Islam.
58. Abū Bakr Ibn 'Arabī, *Ahkām al Qur'an*, 1:189.
59. Ibid., 444.
60. See for example the sūras of Mary 19: 8–20 and The Smoke 44:13.
61. There is disagreement over the meaning of touching whether it is sexual intercourse or all forms of touching. See Abū Bakr Ibn 'Arabī, *Ahkām al Qur'an* 1:444.
62. Abū Bakr Ibn 'Arabī, *Ahkām al Qur'an* 1:444.
63. *Al zhihār* occurs when the husband says to his wife: "You are like my mother's back to me." In doing so, he forbids to himself any sexual intercourse.
64. *Sahīh al Bukhārī*, 3.7:39.
65. "And keep an amicable companionship with them" (Women 4:19) and "And of His signs is that He created for you, of yourselves, spouses, that you might find nest in them, and He has set between you love and mercy" (Romans 30:21).
66. See his hadith, "You are entrusted to treat your wife with kindness," in al Zamakhsharī, *Al Kashāf*, 1:266 and *Sahīh al Bukhārī*, 3.7:34.
67. Al Tabarī, *Ahkām al Bayān*, 4:6.
68. Ahmed Ibn Taymiyyah, *Al Fatāwī al kubrā* 3 (Beirut: Dār al kutub al 'ilmiyya, 1987), 232.
69. Al Tabarī, *Ahkām al Bayān*, 1: 200.
70. Ibn Taymiyyah, 3:106.
71. Abū Hāmid al Ghazālī, *Ihyā 'Ulūm al Dīne* 2 (*Beirut: Dar al ma'rifa*, n.d.), 56.
72. In the shari'a law, the *'iddah* is the waiting period a divorced woman or one who lost her husband waits before getting remarried. The purpose is to ensure the child carries the name of his biological father if the woman turns out to be pregnant. The waiting period is usually set at three months.
73. The question of gifts to the divorced woman is subject of disagreement. While al Shāfi'ī and Abū Hanīfa find it compulsory, the people and the Seven Fuqahā' of Medina do not see it as such. See Fakhr al Dīne al Rāzī, *Mafātīh al Ghayb*, 3.6:149.
74. Ibid., 150.
75. For more information on the choice given to the Wives of the Prophet, peace be upon him, see Al Tabarī's Jāmi' *al Bayān*, 10: 288–91.
76. Abū Bakr Ibn 'Arabī, *Ahkām al Qur'an*, 1:389.
77. Fakhr al Dīne al Rāzī, *Mafātīh al Ghayb*, 5.10:50.
78. Ibid.
79. Ibid., 51.
80. Abū Bakr Ibn 'Arabī, *Ahkām al Quran*, 1:389.
81. Ben 'Āchūr, *Al Tahrīr wa al Tanwīr*, 5:10.
82. Abū Bakr Ibn 'Arabī, *Ahkām al Qur'an*, 1: 389.
83. Fakhr al Dīne al Rāzī, *Mafātīh al Ghayb*, 5.10:54.
84. Ben 'Āchūr, *Al Tahrīr wa al Tanwīr*, 5:10.
85. Ibid., 11.
86. Ibid.
87. Abū al Fadhl 'Alī, Ibn al Hassan al Tabrasī, *Majma' al Bayān fī tafsīr al Qur'an* 4.3 (Beirūt: Dār al Ma'rifa, 1986), 52. In another account, it is "those who fornicate are only a few" (i.e., only a few people).
88. Fakhr al Dīne al Rāzī, *Mafāth al Ghayb*, 5.10:51.
89. Ibid., 55.
90. Al Tabrasī, *Majma' al Bayān*, 3.4:52 and Fakhr al Dīne al Rāzī's *Mafātīh al Ghayb*, 5.10:51.

91. Fakhr al Dīne al Rāzī, *Mafātīh al Ghayb*, 5.10:50–51.
92. Ben 'Āchūr, *Al Tahrīr wa al Tanwīr*, 5:11.
93. Abū Bakr Ibn 'Arabī, *Ahkām al Qur'an*, 1:389.
94. Al Tabrasī, *Majma' al Bayān*, 3.4:52.
95. Fakhr al Dīne al Rāzī, *Mafātīh al Ghayb*, 5.10:55.
96. Ibid.
97. *Sahīh Moslem*, 2: 1080.
98. Ben 'Āchūr, *Al Tahrīr wa al Tanwīr*, 5:11.
99. Grāmī, *Al Ikhtilāf fī al Hadhāra al 'Arabiyya al Islāmiyya*, 673.
100. Abū Bakr Ibn 'Arabī, *Ahkām al Qur'an*, 1:173.
101. Fakhr al Dīne al Rāzī, *Mafātīh al Ghayb*, 3.6:76.
102. This is an allusion to the Almighty's statement, "And they ask you about menstruation. Say, "It is harm, so do not approach women at such times and go not in unto them till they purify themselves" (The Heifer 2:222).
103. Fakhr al Dīne al Rāzī, *Mafātīh al Ghayb*, 3.6:76.
104. Abū Bakr Ibn 'Arabī, *Ahkām al Qur'an*, 1:174.
105. For the different meanings of the word harm or "*adha*," see for example The Heifer 2:262, 263, 264 and Women 2:102.
106. Fakhr al Dīne al Rāzī, *Mafātīh al Ghayb*, 3.6:76.
107. Abū Bakr Ibn 'Arabī, *Ahkām al Qur'an*, 1:181.
108. Fakhr al Dīne al Rāzī, *Mafātīh al Ghayb*, 3.6:77.
109. Al Tabrasī, *Majma' al Bayān*, 1:565.
110. Fakhr al Dīne al Rāzī, *Mafātīh al Ghayb*, 3.6:76. Trans, in the Arabic script, Youssef refers to this same book as *Tafsīr al Rāzī*.
111. Ben 'Āchūr, *Al Tahrīr wa al Tanwīr*, 2:374.
112. Al Tabarī, *Jāmi' al Bayān*, 2:411.
113. Abū al Hassan al Wāhdī al Naysāpūrī, *Asbāb al Nuzūl* (Beirut, *Dār al Kitāb*, 1986), 68. Al Naysāpūrī explains that the word "*mujbiya*" derives from "*tajbiya*" which means to be on one's knees.
114. Al Tabarī, *Jāmi' al Bayān*, 2:405.
115. Trans. The *qibla* is the direction that should be faced by a Muslim during prayer.
116. The Almighty God states: "Yet if thou should bring to those that have been given the Scriptures every sign, they will not follow your *qibla*, nor can you be a follower of their *qibla*; nor are some of them followers of the *qibla* of others" (The Heifer 2:145). As for the Prophet, peace be upon him, he called for shaving one's mustaches and growing one's beard in opposition to the disbelievers" (*Sahīh Moslem* 3:1663).
117. Al Tabarī, *Jāmi' al Bayān*, 2:408.
118. Ismā'īl Ibn al Kathīr, *Tafsīr al Qur'an* 1 (*Dār al Tayyiba li anashr wa al tawzī'*, 1999), 593.
119. Abū 'Abdullah al Qurtubī, *Al Jami' li A h kām al Qur'an* 3 (Cairo: Dar al Kutub al misriyya, 1964): 93–94.
120. Abū Bakr Ibn 'Arabī, *Ahkām al Qur'an*, 1:174.
121. For more information on weak hadiths and the contestation of most of them, see Muhammad Jalāl Kishk, *Khawātir al Muslim fi al Mas'ala al Jinsiyya* (Cairo: *Maktabatu al Turāth al Islāmī*, 1992): 78. In this respect, one of the oddest forms of interpretation and contrivance has been cited by Ibn 'Arabī, who mentioned a group of people who explained the Almighty's statement "And it is not righteousness to enter houses from the back" (The Heifer 2:189) as "the women we have been ordained to come in unto from the front not in the anus." Ibn 'Arabī held this reading to be farfetched asserting, "As for those who hold the intended here to be women, their interpretation is farfetched and can be reached unless with a proof, which was neither found, nor was there a need for it," in *Ahkām al Qur'an*, 1:101.
122. *Sahih al Bukhārī*, 3.7:22.
123. See for example the sūras of He Frowned (80) and Prohibition (66).
124. *Sahīh al Bukhārī*, 7.3:6–7. The story was mentioned in the context of marrying the young to the old.
125. Ibn Sa'd, *Kitāb al Tabaqāt al Kabīr* 8 (Beirut: *Dār Sāder*, n.p.), 59.

126. Ibid., 1:395–96.

127. Ben ʿĀchūr, *Al Tahrīr wa al Tanwīr*, 4:225.

128. *Sahīh al Bukhārī*, 7:4.

129. "Take only what the Messenger gives to you and abstain from what he forbids you. Have fear of God; God is severe in His punishment" (The Gathering 59:3).

130. Trans. Original emphasis.

131. Trans. Original emphasis.

132. Abū Bakr Ibn ʿArabī, *Ahkām al Qurʾan*, 4:1826.

133. Fakhr al Dīne al Rāzī, *Mafātīh al Ghayb*, 15:30.

134. Ben ʿĀchūr, *Al Tahrīr wa al Tanwīr*, 4:242.

135. Sūra of Light 24: 31.

136. Fakhr al Dīne al Rāzī, *Mafātīh al Ghayb*, 12.23:210.

137. See for example, Shihāb UdDīne al Tīfāshī, *Nuzhat al Albāb fīmā lā yūjadu fī kitāb*, ed. Jamāl Jumuʾa (*Riyādh al Rayes li al kutub wa al nashr*: London-Cyprus, 1992), 149–206. Trans. In medieval Arabic texts, this plural masculine word refers to young male servants or pages. Its singular form is *ghulām*.

138. Ibid., 197.

139. Françoise Dolto, *Tout est langage* (Paris: Vertiges du Nord Carrere, 1987), 87.

140. Al Zamakhsharī, *Al Kāshāf*, 4:59. See Maʾrūf al Rusāfī's reading of this account in his book, *Kitāb al Shakhsiyya al Muhammadiyya* (Germany: *Manshūrāt al jamal*, 2002), 361.

141. The reference is to the Almighty's statement, "till he had attained full strength and reached forty years" (The Event 56:15).

142. Abū Bakr Ibn ʿArabī, *Ahkām al Qurʾan* 1:320–322.

143. Trans. It is a Jāhiliyyan marriage practice which allows a woman to take more than one spouse in time of drought and famine so that she can find food.

144. Ben ʿĀchūr, *Al Tahrīr wa al Tanwīr*, 4:5.

145. *Sahīh al Bukhārī*, 3.7:20.

146. For more information about the dispute over the necessity of having a legal guardian in marriage, see Ibn ʿArabī, *Ahkām al Quʾran*, 1:198, 201, 212.

147. "Forbidden to you are your mothers and daughters, your sisters, your aunts paternal and maternal, your brother's daughters, your sister's daughters, your milk mothers who have breast-fed you, your suckling sisters, your wives' mothers, your stepdaughters who are in your care being born of your wives you have been into—but if you have not yet been into them it is not a sin for you—and the spouses of your sons who are of your loins, and that you should take to you two sisters together, unless it be a thing of the past; God is all-forgiving, all-compassionate; and married women, save what your right hands own. So God's Book prescribes for you" (Women 4:23–24).

148. Abū Bakr Ibn ʿArabī, *Ahkām al Qurʾan*, 1:383.

149. Ibid., 382.

150. *Sahīh al Bukhārī*, 7:13.

151. Ben ʿĀchūr, *Al Tahrīr wa al Tanwīr*, 5:6.

152. Al Tabarī, *Jāmiʾ al Bayān*, 4:8.

153. Abū Bakr Ibn ʿArabī, *Ahkām al Qurʾan*, 3:1298.

154. Ibn al Khathīr, *Tafsīr Ibn al Kathīr*, 5:462–63.

155. AbūʾAbadullah al Qurtubī, *Al Jamiʾ li Ahkām al Qurʾan*, 12:107. Trans. Cited as *Tafsīr al Qurtubī* in the Arabic text.

156. Al Tabarī, *Jāmiʾ al Bayān*, 4:212–13.

157. Abū Bakr Ibn ʿArabī, *Ahkām al Qurʾan*, 1:309–10.

158. *Sahīh al Bukhārī*, 7:20.

159. Ibn ʿArabī, *Ahkām al Qurʾan*, 1:310.

160. *Sahīh al Bukhārī*, 3.7 :47.

161. Al Tāhar al Haddād, *Imraʾatuna fī al Sharīʾa wa al Mujtamaʾ* (Tūnis: *Dār al Tūnusiyya li al nashr*, 1989), 55.

162. Grāmī, *Al Ikhtilāf fī al thaqāfa al ʿarabiya al Islāmiya*, 767.

163. Sayyid Qutb, *Fī Dhilāl al Qurʾan* (Beirūt, al Qāhira: Dār al Shurūq, 1988), 1:579.

164. Ben ʿĀchūr, *Al Tahrīr wa al Tanwīr*, 5:226.

165. Ben 'Āchūr, *Al Tahrīr wa al Tanwīr*, 4:226.
166. Abū Bakr Ibn 'Arabī, *Ahkām al Qur'an*, 1:184.
167. It is worth mentioning that *'iddah* has been translated into French as "délai de viduité" (notice of viduity). On the semantic level, this expression requires a time period during which some emptiness is ascertained. In this case, it is the emptiness of the womb.
168. Ben 'Āchūr, *Al Tahrīr wa al Tanwīr*, 28:318.
169. Ibid., 316.
170. Abū Bakr Ibn 'Arabī, *Ahkām al Qur'an*, 1:194.
171. Ben 'Āchūr, *Al Tahrīr wa al Tanwīr*, 28:318.
172. Trans. Italics are the author's emphasis.
173. Abū Bakr Ibn 'Arabī, *Ahkām al Qur'an*, 1:187.
174. Fakhr al Dīne al Rāzī, *Mafātīh al Ghayb*, 3.6:101.
175. Al Tabrasī, *Majma' al Bayān*, 2:466. Trans. Italics are the author's emphasis.
176. Fakhr al Dīne al Rāzī, *Mafātīh al Ghayb*, 3.6:100.
177. Ben 'Āchūr, *Al Tahrīr wa al Tanwīr*, 2:395. Trans. Italics are the author's emphasis.
178. Fakhr al Dīne al Rāzī, *Mafātīh al Ghayb*, 3.6:101.
179. Abū Bakr Ibn 'Arabī, *Ahkām al Qur'an*, 1:208.
180. The Believers 23:5–7.
181. *Tafsīr Ibn al Kathīr*, 5:463.
182. Kishk, *Khawāter Muslim fi al Mas'ala al Jinsiyya*, 74.
183. I say relatively because *nikāh* is a word shared between marriage and sexual intercourse.
184. Badruddīn Muhammad Ibn 'Abdullah al Zarkashī, *Al-Burhan Fi 'Ulūm al Qur'an* 2 (Beirut: Dār al Jīl, 1988), 4.
185. *Sahīh al Bukhārī*, 3.7:3.
186. Ahmed Ibn Hajar al 'Asqalānī (1372–1448), *Fath al Bārī* 9 (Dār al Ma'rifa: Beirut, 2004), 112.
187. *Sahīh al Bukhārī*, 3.7:5.
188. Ibid., 4.
189. *Ibn al Kathīr*, 5:463.
190. An Islamic school of thought.
191. Ibn Taymiyya, 10:573–74.
192. Trans. The reference is to spermatozoids.
193. If one is to say the principle of *qiwāma* goes beyond the condition of providing to include favoring—"Men are in charge of women because of that with which God has distinguished one of them over another and because they financially provide for them" (Women 4:34)—I shall respond that the expression "one of them over another" identifies neither the favored nor the disfavored side.
194. In the context of this joint charge, I shall insert Section 23 from the Tunisian Personal Status Code which binds the wife to provide for her family if she has money.
195. The Tunisian Personal Status Code, Section 13.

Chapter Three

Perplexity over Homosexuality

Lately, homosexuality has been discussed more openly than at any time in the past. This does not necessarily mean that homosexuality as a practice increased; rather, it is its expression or, to use other words, its representation[1] that did. There is no doubt that some concepts such as human rights, difference, responsible freedom, and others played a role in transforming what was once taboo into the open, especially in Western countries where some judicial systems allow the legal cohabitation of same-sex partners. Other systems hold it permissible to have same-sex marriage. Despite the existence of homosexuality in our Muslim and Arab countries, silence over this issue is still quite prevalent. If we go back to what the Qur'an and the Sunnah said about this issue, we find ourselves facing various forms of philosophical perplexity.

PERPLEXITY ONE: BISEXUALITY IN THE QUR'AN

The Great Almighty says: "O mankind! We created you from a male and a female, and made you into nations and tribes, so that you may know one another. The most righteous among you is the noblest in the sight of God. God is all omniscient and knowing" (The Walls 49:13). In her reading of this verse, Rajā Benslāma views that "the divine-gendered order is built on an explicit duality that refuses a third gender."[2] In truth, one does not see this verse as a reference to the gender order but to the common biological distinctions which are difficult to deny. Even if one goes back to the type of gender trouble pointed out by Butler,[3] there is neither third, fourth, nor even a fifth gender to be found. The way an individual imagines his sexual identity cannot totally escape the biological male/female duality, for it cannot be absolutely negated even if one could fall within or outside it. Homosexuals, bisexuals, transsexuals, or those who see themselves as neither women nor men according to Rajā Benslāma's expression,[4] in fact and in most cases, either possess or do not possess a penis in the biological sense. One goes even further than that by postulating that this verse is not referring to the "natural," but to the "cultural." And why wouldn't the Qur'an, in asserting that mankind is created from a male and a female, be pointing to sexual, biological, and psychological duality that distinguishes every human being? The structure of the aforesaid verse ("We created you from a male and a female") permits the possibility of such interpretation, for the use of the preposition "from" which signifies division allows the interpretation of a division of separateness, which is the prevalent explanation (we created people from males in full possession of their masculinity and from females in full possession of their feminineness) as well as the interpretation of a division of connectedness that the Arabic language does not negate (We created people each one of them carrying inside some masculine and female characteristics).

While the sexual duality within each person is a possible interpretation, the Qur'an continues to reveal in other contexts an "original" complementarity between the masculine and the feminine, albeit on an abstract and imaginary level rather than a material and sensory one. Did the Great and Almighty God not assert twice His unity in opposition to the Arabian Peninsula's polytheism? Did He not confirm that he had no *sāheba* or female mate? (The Livestock 6:101 and The Djinn 101:2). One must not dismiss the use of the female gender inflection requiring God to be positioned within a male-gendered language, believed to find complementarity only with a female one. While maintaining that I am not referring in this context to some abstract linguistic statements unrelated to the actual and real being of the Almighty—which no one can represent since nothing looks like Him[5]—I have noticed despite this that a commentator like Tabarī feels no awkwardness shifting from the symbolic context to the biological field. As an explanation to the Almighty's statement "How can He have a child, He who had never had a female mate?" (The Livestock, 6:101), Tabarī says: "The child has to be either a male or a female. It is imperative that the Almighty has no female mate, for he would have a child then."[6] What is important is that in this impossible hypothesis, the Qur'an uses a masculine symbolic language in reference to the Almighty conferring upon Him an impossible hypothetical female mate, who is no other than a feminine-gendered language, rather than a female, reinforcing thus the complementarity of the male and female duality. This pushes us to ponder over the ways the Qur'an itself handles those cases where this supposed complementarity is lost or rather assumes different shapes as in the issue of homosexuality, or the two cases of *sihāq* (female homosexuality) and *liwāt* (male homosexuality), and this by making use of the very terminologies of commentators and religious scholars.

PERPLEXITY TWO: *SIHĀQ* STORIES, OR WHY DID THE QUR'AN REMAIN SILENT OVER *SIHĀQ*?

In the Qur'an, there is an effort to regulate sexual life on the basis of structures that either narrow down or broaden up according to one's gender and social standing. To illustrate, the Qur'an codifies marriage and points out the forbidden sexual relations as seen in the case of *zinā* (fornication or adultery) and the list of incestuous marriages. At this point our purpose is less to dwell over the concept of sex in the Qur'an than to answer the following twofold question. The first part is: Why did the Qur'an remain silent over *sihāq* (سحاق) (i.e., a sexual relation between two women) while pointing to different forms of sexual practice? The second is: Why did the Qur'an remain silent over *sihāq* while it pointed out *liwāt* (لواط) (if we hypothesize that *liwāt* is the sexual relation between two males)?

These two questions derive their legitimacy from the way the Qur'an sees itself and is seen by the Muslim. If the Qur'an is a book of divine wisdom, then it is permissible for the reader to not only raise questions about what is mentioned in it and how it was mentioned, but also about that which was not mentioned yet could have been.[7] Regarding this subject, I shall not fail to mention some had doubted the Qur'an's silence over *sihāq* maintaining that it was the intended *fāhisha* (فاحشة) in the statement of the Great Almighty "As for those of your women who committed abomination, have from you four witnesses against them" (Women 4:15),[8] for the word *fāhisha* is one of those general words that could be applied to "any action that raises abhorrence in the soul and repulsion on the tongue to the utmost degree of its kind."[9] Because of this general meaning and in the absence of linguistic or precedential evidence, one does not see any reason why *fāhisha* should particularly apply to *sihāq*. Even if one assumes the existence of this non-existent particularization and accepts for the sake of argument that *fāhisha* refers to *sihāq*, this hypothetical assumption will not negate the legitimacy of one's previous enquiry, but transform it into one that resembles it: "Why did the Qur'an discuss at length *liwāt* whereas it referred only once to *sihāq* by using a general word that has no relation to it in any way?"

It is important to remember from the beginning that the Qur'an did not address women as a group at all, but only addressed the group of men even in those issues that concerned women.[10] Because these issues have always been closely tied to the world's phallic order which makes woman a subject for the pleasure of man, we assert right away that there are no issues in the Qur'an that concern women in isolation of men, for if menstruations are mentioned, it is because they affect men in forcing them to keep away from women. True, marriage, divorce and the *'iddah*[11] are all questions that concern women, but they also concern men. The Qur'an does not indicate woman is forbidden to pray or fast while menstruating and although this is a question specific to women, not men, it is inferred only from Prophetic tradition. Does all of this allow us to assume that the Qur'an's silence over *sihāq* is one of those instances where women's independent existence from men is absent in the Qur'an? And does this absence go beyond the Qur'an to fall into a medieval cultural tradition which does not see woman as an independent human being and which regulates sexual relations on the basis of a first-rate gender and a subordinate, dependent one? Is this silence over *sihāq* related to the signifier's incomprehension of the feminine as psychoanalytic theories suppose? Indeed, as Lacan explains, the phallic sign expresses man but it cannot wholly represent the feminine declaring that a woman can only be excluded in view of the nature of things, which is also the nature of language.[12]

But is it possible that this silence over *sihāq* is the language of any signifier? Is it one way of making *sihāq* absent because by excluding man, this sexual practice has fallen outside the world's phallic order that makes woman a subject for the pleasure of man? Is it possible that the silence over *sihāq* is in itself a language signifying that this practice is not a threat to the maintenance of the patrilineal order? The absence of *sihāq* could also be a form of disapproval (a sexual practice outside the phallic order is not worth mentioning) or condemnation (a sexual practice outside the phallic is punished by not mentioning it). Whether *sihāq* was concealed because of disapproval or condemnation, it remains in either case a recognition of a prototypical first-rate sexual practice, which makes all others inconceivable. The concealment reveals a discrepancy which is at the same time important and profound in that from the standpoint of those who disapprove it, *sihāq* is a trivial relationship because it does not fall within the phallic order, and whatever does not concern man is of no concern to the human being because only man is a human being. In addition, *sihāq* is a trivial relationship because it does not threaten the established social order that is built on patrilineal lineage. However, from the point of view of those who condemn it, *sihāq* itself is an abominable relationship not to be mentioned and why not since by excluding man from sexual intercourse, it is threatening his phallic and masculine narcissism?[13] Doesn't this discrepancy between disapproval and condemnation remind us of another discrepancy in the collective imaginary which disapproves of woman by considering her weak, yet at the same time condemns her by viewing her as the holder of inordinate wiles?

PERPLEXITY THREE: *SIHĀQ* IN QUR'ANIC RULINGS

In addition to its absence in the stories, *sihāq* is absent in the rulings of the Qur'an. Despite this, verse 14 in the sūra of The Amramites cannot not call upon the modern reader, for stating, "Alluring to the people are worldly pleasures such as women, having children, piles upon piles of gold and silver" (The Amramites 3:14). It is clear that the Great and Almighty God assigns the love of the cited pleasures to all people and that woman is among these pleasures. Since women are included in the word "people," does this mean that this verse is proclaiming that women too are attracted to the women among those lovely pleasures?

The perplexity which overwhelms the Qur'an's modern reader does not seem to have left any trace among the classical commentators who did not stop to examine the word "people" despite its broad and inclusive etymological significance. According to Arabic dictionaries, this word cannot be used to refer exclusively to one sex or one group of people. And in contrast with the word "*qawm*" in the Arabic language, originally used to refer to a group of men only, this usage is confirmed in dictionaries as well as in His statement: "O you who believe! Let not a people [*qawm*] deride other people, for they may be better than they. Nor shall any women ridicule other women, for they may be better than they" (The Walls 49:11).

This peaceful vision in the Almighty's statement "alluring to the people are worldly pleasures such as women, having children, piles upon piles of gold and silver" has been echoed by many commentators. To cite a few examples among them, al Rāzī says: "Know that there is great wisdom in the love of wife and child the Great Almighty placed in the heart of man. Had not been this love, [original] reproduction and procreation would not have happened."[14] The author of *Mafātīh al Ghayb* is unproblematically substituting man for a human being—unless one presumes al Rāzī may be open to the possibility of marriage between two women, which can neither be imagined nor be. From this same perspective, Tabarī just affirms: "Alluring to the people is the love of worldly pleasures such as women, having children and what has been listed."[15] Even Ibn 'Arabī who relies on an iconic and gnostic reading did not find in the aforesaid verse anything that would raise either perplexity or enquiry.[16] One may explain this serenity by what was previously stated about the view of holding the male to be the ideal human being, which allowed these commentators to create by force an interchange between the word "*ennās*" (people) as signifier and the word "*al rijāl*" (men) as signified. As a result, women and the rest of what was enumerated in the sūra could be subjects for the pleasure of men only.

One expected modern commentators to pause on the generality of the word "people" and especially women's desire, but Ben 'Āchūr is found observing that the desire for women was one of those original human desires: "The statement about the desire for women and children and what follows them is a statement about the origins of human desires and they include numerous desires which are not different across nations, centuries, and countries. The penchant for women is the foundation of human nature. It is prescribed by God for a wise reason which is the preservation of the human species through procreation." This generalization erases woman as a desiring subject and refers to her of course as a desired one only. In contrast with the generalization in the field of sexual desire, there are, however, details on both sexes when the commentator addresses the desire for children. He says: "The love of children is embedded in one's nature, for God instilled in men and women an affective sentiment that makes them see the child as part of them."[17] Details on both sexes continue afterwards in regard to the desire for gold and silver: "Gold and silver are two beautiful things and so is the jewelry made for men and women from them."[18]

Notice the feeling of serenity when the common word "people" preserves its general meaning in the context of the desire for procreation and the desire for gold and silver. Also noticeable is the feeling of serenity when this word is transformed, as if with a magic hand, into a specific word that is restricted to men in the field of sexual desire. This feeling of serenity is odd because it is not substantiated by any linguistic or contextual evidence. What is even more surprising is that this feeling of serenity recurs even in the writings of those who are modernists in methodology and thought. This is the case of Tunisian researcher Grāmi whose curiosity is not triggered by the fact that in this verse the desire for women is assigned to people, not men. From a feminist perspective, Grāmi limits herself to the view that in religious texts women are associated with objects.[19] There is no doubt that any reading of the verse that gives serenity about the naturalness of its meaning is a weakness that impoverishes the reading of the Qur'an in its multiple and various dimensions.

And from one of these, it is possible to wonder: Why can't the choice of the general word "people," to whom women are assigned because they are among the desired objects, have a more insightful and deeper significance that goes beyond sexual desire or sexual intercourse to include the possibility of an inherent and symbolic desire between two females? Because it is by force that they are made mothers, women are the matrix for that original desire which in the beginning stirs every child, male, or female toward the mother. Since Freud, psychoanalytic theories showed that the Oedipal stage in which the male longs for his mother and the female for her father was preceded by a "pre-Oedipal" stage (*pré-oedipe*), in which both the male and female child desire the mother. The daughter's desire for the mother is what pushed Freud to proclaim that there is some naturalness in female homosexuality.[20] Is it possible that the "natural" relationship of desire between the female child and her mother and the absence of threat that female sexuality poses to the phallic symbolic order are the two factors which explain why the number of women who go see a doctor because of the "symptoms" of sexuality is less than that of men who go see one because of those same symptoms?[21] Or is it this "natural" relationship with the mother which makes

Lacan include as transsexual anyone who takes woman as the subject of desire, regardless of gender, male or female?[22]

PERPLEXITY FOUR: LIWĀT STORIES

In the Qur'an, many verses mention the abomination of the People of Lot that was never committed in the world before. Among these: "And Lot said to his people, 'you commit an abomination that no one in the world has ever done before! You lust after men and not women. Surely a wanton people you are'" (The Purgatory 7:80–81); "Do you lust after men of all people and leave your wives which God created for you? Surely a transgressing people you are" (The Poets 26:165–166); "And Lot said to his people, 'How could you knowingly commit such an abomination? You lust after men and not women. Surely an ignorant people you are'" (The Ant 27:54–55); and "And Lot said to his people, 'You commit an abomination that no one in the world has ever done before. You lust after men and commit robbery on highways and evil in your meetings'" (The Spider 29:28–29).

The reader cannot not notice the clearly different ways the *sihāq* and *liwāt* stories are told in the Qur'an. In contrast with the absence of *sihāq*, the Qur'an refers to *liwāt* in several contexts. This is not surprising for if *sihāq* falls outside the world's phallic order—by affecting masculine narcissism, providing a different view of a woman's sexual pleasure and repudiating the view that holds her a mere subject for male pleasure[23]—it does, however, preserve the possibility of having woman as subject for male pleasure, albeit with power, not action. In contrast, male homosexuality does not only go beyond the world's phallic order, but also destroys this order whose existence is possible only if one subject, woman, is available for masculine pleasure.

The social rejection of the female because she is merely subject for male pleasure is what explains the "repugnancy" and denunciation felt towards *liwāt*. If commentators denounce it, it is because it transforms the male into a subject for male pleasure and from there, it makes the male acquire feminine features, destroying therefore the phallic symbolic order that most commentators view as natural. Al Rāzī, for instance, says: "masculinity is believed to be action and femininity is believed to be reaction. If the male starts to react and the female to act, this would be against nature and divine wisdom."[24] Male homosexuality is dangerous because it makes the male who is active, superior, and the best, acquire some features of the denunciated and reactive female.

This is why to this day, we find that despite their disapproval of *liwāt*, Muslim societies prefer, in case there is homosexual relationship between two men, the active rather than the reactive partner, who by performing what is in the social imaginary the function of a woman lowers men's status.[25]

PERPLEXITY FIVE: *LIWĀT* IN QUR'ANIC RULINGS

The previous section (Perplexity Four) viewed *liwāt* as an abomination and its meaning was clear: it was lusting of all people after males, as confirmed and emphasized in most commentaries. However, if one takes a look and contemplates the verses addressing *liwāt*, she or he finds out that what the abomination of the People of Lot delineates as lusting after men is in fact desiring men sexually, at the exclusion of women: "And Lot said to his people, 'you commit an abomination that no one in the world has ever done before! You lust after men and not women. Surely a wanton people you are'" (The Purgatory 7:80–81) and "And Lot said to his people, 'How could you knowingly commit such an abomination? You lust after men and not women. Surely an ignorant people you are'" (The Ant 27:54–55). In other verses in the Holy Qur'an, the abomination of the People of Lot consists of lusting after men, highway robbery, and committing evil acts in gatherings: "And Lot said to his people, 'You commit such an abomination, no one in the world has ever done it before you. You lust after men and commit robbery on highways and evil acts in your meetings" (The Spider 29:28–29).

While the lusting after men may appear as a clear reference, with initially a sexual dimension suggesting sexual relations between men, there was a strong disagreement among commentators over the highway robbery and the committing of vicious acts. Some of them read the highway robbery in its literal meaning which is to rob people who are traveling like highway robbers do.[26] Despite the absence of any contextual or textual evidence, some other commentators read the highway robbery with symbolic meanings such as "cutting out the usual way of having sex with women which includes the greater good of preserving the human species,"[27] or cutting out the influx of travelers to them (the People of Lot) due to their vicious behavior. Indeed it was reported that they used to do that with the travelers they crossed path with and the foreigners who came to their land.[28] Adding some details, al Tabrasī stated that the People of Lot "used to mark those traveling by as hitting targets: "He who hits one down with a stone gets first pick. They would take his money, have sex with him, and give him a three dirham fine—a verdict that used to be issued by a judge."[29]

Given the general and foggy nature of the word "*munkar*"(vice or wickedness), the "committing of vicious acts" was not spared the disputes of commentators, for what "vice" referred to was different from one commentator to another. For al Tabarī, "commentators disagreed over the meaning of vice which God meant and which was committed in their gatherings. Some said that they used to hold farting contests in their gatherings. Others said that they used to throw stones at passersby. Some others said they used to commit abomination in their *majālis* (meetings)."[30] Tabrasī also mentioned that their "meetings incorporated a variety of vices and abominations such as insults, derision, slapping, gambling, playing *mikhrāq*,[31] using travelers as shooting targets, and playing the flute and other musical instruments."[32] As for al Rāzī, he considered that an evil act was "the exposure of what is obscene"[33] (i.e., the exposure of abomination). As Mujāhed put it: "At their meetings, they [men] used to lust after men and see one another."[34] Some commentators preferred one explanation over the others such as al Tabarī who asserted that "the explanation that is most likely to be correct is the one which says that in your gatherings you are taking the passersby as shooting targets and deride them as an account by the Prophet, peace upon him, has reminded us."[35] What is important is not settling over one single explanation for the meaning of highway robbery or vice, for each has her/his arguments and readings, and the Qur'an carries various meanings especially when it comes to interpreting such vague and foggy concepts, literally or symbolically. What is important, in my opinion, is that the abomination of the People of Lot was not simply lust after men, but also included other acts that threatened the safety of others as well as their physical and psychological well-being. It is even possible to go further than that and wonder: Was the abomination of the People of Lot lusting after men or forcing men into non-consensual sex, aside from hitting them, throwing stones at them, and insulting them?

The Qur'anic story mentioned in the sūra of Hūd, sūra of the Valley, sūra of the Winnowing Winds, and sūra of the Moon makes us lean toward this conclusion as in His divine statement: "And when our messengers, who had been harmed, came unto Lot, powerless to do anything, he said: 'This is a difficult day.' And when His people, who had grown accustomed to their sinful acts, came rushing unto him, he said: 'O my people, it would be purer for you, if you take my daughters instead. Be fearing of God. Do not shame me in front of my guests. Have you not one reasonable man among you?'"[36] (Hūd 11:77–78). In the sūra of Hūd as well, the Great Almighty also says: "And the people of the city came, rejoicing at the news. He said: 'These are my guests. Embarrass me not! Be fearing of God and shame me not!'" (The Valley 15:67–68–69). The same story recurs in the sūra of the Winnowing Winds (51:24–37) and sūra of the Moon (53:37). All the stories converge that the angels who had come to announce to Abraham the birth of his son immediately told him about the severe punishment that would befall the People of Lot. The commentators point out that the People of Lot, mistaking the angels for nice-looking men, rushed to his house to seduce them. The text of the Holy Qur'an asserts two important things: the first is the correlation between the angels and the law of hospitality in that we find the words "guest" and "Abraham's guest" repeated in every verse the story is men-

tioned. The second is Lot's[37] fear and worry when he learned about the visit
of his people. Inviting them not to dishonor and shame him through his
guests, and wishing for a force to repel them, "he said: 'I wish I were strong
enough to face you, or could seek protection from a powerful ally!'" (Hūd
11:80). It is clear from what preceded that they were not coming to Lot's
house to give his guests a proposal they may either accept or reject, according to a view of sexuality that is based on the principle of consent and
rejection, but rather to force his guests into sex acts against their will (i.e., to
bring him shame and dishonor in a land which holds hospitality to be one of
its moral foundations). This is what many commentators have asserted.
Tabarī, as a matter of fact, emphasizes that Lot was worried about his guests
and knew that he had to defend them.[38] It is obvious that defense can be only
for those who are the target of a particular harmful action and not for those
who have the choice of doing or not doing an action. From that same perspective, al Rāzī indicates that Lot "was worried about them (the guests)[39]
from his people's wickedness and that they may be unable to defend themselves."[40] And resistance from one who desires to do an act or is consenting
to it is not conceivable.

In explaining Lot's statement, Tabarī transforms and makes the implied
meaning of rape explicit: "Do not shame me through my guests": "Do not
humiliate me! In riding my guests against their will, you are riding me."[41]
Tabarī also emphasizes the guests' hatred to what the People of Lot wanted
to do with them, "Lot said to his people: 'Those you came for to rape are my
guests. It is a man's duty to honor his guest. Do not shame me, o people,
through my guests. Honor me by renouncing your intent to harm them.'"[42]

We infer from what precedes that the abomination of the People of Lot
could go beyond beating, stone-throwing, and insults to non-consensual sex
with men (i.e., raping them). This is what Ben 'Āchūr asserts in declaring
that one way through which the People of Lot have committed abomination
has been by forcing passersby into it.[43] It seems that guests (i.e., the foreigners who pass by the village), are the primary target of rape. This may explain
the allusion to the highway robbery in the Qur'an, the focus on the protocol
towards guests in the Qur'anic story, and Tabarī's statement that the People
of Lot "raped" only those who came as guests, for they told Lot: "We will
not leave our practice. Beware of having, hosting, or inviting someone to stay
with you. We shall leave neither him nor our practice."[44] Ben 'Āchūr also
asserts that the People of Lot used to hang out on the roads to choose whom
to pick among the passersby.[45]

Perhaps the stretching of the abomination of the People of Lot beyond the
prevalent and explicit meaning, which is the lust after men, manifests itself in
the views of some commentators who considered that "the People of Lot
were punished for blasphemy (*kufr*)," this is why the punishment included
the elderly and the young.[46] However, let's study how the abomination of the

People of Lot has been delineated in the Qur'anic narrative, for if we had easily agreed on the reason why *liwāt* had been prohibited—which is causing harm to others by beatings, insults, and rape—it is difficult for the prudent reader not to wonder why the Qur'an focused on the prevalent meaning for the abomination of the People of Lot. Being also the common denominator between these verses, this abomination consists of lusting after men and not women. This specific designation is illustrated in the use of coordinating conjunctions or the conditional mode as seen in His statement, "Do you lust after men of all people *and*[47] leave your wives which God created for you? Surely a transgressing people you are" (The Poets 26:165–166). If one is to follow the linguistic rule on coordinating conjunctions, s/he would find that the condemnation of lusting after men is linked to the condemnation of leaving the spouses that the Almighty had created. This is similar to the statement, "You eat bread and leave the apple," which condemns both the eating of bread and the leaving of the apple, not just the eating of bread. As for the conditional mode, its use is evident in the words of the Great Almighty who repeats that they lusted after men and not the women: "And Lot said to his people, 'you commit an abomination that *no one in the world has ever done*! You lust after men and not women. Surely a wanton people you are'" (The Purgatory 7:80–81) and "And Lot said to his people, 'How could you *knowingly* commit such an abomination? You lust after men and not women. Surely an ignorant people you are'" (The Ant 27:54–55). The expression "and not women" is a conditional clause which suggests that the abomination of the People of Lot takes form only when two conditions are met (i.e., lusting after the men on the one hand, and lusting after them and at the exclusion of women on the other hand). As a matter of fact, lusting after men—from a linguistic viewpoint—cannot be reckoned as a prohibition unless women are turned away from and avoided. Rather, it is having them together that is prohibited.[48] This is similar to the Almighty's statement, "You command people to be righteous and yourself, you forget and you are reciting the Book. Have you any common sense?" (The Heifer 2:44). The condemnation is not just for the command of righteousness but also for forgetting at the same time the self.

Whether the Qur'an uses coordinate conjunctions or conditional clauses, the connection between the lust after men and the avoidance of women cannot be arbitrary, especially given that it creates two linguistically possible readings: the first reading is "instantaneous" and hypothesizes that the expression "and not women," which means the avoidance of sex with women, is a mere assertion of the expression "lust after men," which means having sex with men. This is because at the very instant a man approaches another sexually, he is, at least in principle, avoiding woman. As for the second reason, it is temporal in that it views the expression "and not women" as a temporal designation so that a man can sexually approach another, for some men may have sex only with men during their lifetime while others may have sex with both men and women in different periods of their lives. These are the bisexuals (i.e., those who do not belong to that group which lusts after men and forsakes women).

My purpose is not to top one viewpoint over another. In fact, it is not the nature of this work to make final judgments, for I always remember that only God knows the true meaning of the Qur'an. Rather, my purpose is to announce a philosophical perplexity that calls for investigation and elucidation. Because God commands me to observe and reflect, I wonder what brought the words of the Great and Almighty God, which are wise and valid at any time and place, to follow the lust after men with the avoidance of women.

Homosexual relations between men necessitate two elements. The first is desire for men and the second is either the temporary or total avoidance of the opposite sex (i.e., women). In the Qur'an, the focus is on the second element. Does the emphasis on this element (i.e., the avoidance of women), which is seen as the complete picture of the abomination, have any profound and subconscious significance?

To answer this question, it is necessary to have a quick reminder of the unconscious representation of the sexual relation between man and woman as explained in Lacanian psychoanalysis (*Lacanian*). This relationship rests upon a clear discrepancy between two elements: the first is symbolic, appears in verbal discourse, and is built on complementarity. The second is real (*réel*),[49] appears on the unconscious level, and is built on separation. As for linguistic discourse, the latter paints a relationship of complementarity between the active man who possesses the penis (*pénis*) and the passive woman who receives it. As for the unconscious manifestation of the sexual order, it defines man as a desiring subject (*désirant*) and woman as desired object (*objet du désir*). This duality may seem to rest on complementarity were it not for the knowledge that the phallus is the only subject of desire in any person, male or female.[50] Given especially the knowledge that woman represents the phallus for man, the contradiction between the manifest complementarity and the actual separation becomes noticeable. This is because when a man desires a woman, his desire is, in fact, for the phallus (i.e., for what he lacks), but in this desire of his, it is expected from him who suffers from lack, to fill the lack of the Other (i.e., the woman's lack of a penis). Hence, the man is at the same time lacking and required to fill in the Other's lack. This is what makes the ideal of complementarity become, on the level of discourse turn, in the ordeal of encounter, suddenly complex.[51] This original split in man between an original lack in him and the call to desire a woman, who herself, lacking, is begging him to fill in her lack, explains the anxiety that the desire for woman elicits in man.

In a famous expression, Lacan asserts that "there is no sexual relationship." This expression, in our opinion, goes beyond negating the complementarity of the sexes to remind one of the human being's original lack, that is, of the void in the original desire, which no object of a passing need can ever fill. In her/his essence, a human being is a desiring creature who is lacking in relation to what constitutes wholeness, that is, the non-divine (from a psychoanalytic standpoint)[52] and God from a religious standpoint.[53]

The Great and Almighty God wants human beings to accept their original lack given that it is an embodiment of them as creatures and of Him as creator and of them as worshipers and of Him as the worshiped. If this complementarity[54] is reached more easily through same-sex relations, and if the essence of the sexual relation with the opposite sex is a reminder of this lack, it is only logical that the Qur'an denounces the avoidance of the opposite sex—including the anxiety and fear of castration one confronts in such a relation—for it is a form of escapism from the original lack that characterizes her/him. Perhaps, this is the highest point one can reach to defy that lack and refuse the limits of one's human nature.

PERPLEXITY SIX: WHY WAS LOT'S WIFE PUNISHED?

The Qur'an tells that the People of Lot were all punished except him and his family. Some commentators maintain that those who were saved were Lot and his two daughters while others hold them to be his followers or those related to him by in-law ties.[55] As for those who are punished, most of them are from the People of Lot, despite the fact that the Great and Almighty God singled out his wife, which the Qur'an cites again and again as if to emphasize her punishment: (1) "And we rescued him and his household, *save his wife who was among the doomed*" (The Purgatory 7:83)[56]; (2) "The messengers said: 'O Lot, we are your Lord's messengers, and these people cannot reach you. You shall leave with your family during the night, and let not anyone of you look back, *save your wife who will be stricken with what will strike them.* Their tryst is the morning and is not the morning imminent?'" (Hūd 11:81); (3) "He said, 'What is your mission, O messengers?' They said, 'We are being dispatched to evildoers. As for Lot's family, we will save them all *except his wife whom we counted with the doomed*'" (The Valley 15:57–60); (4) "And we saved him and his family, *except his wife; we counted her among the doomed*" (The Ant 2:57); and (5) "He said, 'But Lot is living there.' They said, 'We are fully aware of who is there. We shall save him and his family, except his wife; she is doomed.' When our messengers who had been mistreated, came unto him, he was embarrassed he could not protect them. But they said, 'Have no fear, and do not worry. We will save you and your family, *except your wife; she is doomed*'" (The Spider 29:32–33).[57]

Many commentators have wondered why Lot's wife had been excepted from the rescue for she could not have been involved in the abomination of *liwāt*, given that it is a male abomination that is beyond women's reach. Her punishment could not have been indiscriminate or arbitrary either, for in His Wisdom, He punishes only he who deserves it. Commentators provided two explanations for the punishment of Lot's wife.

The first explanation relies on historical accounts, no traces of which are in the Qur'an. They indicate that Lot's wife used to inform the People of Lot about the handsome male guests who came to their house, which could have made them the possible "victims" of rape. This is asserted for example in the accounts of Tabarī and al Rāzī. For Tabarī, "The wife's desire is the same as theirs . . . when his wife saw them, she liked their handsomeness and beauty, and sent out to the villagers that no one handsomer or more beautiful than their guests had ever been seen, until the news was on everybody's lips." In a different section, the author of *Jāme' al Bayān* states: "When they arrived, the wicked old woman climbed up and waved with her cloth. So, the degenerate hurried in hastily and said: 'What do you have?' She said: 'Lot is having guests tonight. I have never seen more nice-looking faces or a better smell than theirs.'[58] In his usual stern style which recalls that of al Hajāj Ibn Yūsuf, al Rāzī states: "The People suffered because of the abominations they committed, and if his wife did not do any of this, then how come she is among those who are doomed? We say he who incites to evil has the same share of responsibility as he who commits evil. Also he who incites to good is just like he who does it. And she used to inform the People of Lot about Lot's guests so that they could take them as targets. Through the passing on of information, she became one of them."

Commentators gave a second explanation for the demise of Lot's wife which is closer to the Qur'anic text in that it asserts that the Great and Almighty God ordered Lot and those who were saved among his people to not look back at where the oppressors were:

> The messengers said: "O Lot, we are your Lord's messengers, and these people cannot reach you. You shall leave with your family during the night, and let not anyone of you look back, save your wife who will be stricken with what will strike them. Their tryst is the morning and is not the morning imminent?" (Hūd 11:81)

This statement is open to two readings depending on the grammatical function of "your wife." If the word is read in the accusative case, she is the exception amidst his family, which means Lot can start leaving without his wife. If the word is read in the nominative case, she would be the exception in relation to "anyone" and this means that Lot was ordered to make his wife leave (i.e., to save her), but in looking back (i.e., in disobeying the divine order), she caused her demise.[59] Regarding this, Tabarī states:

> At the time they were all destroyed, Gabriel spread in his wing and lifted her up until those in Heaven heard the chants of roosters and the barking of dogs. Then, he put things upside down and made the sky rain with *sijjīl* rocks, and when upon hearing quiet, Lot's wife said, "O my people!" A stone hit her and she was killed.[60]

The first explanation for the death of Lot's wife relies on the fact that she helped the People of Lot commit an "abomination" while the second relies on her looking back at her people (i.e., somehow on her compassion toward them). This compassion toward the "evildoers" sends one back to what was mentioned in the verse decreeing the necessity of not showing pity for the adulterous sinner,[61] notwithstanding the fact that whether *liwāt* is adultery remains the subject of debate among religious scholars as shall be seen.

What is important is that the punishment of Lot's wife for disobeying the order not to look back cannot not remind us of the mythical equivalent of this punishment—at least as far the causes are concerned—for in the well-renowned Greek myth, Orpheus was punished because he had looked back at his beloved which was forbidden by the gods. While the one who dies in the myth is the beloved, the one who is punished is no less than Orpheus who is deprived of her. In the Greek myth and the Qur'anic story, it is the forbidden glance[62] that leads to punishment as if the gaze had frontiers that could not be trespassed. These are the frontiers of what can be seen, that is, the frontiers of what the relative capacity of the eye allows one to see, for mankind can see the picture, but cannot see what cannot be represented. In other words, mankind cannot see the Real (le Réel). The most evident example is when Moses asked to see God and the shocks that befell him afterwards until he repented.[63] Gazing at that which is not permissible is beyond the human dimension and an anticipation of Resurrection Day[64] when the veil shall be lifted over the eye. This is why it is one of the causes that call for punishment.

Relying on either the interpretation of the explicit text or miscellaneous accounts, commentators mentioned two reasons for the punishment of Lot's wife. I hold the Qur'an to be open to interpretations other than to the ones which are textual and linguistic or to the ones historical and contextual—this is the symbolic interpretation. Commentators have explained the reference to Lot's daughters in Lot's statement in the Qur'an, "O my people, it would be purer for you, if you take my daughters instead," as a biological reference to Lot's own blood daughters. It is also possible that the paternity reference is symbolic given that Lot is the Father of the People, which would make the cited daughters here the women in his *umma*.[65] From this perspective, we view Lot's wife as representative of the Mother of the People of Lot, just as

Lot is their Father. The Qur'an's choice of eliminating the Symbolic Mother to save the Symbolic Father and Prophet reminds us of the claim of many psychoanalysts who argue today that the choice of one's sexual subjectivity, heterosexual or homosexual, manifests itself in the pre-Oedipal stage, which is essentially characterized with the relationship with the Mother.[66]

PERPLEXITY SEVEN: PUNISHMENT FOR *SIHĀQ* AND *LIWĀT*

Both the Qur'an and the Sunnah take part in clarifying some of the punishments meted out to sinners in Islam. Even if commentators generally agree on the punishments mentioned in the Qur'an such as the punishment for fornication and thievery, they disagree over punishments attributed to the Prophet, and chief among these is the death penalty by stoning for the married fornicator. This punishment does not exist in the Qur'an despite some people's claim that the verse supporting it has been abrogated and that its ruling remained effective. At this point, my objective is not to study in detail the areas of dissention.[67] Rather, I would like to point out that the absence of an absolute and explicit punishment in the Qur'an for *liwāt* and *sihāq* has engendered disagreement between religious scholars and commentators, for such hypothetical issues are based on interpretation and analogy. One aspect of these interpretations is the attitude of those commentators cited earlier, who held that the Qur'an mentioned and referred to *sihāq* through the word abomination in His divine statement: "Those who commit abomination among your women, you must have from among you four witnesses against them. If they do bear witness against them, then you shall keep such women in their homes until they die, or until God provides a solution for them" (Women 4:15). One of those commentators is Abū Muslim al Asfahānī who saw that the punishment for *sihāq* was imprisonment until death.[68] From within that same perspective, they saw that the punishment for *liwāt* was harming through rebuke or name-calling in view of the Great and Almighty's statement: "And as for those among you, who are guilty of committing it, have those both punished. And if they repent and straighten up, then leave them alone. God is ever redeemer and merciful!" (Women 4:16).

Even though it is the vagueness of the word abomination in the two cited verses which explains the dissimilar positions in the interpretations of this verse, a hadith by the Prophet, peace be upon him, supports the idea that verse 15 in the sūra of Women is about adulterous women, not *sihāq*, in that the Prophet said: "Take it from me that God has made a last recourse about them. The maiden is flogged and the non-virgin is stoned." This hadith caused some to be astonished for if God had provided a last recourse for s/he who committed abomination, the sentence should be lighter not harsher, as death by stoning is harsher than imprisonment.[69]

It is clear thus that there is disagreement over the punishment for *sihāq* and *liwāt* in the Qur'an. This is because of the divergence among commentators and religious scholars between those who seek to link *sihāq* and especially *liwāt* to adultery, whose punishment is clear in the Qur'an, and those who search in the hadiths of the Prophet, peace be upon him, for punishment for *sihāq* and *liwāt*. Those who seek to link *sihāq* and *liwāt* to adultery have contended that *liwāt* is equal to adultery in name, which is abomination, and shares its meaning because "its meaning is legally forbidden and naturally desired. If there is penetration, punishment is permissible."[70] Even though the attribute of abomination qualified both the adultery and male *liwāt*, this common meaning is relative and does not mean they are equal in punishment, for in language abomination is an expression for anything abhorrent to the soul and offensive to the tongue until it reaches the limit of its kind. Given its general usage, abomination goes beyond adultery and *liwāt* and other deeds, as confirmed by many religious scholars in their readings of the word abomination in the Qur'an, such as the statement of the Mighty and Majestic He: "O you who believe! It is not lawful for you to inherit the women nor should you force them to give up anything you have given them, unless proven guilty of abomination" (Women 4:19). There was no agreement among commentators that the abomination which allowed husbands to prevent their wives from marrying (i.e., to remain married to them in order to take their money) is adultery, but they believed this was a recalcitrance that could not be lived with, peevish behavior, or offensive conduct to the husband and his family.[71] From here, it seems because it is a general term, abomination, rather than signifying one meaning, designates adultery, recalcitrance, as well as *liwāt* taken as the sum of those negative deeds mentioned by commentators that would culminate in the rape of guests.

It is no surprise that the equivalence in meaning between adultery and *liwāt* is the subject of disagreement between commentators. While some see that *liwāt* is linked to what is legally forbidden and naturally desired, others see that "treading into a private part not bidden by any permissible obligation, marriage contract, dowry or proof of lineage has not been linked to any punishment."[72] What is strange is that in the view of most commentators adultery is tied to penetration (i.e., to the presence of the male organ in the vagina), which is analogous to the absence of an eyeliner in a kohl bottle and that of a rope in a well. If sexual encounter occurs in a different form, then that is not considered adultery. From a logical perspective, it is likely that these delimitations are tied to the fact that penetration could cause pregnancy (i.e., it could imply the comingling of lineage), and it is this impossibility in the sexual relation between two men that made some religious scholars abnegate death by stoning for *liwāt*, since the comingling of lineage is not to be feared.[73]

Even though al Rāzī departs from that same angle (i.e., the absence of the possibility of procreation), he asserts that *liwāt* is an abomination like adultery. For this commentator, had not God created it for a good reason, desire would have been a repulsive trait in mankind. A good reason for desiring the vulva is to preserve the species through procreation and the protection of one's lineage. Because it achieves only procreation and squanders away lineage, adultery is repulsive on the manifest level. As for *liwāt*, it is even more repulsive because it does not lead to procreation.[74] In seeking to bring homosexuality closer to adultery, or rather in explaining that *liwāt* is more immoral than adultery, al Rāzī is so contemptuous of sexual desire that he sees it as a necessary evil and additionally ties it only to procreation. This attitude is closer to Christian beliefs because Islam does not make any necessary link between sex and procreation, but rather welcomes sexual pleasure in itself provided that it is halal.[75] Otherwise how can we account for what the Prophet, peace be upon him, asserted when he stated that it was charitable penance for a man to sexually approach his wife and for a Muslim to fulfill his sexual desires? How can we explain the Islamic marriage to one's slaves, whose purpose is less procreation than the pursuit of sexual pleasure?

What is important is that al Rāzī and many other commentators, rejecting the absence of any punishment for *liwāt* in the Qur'an, took it upon themselves to provide arguments to prove there is one even if at the expense of the language of the Qur'an and the explicit words of the Almighty. In his distortion of the Qur'an, al Rāzī held the view that the punishment of Lot's People is evidence that this same punishment should be carried out in this worldly life.[76] Regardless of the absence of any correlation between the People of Lot who committed the abomination of highway robbery, vicious acts, and rape and the "sin" of having two men willfully engage in a homosexual relationship, there is no proof that divine punishment for a people who have been wiped out for their sins or disobedience is the model for human punishment. If this were the case, we should punish by drowning anyone who accused Muhammad of falsehood because this was the same punishment that the Great and Almighty God inflicted on those who rejected the message of Noah. Is not the sin the same (i.e., accusing prophets of falsehood)?[77] Even if we concede hypothetically that there is a rationale for an analogy between the penalty against the People of Lot in a court system and the way God punishes those people who are non-believers, the question of the People of Lot will not easily be solved because here is no consensus over the divine punishment which befell them, for the Qur'an says: "And a heavy rain we rained upon them. See the end of evildoers" (The Purgatory 7:84). Although Ben 'Āchūr indicates that the word "rain" refers to the water descending from the clouds, he leans towards the Torah in explaining that what befell the People of Lot were "either stones and sulfur or lightning strikes or earthquakes."[78] There was also disagreement over the meaning of "*rejs*" in the

Great and Almighty's statement: "And we are about to bring down on the people of this town a fury (*rejs*) from the sky as a consequence of their wickedness" (The Spider 29:34). "Some of them said it referred to a stone and it is said to be a fire and an eclipse to others. Despite this, its source cannot be the Heavens but rather it is the order to eclipse or its ordinance that comes from the Heavens."[79] The Great and Almighty God mentions in other verses similar types of punishment in that He says: "And when it was time for our ordinance, we turned it upside down and made the sky rain with a pile of devastating rocks (*sijjīl mandhūd*)" (Hūd 11:82). An in another verse, He says, "And we turned it upside down and rained upon them *sijjīl* rocks" (The Valley 15:74). While commentators agreed on the meaning of turning it upside down, they disagreed on whether the word "*sijjīl*" attributed to the rocks was referring to a very hard rock, some clay rock, or the name of the earthly sky that God had brought down on the People of Lot.[80] In addition to the types of punishment that befell the People of Lot, one finds another punishment embodied in His statement: "And they even asked to have sex with his guests. So, we blinded them. Now suffer my punishment after you have been warned" (The Moon 54:37). That this punishment consists of transforming into blind those who are all-seeing is asserted in Tabarī's statement, "When they came to Lot to have sex with his guests, the messengers struck them and blind they returned."[81] Does this verse necessarily imply by analogy gouging out the eyes of those proven guilty of the sin of *liwāt*?

What is important in all of this is that even if we hypothetically concede that the Sharia Law punishment only replicates the divine law that wiped out nations which has been proven erroneous and impossible in practice (for how can a man turn earth upside down or send rocks or clay from the sky?), one can only wonder about one's ability to choose one of these various punishments over which there is disagreement. Interpreting His divine statement, "And a heavy rain we rained upon them. See the end of evildoers" (The Purgatory 7:84), Al Rāzī states,

> What is intended from this punishment is the bringing down of rocks upon them. So the verse came to mean as a result, come see how God brought down stones on him who does such a specific action. And the citation of the sentence just after the appropriate description is proof that the latter is the cause for that sentence. This verse requires that this specific wrongdoing is the cause for this specific deterrent. Whenever the cause occurred, that sentencing had to follow wherever that cause may have happened.[82]

It is not known if al Rāzī leaned towards sentencing the *lāta*[83] to death by stoning and neglected most deterring measures previously cited because it was easy to throw stones or rather because it was feasible, contrary to causing earthquakes or pouring clay rain from the sky, which may not only be difficult or beyond man's ability, but could also hurt groups of people, not a few individuals. Al Rāzī has perhaps opted for the stoning to death by analogy with the death by stoning for the married adulterous spouse, a ruling most commentators not only asserted without any well-founded Qur'anic text, but over which these same commentators were also unsure if such an abrogation of the Qur'an by the Sunnah should be considered as one of the consensuses reached by the disciples or as a source of jurisprudence that would be more important than the Qur'an.

What is substantiated is that the Qur'an has only a hundred lashes for the adulterous man and woman as explicitly asserted in the sūra of Light. What is also substantiated is that the Qur'an has no explicit provisions for *lāta* (homosexual men), not to mention any punishment for *musāhiqāt* (homosexual women)[84] over which the Qur'an remains silent, unless we viewed verses 15 and 16 in the sūra of Women[85] as referring to *lāta* and *musāhiqāt* which would make scolding and rebuke the punishment for the first as Abu Hanīfa had suggested, and house imprisonment for the second. The Sunnah, however, may indicate some punishments for him who engages in the acts of Lot's People. Among these is a statement that has been attributed to the Prophet, peace be upon him, "Whoever you find doing the action of the people of Lot, execute the one who does it and the one to whom it is done."[86] And since the misdeeds of the People of Lot are general such as committing wickedness, highway robbery, throwing stones, and rape and since this hadith is leaning towards the meaning of rape—since there is a one who does it and another to whom it is done—that hadith allows the killing of the one who is acted upon even if a helpless victim of rape. This matches another hadith by the Prophet told by Abū Dāwūd, al Thirmidhī, al Nisā'ī, and others, and which states: "He who is found having sex with a female donkey, he and the female donkey shall be put to death."[87] The female donkey who is a victim is also killed. This "logical" embarrassment is what made some decree the killing of the man, but not the female donkey. Ibn Arabī is of the opinion of completely denying the second hadith about the female donkey and considered it a hadith matrūk (discarded) by consensus. One does not know how a hadith can be discarded by consensus. Does it mean that it was not said, and in this case it becomes a fabricated hadith which escaped many of the best religious scholars? Or does it mean it was said then discarded by consensus? Why would this be surprising, after one saw how in matters of inheritance and marriage consensus had become a substitute for the explicit word of the Almighty in the Qur'an, whenever some of the commentators fancied? If it is confirmed that consensus is a substitute for the Qur'an, then the opinion of commentators has priority sometimes in being the substitute for the Prophet's statement. Is not the Sunnah of the Prophet the second source of law after the Qur'an?

It is odd that the entire Prophet's hadiths which condemn *liwāt* and decree punishment for them who commit it have been attacked for their lack of authenticity. For instance, al Tirmidhī finds the hadith, in which the Prophet, peace upon him, cursed three times those who commit *liwāt* and stated: "Verily, what I fear most for my nation is the deed of the People of Lot." Commentators also rejected the hadith, "Whoever you find doing the action of the People of Lot, execute the one who does it and the one to whom it is done" on the basis of some disagreement over its attribution to 'Akrama 'an Ibn 'Abbā in the chain of transmission (*isnād*). They also said that the hadith that "*sihāq* among them [was] adultery" had a weak chain of transmission. The hadith that "when a man rides a man, God's throne is shaken" was described as weak and meager in content. The narrator in Ibn 'Abbas's hadith, "If a *lūtī*[88] were to die without repentance, he is transformed in his tomb into a pig" was described as mentioning unknown people, and one of its sources, Ismaīl Ibn Um Dirham, was not an authoritative voice. Ibn al Jawzī has even included this hadith in the list of fabricated hadiths.[89]

If one is to look today at the rampant fatwas on the internet, s/he will find out that the sheikhs who make them use these weak hadiths to justify the punishment for *liwāt*. If one is to consider those hadiths by the Prophet to be authentic and hypothetically concede, for the sake of argument, that they do not refer to the actions of the People of Lot, which are described in the Qur'an and by commentators as oppression, aggression, and rape, but to a homosexual relation between two men based on acceptance and consent, it is permissible to wonder: If these hadiths had been cut off, what would make a commentator like al Rāzī rely on logical arguments and logical analogies to pronounce death by stoning as the penalty for adultery? Would not the use of explicit hadith have been easier? What would make a noble religious scholar like Abū Hunaifa dismiss this hadith if it were an authentic and trustworthy hadith? Did not Abū Hanīfa limit the punishment for homosexuality to rebuke?[90]

The objective of writing this book is not to prove or disprove the existence of a punishment for homosexuality, nor is it our purpose to define the type of that punishment if found. Other religious scholars and lawmakers are more apt to do this job than I am. What I wish to look at and interrogate are religious sources and the texts of Islamic jurisprudence to show that what some may consider final and explicit is only a belief that lacks observation, examination, and precision. If observation, examination, and precision are necessary to the field of academic research and theoretical issues, they can only be all the more necessary in the field of judicial theory and practice, for they have a strong bearing on the lives of others. Is it a trifle to have an Egyptian court give in the twentieth century the death penalty to a group of gay people while no such punishment against them is indicated in the Qur'an, and while there is no consensus among Islam's religious scholars to confirm any tradition that calls for the killing of gay people? Did those not take into consideration the astonishing and huge difference between the Hanafī punishment by rebuke and Malekī punishment by killing, not to mention stoning to death? Is the court sure that the verdict it announced without any Qur'anic supporting evidence is not a murder of an innocent person? Isn't the spilling of people's lives without any legitimate cause itself the wickedness on Earth? Or did those consider suspended the words of Abū Hanīfa and others? Did they perhaps believe that it was not for the greater good that the Great and the Almighty God decreed certain things in his Book and remained silent over others, which is to distinguish mankind from one another and elevate the position of those *mujtahedīne* who use reason?

PERPLEXITY EIGHT: ARE THE *GHILMĀN* OF HEAVEN FOR SEXUAL SERVICE?

In many verses, the Qur'an points to the Heavenly bliss that the Great and Almighty God promised for the pious among His people. Among this bliss are rivers of wine for the pleasure of those who drink it,[91] the wide-eyed *hūris*,[92] and the *ghilmān* or young men that the Qur'an refers to in three places: (1) "And waiting on them are *ghilmān* as if they were hidden pearls" (Mount Sinai 52:24); (2) "And waiting on them are immortal youths with cups, pitchers and pure drinks" (The Event 56:17–18); and (3) "And waiting on them will be immortal youths you shall take for scattered pearls upon seeing them" (Mankind 76:19). It seems the Qur'an has put these pages at the service of the dwellers of Paradise, as they wait on them with cups and pitchers. The hadiths of the Prophet, peace be upon him, assert the meaning of service in that a man told the Prophet, peace be upon him: "'O Prophet of God! If this is the servant, then how about He who is served?' He replied: 'I swear by God, who holds in His hand Muhammad's soul that the supremacy of the one being served over the one serving is like the supremacy of the full moon over other stars.'"[93] Commentators have raised the issue of the nature of those servants. While some believed that the children of those who worshiped beings other than God were the servants for the Dwellers of Paradise, 'Alī and al Husseyn held that the children of Muslims had neither sins to be accounted for nor good deeds to be rewarded for. Others proposed that out of all servants, those young men were specifically created to serve the Dwellers of Paradise.[94]

Some commentators, especially the modern ones, were undoubtedly embarrassed by the idea of a paradise having children as servants. Ben 'Āchūr, for example, trying to justify why children were chosen to be Heaven's servants, proclaimed that *wildān*—plural of *walīd*, that is, *sabi* (a young man)—are the best servants one can take because they are quicker to move, faster to work, and the one who is served is not embarrassed to restrain or give them orders.[95]

The inquiry into the nature of those children or into the reason for choosing children pales in comparison with the proclaimed nature of the service those children rendered to the Dwellers of Paradise. While the Qur'an mentioned the service of attending the Dwellers of Paradise with cups of wine, some commentators saw that underneath the emphasis of describing those *ghilmān* with appealing and seductive features may lie the intent to use them for sexual service, especially because those youths were depicted as immortals. What this attribute means is that either they are here forever—they do not die, get old, nor change—or that they are bejeweled, for the word *khalad* means *al qirt* (earring). One is said to have *khalada* his slave concubine when he adorns her with earrings. Muhammad Jalal Kishk considered the description of the *ghilmān* with earrings and bracelets significant "for the wearing of jewelry is fitting of women, but reprehensible for men. How come God mentioned that in the context of seduction? The answer is that since the Dwellers of Heaven are associated with youth, it is reasonable that they are adorned with gold and silver even if they were men."[96] In Kishk's view, their immortality at the age of *ghilmān* is related of the fact that they are the source of sexual pleasure, "And given there is an agreement among commentators over their eternal youth and immortality at the age of *ghilmān*, we have concluded that the text's emphasis on earrings is an assertion of the eternal pleasure of those who desire them, and this contrary to the disappearance in this worldly life of *al fitna* once the *ghulām* turns into a man"[97] Indeed, Kishk asserts that the choice of *ghilmān* of all others to serve can be explained only by the motive of a desired sexual pleasure for him who rose above it in this Earthly Life: "Why does the text emphasize that they are *ghilmān* and male youths? If the goal had been sensory pleasure and nice looks only, why were not they angels? Is there anything more beautiful and magnificent than an angel? Is there a service more excellent than that of an angel?"[98] He even declared that it was our right to interpret from His statement "*ghilmān* for them" that these were their *ghilmān*, the ones over whom they rose, and who protected them from worldly abomination. Now that they are eternally reunited in Paradise, they are forever at the moment when desire was repressed as consequence of religiosity.[99]

My intent is neither to refute the view of those who upheld that these male youths were for sexual pleasure, not is it to confirm their assertion. It is true that there is no explicit indication in the Qur'an to take these male youths as sex objects, however the principle of *al qiyās* (analogy) may lead to this interpretation on the basis that wine which was forbidden in this worldly life would become a reward in the afterlife and that silk forbidden to men to wear in a hadith would become permissible in the afterlife as seen in his statement, peace be upon him, "He who is delighted that the Great and Almighty God will serve him wine in the afterlife, let him leave it in this worldly life. And he, who is delighted that the Great and Almighty God will clothe him in silk in the afterlife, let him leave it in this worldly life."[100]

One may forgo the questions of al Ma'arrī who was mystified that what was forbidden in this worldly life would become lawful in the afterlife. One may also forgo the expediency of some Muslims who construct delights in the afterlife to receive them in the worldly life as is the case of Yaḥyā Ibn Aktham who said: "God blessed the Dwellers of Paradise by serving them male youths He placed above slave girls in service. Who shall now pull me away from the honor He tailored for the Dwellers of Paradise?"[101] One shall forgo the questions of al Ma'arrī and of those who shared his pathway, because as the word of a wise God, the Qur'an cannot be held accountable for the reader's confusion between the worldly life and the afterlife, even though the Great and Glorious He made distinctions between the enjoyments of this worldly life and the blessings of the afterlife as in His statement "And all that is nothing but the enjoyment of worldly life. And the Hereafter, to your Lord, is for the righteous" (The Ornaments 43:35). One shall also forgo the words of Ibn Aktham and Kishk, for the Qur'an can be held accountable neither for the fantasies nor the deep-seated desires that some want to antici-pate in this worldly life and that others rise above only out of cupidity for the afterlife.

I seek neither to assert nor refute the hypothetical issue of the *ghilmān's* involvement in some sexual service. Rather I seek to raise a deeper perplex-ity regarding some commentators' strong propensity to anticipate what is in Heaven and present it in a detailed, clear, and sensory picture. What one cannot ignore is this frenzied rush to present final and ready-made answers in anything that relates to religion. Although things could be dangerous, one may take it easy in matters of law despite the differences and the range of opinions which have been pointed out. One may take it easy in matters of law, especially given that the need for a resolution, even a partial one, im-poses itself to answer the call for social coexistence on the basis of laws which would regulate interaction between people. What is strange, however, is that the frenzy to find ready-made answers goes beyond worldly matters to persist in the context of the afterlife, toward which perhaps the simplest form of human humility invites us to stop, fully conscious of our limits and lack. Is it not strange that many commentators ignore this possible explanation for the Almighty's statement, "Such as the symbol of the Heaven promised for the righteous beneath which rivers flow, its fruit and shade everlasting" (The Thunder 13:35) or the statement of the Great and Glorious He, "Such as the symbol of Heaven promised to the righteous wherein are rivers of pure water" (Muhammad 47:15). This explanation is based on the belief that the Heaven cited in the Qur'an is only a symbolic picture to a Heaven that the human mind cannot fathom because of its limits. What further supports this explanation is the statement of the Prophet, peace be upon him, that "Heaven consists of that which no eye has ever seen and no ear has ever heard, without any harm done to the human heart."[102] But it is doubtful that the commentators, who count the deflowering of maidens as the mission of the Dwellers of Heaven, would adorn themselves with some humility, or rather modesty which would invite them to be silent over that which cannot be articulated.

THAT WHICH LIES AFTER PERPLEXITY

I have demonstrated that in the Qur'an *sihāq* is missing and presented different explanations for this absence. I also tried to explain that *liwāt* was not synonymous with homosexuality. The abomination of the People of Lot comprises anything that harms others, and in the context of sexuality, it specifically refers to the raping of men by men. Are we ignorant or do we pretend to be ignorant when we delude ourselves with the common view that sexual encounters between two men and between two women are the same thing as homosexuality? Are we forgetting or pretending to forget the psychological and unconscious dimensions of the sexual act which reveal the child's relation to the mother as well as the deep-seated basis for a man's relationship with a woman? If this condemnation and denunciation of homosexuality on the basis of subjective rulings reveals anything, it is one's psychological anxiety and refusal of difference, not to mention one's psychological dividedness on the unconscious level.

In many Muslim countries, it is an embarrassment to speak about homosexuality. And if in the end I tied the various types of perplexity to the question of the *hudūd* against *liwāt* and *sihāq*, clarified that these punishments were missing in the explicit text of the Qur'an, and pointed to the divergence of opinions on this issue between religious scholars, my purpose is to highlight the big or rather the enormous difference in attitude toward homosexuality between the old religious scholars and commentators on the one hand and common Muslims today on the other hand. Even if one is to include her/himself in the conservative opinion that all those who practice *liwāt* must necessarily be killed or stoned to death, it is necessary to raise the following question: is the killing of all those who practice *liwāt* going to put an end to homosexuality? Is *liwāt*, as any other form of sexual behavior, a conscious and rational choice that can be eliminated through mere rebuke? Do not many of those who practice *liwāt* in the Muslim world wish to be part of the predominant sexual matrix? Do not many of them wish to marry for the sake of psychological and sexual stability and social approval? Is this not difficult at times and impossible at others? Is it on the basis of horror, fear, and threat that Muslims can show love for other Muslims and help one another achieve inner peace? Has the concept of a Muslim changed from being, he who says there is no God but God and Muhammad is his Prophet, to becoming s/he who applies what this so-called religious scholar or sheikh said? Have some of us perhaps fallen into idolatry in substituting themselves for the Almighty God, distinguishing the Kaffir from the Muslim and penetrating people's heart to determine the degree of divine blessing upon them and the possibility of their inclusion in the vast mercy of the Great and Almighty God?

NOTES

1. Gisèle Chaboudez, *Rapport sexuel et rapport des sexes* (Paris: Denoël, 2004), 363.
2. Raja Benslāma, *Bunyān al Fuhūla: Abhāth fi al mudhakar wa al mu'anneth* (Tunis: Dar al Ma'rifa li al nashr, 2006).
3. Judith Butler, *Trouble dans le genre, pour un féminisme de la subversion* (Paris: Editions la Découverte, 2005).
4. Rajā Benslāma, *Bunyān al fuhūla*, (The Foundations of Virility) (Tunis: Dar al Ma'rifa li al nashr, 2006), 28. Dolto holds a similar interpretation when she argues that Adam and Eve could be symbolic representations of the active and passive polarities we find in one person, be it male or female. Françoise Dolto, *Le Féminin* (Paris: Gallimard, 1998), 25. To these two interpretations, add a third one which considers that the preposition "from" does not mean in this context splitting but origin. The meaning of the verse is that all people were created starting from one male and one female who are Adam and Eve. See Fakhr al Dīne al Rāzī, *Mafātīh al Ghayb*, 14.28:137.
5. "Nothing is like Him and He hears and sees everything" (*Consultation*, 42:11).
6. Al Tabarī, *Jāmi' al Bayān*, 5:293.
7. A large number of commentators raise questions about the reason for mentioning it in view of an already existing text rather than a hypothetical one. This type of explanations is predominant in what is characterized as the school of rationalist interpretation amplified in the commentaries of al Zamakhsharī or al Rāzī.
8. Ibn 'Arabī, *Ahkām al Qur'an*, 1:354 and *Mafātīh al Ghayb*, 5.9:239.
9. Ibn 'Arabī, Fakhr al Dīne al Rāzī, *Ahkām al Qur'an*, 1:354.
10. Women as a group are not addressed in the Qur'an but some groups of women or a few individuals make partial appearances in some verses. See for example The Amramites 3.42–43 and The Parties 33:33). In *Weak in Mind and Religion*, I tried to explain the absence of the direct address to women with the use of psychoanalytic concepts. See Youssef, *Weak in Mind and Religion*, 88–89.
11. Trans. The three month period following divorce during which a Muslim woman is not allowed to remarry is for the purpose of making sure that she does not get married while carrying a child from the first husband.
12. Vladimir Granoff et al., 12.
13. Old accounts present to us at the same time images which disapprove of, and others which condemn *sihāq*. Within the disapproval category is the following story: "A man was told, 'your wife is having a sexual relation with another woman.' His reply was: 'If she spares me that, which would quench the fire inside, let her do whatever she likes'" (al Tifāshī, 242). Among the forms of condemnation is this poet's statement: "Say to her who likes sex with women that God forbade it because no good is in it/ O perfect beauty! So wrong are you to

elevate *sihāq* above the sword" (*al Tifāshī*, 247). Trans. The two internal quotations in the first quote are added by translator for the purpose of clarification.

    14. Fakhr al Dīne al Rāzī, *Mafātīh al Ghayb*, 4.7:212. Trans. The word between brackets in the quotation is added by translator for clarification purposes.

    15. Al Tabarī, *Jāmi' al Bayān*, 3:198.

    16. Ibn Arabī happened to have used in the past a figurative and symbolic reading of signs, which referred in their original meaning to both the male and female gender. See Muhieddīne Ibn 'Arabī's *Tafsīr al Qur'an al Karīm* (Beirut: Dār al Andalus, 1981), 255–256.

    17. Ben 'Āchūr, *Al Tahrīr wa al Tanwīr*, 3:181.

    18. Ibid.

    19. *Ikhtilāf fī al thaqāfa al 'arabiyya al islāmiyya*, 629.

    20. Serge André, *Que veut une femme?* (Paris: Seuil, 1995), 178.

    21. Granoff et al., 22–23.

    22. Chaboudez, 370.

    23. From a patriarchal perspective, the lesbian still remains a subject for male pleasure. See for example the stories about the transformation of lesbians into transsexuals in *al Tifāshī*, 245.

    24. Fakhr al Dīne al Rāzī, *Mafātīh al Ghayb*, 7:176.

    25. Malek Chebil, *L'Esprit de sérial: Mythes et pratique sexuels au Maghreb* (Paris: Payot, 2003), 75.

    26. Al Tabarsī, *Majma' al Bayān*, 7–8:440.

    27. Fakhr al Dīne al Rāzī, *Mafātīh al Ghayb*, 25.13:59.

    28. Al Tabarī, *Jāmi' al Bayān*, 10:135.

    29. Al Tabrasī, *Majma' al Bayān*, 7–8:440.

    30. Al Tabarī, *Jāmi' al Bayān*, 10:135–136.

    31. Trans. This game consists of wrapping a towel or a piece of cloth to hit someone. It is usually played by male children.

    32. Al Tabrasī, *Majma' al Bayān*, 78:441.

    33. Fakhr al Dīnee al Rāzī, *Mafātīh al Ghayb*, 13.25:59.

    34. Al Tabarī, *Majma' al Bayān*, 7–8:440–441.

    35. Al Tabarī, *Jāmi' al Bayān* 10:137.

    36. The quotes within this quote are not in the original Quranic text. They have been added by translator for clarification purposes.

    37. In the original Arabic text, Youssef wrote "Abraham's fear" by mistake.

    38. Ibid., 7:79.

    39. Trans. Parentheses are in the original Arabic text.

    40. Fakhr al Dīne al Rāzī, *Mafātīh al Ghayb*, 9.18:32.

    41. Al Tabarī, *Jāmi' al Bayān*, 7:84.

    42. Ibid., 526.

    43. Ben 'Āchūr, *Al Tahrīr wa al Tanwīr*, 20:240.

    44. Al Tabarī, *Jāmi' al Bayān*, 11:564.

    45. Ben 'Āchūr, *Al Tahrīr wa al Tanwīr*, 20:240.

    46. Abū Bakr Ibn 'Arabī, *Ahkām al Qur'an*, 2:777.

    47. Trans. Words in italics are the translator's and they show the conjunctions and the conditional mode the author is referring to in the text.

    48. Fakhr al Dīne al Rāzī, *Mafātīh al Ghayb*, 2.3:50.

    49. The real is one of the three Lacanian stages. The others are the symbolic and the imaginary. It includes that which cannot be included in the linguistic representation that is symbolic.

    50. There is a reminder here that the phallus is not the male organ but its symbolic representation. This is why the mother represents for the child an imaginary phallus.

    51. Chaboudez, 95.

    52. Trans. Parentheses exist in the original Arabic text.

    53. To study the relation between the non-divine and God, see Denise Vasse, *L'Autre du désir et le Dieu de la foi, Lire aujourd'hui Thérèse d'Avila* (Paris: Seuil, 1991), 209.

    54. Chaboudez, 364.

    55. Fakhr al Dīne al Rāzī, *Mafātīh al Ghayb*, 7.14:178.

56. Trans. Emphasis in italics is in the original Arabic text.
57. Italicized passages are the author's original emphasis in the Arabic text.
58. Al Tabarī, *Jāmi' al Bayān*, 7:89–90.
59. Fakhr al Dīne al Rāzī, *Mafātīh al Ghayb*, 13.25:63.
60. Ibid., 88.
61. The Almighty says: "The adulteress and the adulterer you shall give each of them a hundred lashes. Be not swayed by pity from carrying out God's law, if you truly believe in God and the Last Day" (The Light 24:2).
62. Alain Didier-Weil, *Les trois temps de la loi* (Paris: Seuil, 1995), 69–70.
63. The Purgatory 7:143.
64. "We lifted the veil over you and your vision became of steel" (Qur'an 50:22).
65. Fakhr al Dīne al Rāzī, *Mafātīh al Ghayb*, 9.18:33–34. Trans. The word umma means nation.
66. This idea is inspired by Muhammad Amine al Trīfī who gave us permission to develop it and publish it. Marie Christine Hamon, *Féminité et mascarade* (Paris: Seuil, 1994), 267–295.
67. For s/he who wants to expand on this point of dissension, please see Muhammad Jalal Kishk's *Khawāter Muslim fi al Mas 'ala al Jinsiyya* (*Meditations of a Muslim Regarding the Issue of Sexuality*) (Cairo: Maktabat al turāth al Islāmī, 1992), 67–72.
68. Fakhr al Dīne al Rāzī, *Mafātīh al Ghayb*, 5.9:239.
69. Ibid., 242.
70. Abū Bakr Ibn 'Arabī, *Ahkām al Qur'an*, 2:776. The mentioning of penetration asserts the predominant silence over *sihāq* and the excessive preoccupation with male homosexuality which even though horrendous, it is indicative of male pleasure.
71. Abū Bakr Ibn 'Arabī, *Ahkām al Qur'an*, 1:363; Fakhr al Dīne al Rāzī, *Mafātīh al Ghayb*, 5.10:12; Ben 'Āchūr, *Al Tahrīr wa al Tanwīr*, 4:286.
72. Abū Bakr Ibn 'Arabī, *Ahkām al Qur'an*, 2:777.
73. Ibid., 776.
74. Fakhr al Dīne al Rāzī, *Mafātīh al Ghayb*, 13.25:59.
75. Abdelwahāb Bouhdība, *La Sexualité en Islam* (Tunis: Cérès, 2000).
76. Fakhr al Dīne al Rāzī, *Mafātīh al Ghayb*, 7.14:179.
77. The Purgatory 7:64.
78. Ben 'Āchūr, *Al Tahrīr wa al Tanwīr*, 8:327.
79. Fakhr al Dīne al Rāzī, *Mafātīh al Ghayb*, 13.25:63–64.
80. Al Tabarī, *Jāmi' al Bayān*, 7:92.
81. Ibid., 91.
82. Ben 'Āchūr, *Mafātīh al Ghayb*, 7.14:179.
83. Trans. This plural word derives from *Liwāt*. It designates men who practice *liwāt*.
84. Trans. This plural feminine word derives from *sihāq*. It designates women who practices *sihāq*.
85. "Those who commit abomination among your women, you must have from among you four witnesses against them. If they do bear witness, then you shall keep such women in their homes until they die, or until God provides a solution for them. And as for those among you, who are guilty of committing it, have those both punished. And if they repent and straighten up, then leave them alone. God is ever redeemer and merciful!" (Women 4:15, 16).
86. Abū Bakr Ibn 'Arabī, *Ahkām al Qur'an*, 2:777.
87. Ibid.
88. Trans. It is a singular masculine noun referring to a man who commits *liwāt*. Its female equivalent is *sāhiqa*.
89. Kishk, 191, 192.
90. Abū Bakr Ibn 'Arabī, *Ahkām al Qur'an*, 1:776.
91. Muhammad 47:15.
92. The Smoke 44:54; Mount Sinai 52:50; Most Gracious 55:72; and The Inevitable 56:22.
93. Al Tabarī, *Jāmi' al Bayān*, 11:492.
94. Al Tabarsī, *Majma' al Bayān*, 9.10:327.
95. Ben 'Āchūr, *Al tahrīr wa al Tanwīr*.
96. Kishk, 200.

97. Ibid., 201.
98. Ibid., 205.
99. Ibid., 201.
100. Ibid., 209.
101. Al Tīfāshī, 174.
102. Ben 'Āchūr, *Al Tahrīr wa al Tanwīr*, 8:133.

Conclusion

Looking at the situation of Islam and Muslims today, it is impossible for one who is endowed with the capacity to think—even a minimal one—not to wonder: What happened to Muslims such that Islam became synonymous with closed-mindedness and extremism? What happened to Muslims such that Tabarī and al Rāzī turned out at times more open-minded than the sheikhs of Al Azhar Mosque or other official religious institutions that attempt to institutionalize a religion based on a man's individual relation with her/his Creator? What happened to us such that we worship the religious scholars and commentators, idolize their words, and forget that they are like us, that is, human beings who are fallible and successful in their independent thinking and that the Almighty God offered us His trust as He did with them? What happened to us so that TV channels become "our path to Heaven" as if the Almighty God, out of love, gave the key to His Garden exclusively to their TV directors? What happened to us such that we failed to "produce" the glorious Islam—the Islam of the freedom of belief, love, and tolerance—and substituted it with "an Islam" which is strange, scary, and that sees in woman only "'awra" that must be covered and sees in man only a greedy animal, who day and night thinks only of sex to the point that a woman's hair could distract him from his religious and worldly duties? What befell us such that we offered our youths only the picture of a screaming sheikh who forbade singing, representation, arts, shaving, and who threatened with the suffering of the tomb anyone who did not observe what he prohibited and provided without any doubt the list of those entering Hell and Heaven with people's first and last names, and at times their national identification card numbers? What happened to us such that we present to the West only the image of a Muslim activist who thinks about jihad by blowing himself up, killing the soul that God forbade to kill, because of a difference of opinion or faith?

This book seeks to grasp only part of the answer. If I was asked to write in one sentence what I included in this book, I would say: Huge is the divide between the Qur'an's capacity for open explanations and interpretations on the one hand, and the closure in the opinions and attitude of most religious scholars and sheikhs on the other hand.

My examination of the contrived deductions of commentators and exaggerations of religious scholars is not in any case an insult to them, nor is it a claim that I have the ultimate truth. Because all of us are subjective, my reading—just as theirs and the readings of those who will come after me—comprises contrived deductions and weaknesses. Perhaps in those many instances in the Holy Book where the Almighty emphasizes what is commonly known in verb and action, He is referring us to the quintessential concept of human subjectivity, for what is *ma'rūf* or commonly known is only that which people have known. As such, it not only differs in space, time, and location, but also varies to suit the diversity in people's views and inclinations. The interpretation of the Qur'an cannot escape "what is commonly known," that is, the ever changing human knowledge that is always in renewal.

Aloud, I raise my voice to ascertain that only the Qur'an is appropriate to any time and space, not the human readings of the Qur'an which are subjective and tied to the affiliations, historical contexts, and psychological complexes of those who hold them. Indeed, I raise my voice to say that Tabarī, al Rāzī, or Ben 'Āchūr—perhaps we shall add for our youths 'Amru Khāled or Yūssef al Qardhāwī—do not possess an absolute and ideal reading of the Qur'an, and in fact, they represent only their subjective and limited selves, just as I only represent my own subjective and limited one. It is always this human subjectivity which leaves the door open for *ijtihād* and which makes every reading of the Qur'an an everlasting adventure that longs for the original meaning that only He, the Almighty, knows.

Appendix A

Index of Qur'anic Verses

THE AMRAMITES / ĀLI 'IMRĀN

"No one knows its interpretation but God" (The Amramites 3:7), v, 2.

"Alluring to the people are worldly pleasures such as women, having children, piles upon piles of gold and silver" (The Amramites 3:14), 104–105.

THE ANT / AN-NAML

"And Lot said to his people, 'How could you knowingly commit such an abomination? You lust after men and not women. Surely an ignorant people you are'" (The Ant, 27:54–55), 107, 108, 110.

"And we saved him and his family, except his wife; we counted her among the doomed" (The Ant 2:57), 113.

THE BANQUET/AL-MĀ'IDAH

"Permitted to you is the meat of the female donkey in your livestock" (The Banquet 5:10), 46.

"Permitted to you this day are all things good. The food of those who received the Scriptures is permitted to you and permitted to them is your food. Also permitted to you is marriage with believing married women and the married women who received the Scriptures revealed before, provided that you pay them what is due to them in wedlock, not as prostitutes or secret lovers" (The Banquet 5:5), 47.

THE BELIEVERS / AL-MU'MINŪN

"Successful indeed are the believers, who are humble in their prayers, who turn away from idle talk, who give charity, and who guard their private parts save for their spouses or those their right hands possess, for no blame is to be laid on them" (The Believers 23:1–6), 76.

THE DISPUTE / AL-BURŪJ

"And those who say to their wives, 'Be as my mother's back,' and then take back what they have said, they shall set free a slave, before the two of them touch one another" (The Dispute 85:3), 112.

DIVORCE/AT-TALĀQ

"As for your women who have despaired of further menstruating, if you are in doubt, their *'iddah* waiting period shall be three months; and those who have not menstruated as yet. (Divorce 65:4), 71, 81.

"And for those with child, their term shall be when they bring forth their burden" (Divorce 65:4), 86.

THE EVENT/AL-WĀQIAH

"And waiting on them are immortal youths with cups, pitchers and pure drinks" (The Event 56:17–18), 122.

"We have created them anew and virgins we made them" (The Event 56:35–36), 72.

". . . till he had attained full strength and reached forty years." (The Event 56:15), 98n141.

THE GATHERING/AL-HASHR

"Take only what the Messenger gives to you and abstain from what he forbids you. Have fear of God; God is severe in his punishment." (The Gathering 59:3), 98n129.

THE HEIFER / AL-BAQARAH

"That is the Scripture whereof there is no doubt, a guidance for the righteous, who believe in the unseen, observe the prayers, give charity from what We bestowed upon them, believe in what is revealed to you and those before you, and have certitude in the afterlife. Those are guided by the Lord. Those are the successful" (The Heifer 2:1–5), 23.

"You command people to be righteous and yourself, you forget and you are reciting the Book. Have you any common sense?" (The Heifer 2:44), 110.

"During fasting, permitted to you is sex with your wife at night" (The Heifer 2:187), 46.

"When they have purified themselves, then come unto them from wherever God has commanded you" (The Heifer 2:222), 66.

"Your women are a tilth for you, so go to your tilth as you please" (The Heifer 2:223), 56, 57, 65, 66.

"Divorced women shall wait by themselves for three cycles" (The Heifer 2:228), 84.

"It is not lawful for them to hide what God has created in their wombs; if they believe in God and the Last Day" (The Heifer 2:228), 84.

"And their husbands have better rights to take them back if they desire to set things right" (The Heifer 2:228), 84–85.

"Divorce must be twice: Either a woman is kept in honor or released in kindness (The Heifer 2:229), 83.

"And do not keep them, intending harm, to transgress against them" (The Heifer 2:231), 83–84.

"And those of you who die leaving behind wives, they [the wives] shall wait by themselves for four months and ten nights" (The Heifer 2:234), 81–82.

"You are not to blame, if you divorce women while as yet you have not touched them nor determined what is owed to them. Yet give them generous gifts, the affluent man and the needy man each according to his needs—an obligation on the righteous" (The Heifer 2:236), 59.

"If you divorce them before touching them, but after you had set the dowry for them, give them half of what you set for them, unless they forfeit their rights, or the rights of the party in whose hand the marriage tie is are forfeited" (The Heifer 2:237), 50.

"God permits trading and forbids usury" (The Heifer 2:275), 23.

"And they ask you about menstruation. Say, "It is harm, so do not approach women at such times and go not in unto them till they purify themselves"" (The Heifer 2:222), 97n102.

"Yet if thou should bring to those that have been given the Scriptures every sign, they will not follow your qibla, nor can you be a follower of their qibla; nor are some of them followers of the qibla of others" (The Heifer 2:145), 2n116.

"And it is not righteousness to enter houses from the back" (The Heifer 2:189), 2n121.

THE HEIGHTS / AL-MA'ĀRIJ

"And in whose wealth there is a right acknowledged for the beggar and the destitute" (The Heights 70:24–25), 23.

HUD / HŪD

"And when our messengers, who had been harmed, came unto Lot, power-less to do anything, he said: 'This is a difficult day.' And when His people, who had grown accustomed to their sinful acts, came rushing unto him, he said: 'O my people, it would be purer for you, if you take my daughters instead. Be fearing of God. Do not shame me in front of my guests. Have you not one reasonable man among you?'" (Hūd 11:77–78), 109.

"He said: 'I wish I were strong enough to face you, or could seek protec-tion from a powerful ally!'"(Hūd 11:80), 109.

"'O Lot, we are your Lord's messengers, and these people cannot reach you. You shall leave with your family during the night, and let not anyone of you look back, save your wife who will be stricken with what will strike them. Their tryst is the morning and is not the morning imminent?'" (Hūd 11:81), 113, 114.

"And when it was time for our ordinance, we turned it upside down and made the sky rain with a pile of devastating rocks (*sejīl mandūd*)" (Hūd 11:82), 118.

THE IRON / AL-HADĪD

"And spend of that over which He made you trustees." (The Iron 57:7), 23.

THE LIGHT / AN-NŪR

"The adulteress and the adulterer you shall give each of them a hundred lashes. Be not swayed by pity from carrying out God's law, if you truly believe in God and the Last Day." (The Light 24:2), 128n61.

THE LIVESTOCK / AL-AN'ĀM

"How can He have a child, He who had never had a female mate?" (The Livestock 6:101), 102.

"And He has set forth in details that he had forbidden you . . . " (The Livestock 6:119), 90.

MANKIND / AL-INSĀN

"And waiting on them will be immortal youths you shall take for scattered pearls upon seeing them" (Mankind 76:19), 122.

THE MOON / AL-QAMAR

"And they even asked to have sex with his guests. So, we blinded them. Now suffer my punishment after you have been warned" (The Moon 54:37) 118.

MOUNT SINAI / AT-TŪR

"And waiting on them are ghilmān as if they were hidden pearls" (Mount Sinai 52:24), 122.

MUHAMMAD / MUHAMMAD

"Such as the symbol of Heaven promised to the righteous wherein are rivers of pure water" (Muhammad 47:15), 124.

THE ORNAMENTS / AZ-ZUKHRUF

"And all that is nothing but the enjoyment of worldly life. And the Hereafter, to your Lord, is for the righteous" (The Ornaments 43:35), 124.

THE PARTIES / AL-AHZĀB

"O Prophet! Tell your wives: "If you want this worldly life and its glitter, then come. I shall allow you to enjoy it and handsomely set you free" (The Parties 33:28), 59.

"O you who believe! If you wed believing women and divorce them before you have touched them, then the *'iddah* (عدة) period shall not be required of them. But indulge them and handsomely set them free" (The Parties 33:49), 113.

THE POETS / ASH-SHU'ARĀ'

"What! Of all creatures do you come unto the males, leaving your wives that your Lord created for you? Nay! You are but a transgressing people." (The Poets, 26:165–166), 69.

THE PURGATORY / AL-A'RĀF

"And Lot said to his people, 'you commit an abomination that no one in the world has ever done before! You lust after men and not women. Surely a wanton people you are'" (The Purgatory 7:80–81), 107, 108, 110.

"And we rescued him and his household, save his wife who was among the doomed" (The Purgatory 7:83), 113.

"And a heavy rain we rained upon them. See the end of evildoers" (The Purgatory 7:84), 118, 119.

THE SPIDER / AL-'ANKABŪT

"And Lot said to his people, 'You commit such an abomination, no one in the world has ever done it before you. You lust after men and commit robbery on highways and evil acts in your meetings" (The Spider, 29:28–29), 107.

"He said, 'But Lot is living there.' They said, 'We are fully aware of who is there. We shall save him and his family, except his wife; she is doomed.' When our messengers who had been mistreated, came unto him, he was embarrassed he could not protect them. But they said, 'Have no fear, and do not worry. We will save you and your family, except your wife; she is doomed'" (The Spider 29:32–33), 113.

"And we are about to bring down on the people of this town a fury (*rejs*) from the sky as a consequence of their wickedness" (The Spider 29:34), 118.

THE TEST / AL-MUMTAHANAH

"O you who believe, when immigrant women who are believers seek asylum with you, you shall test them. God knows their faith best. Once you establish that they are believers, you shall not return them to the disbelievers. They are neither lawful for the disbelievers, nor are the disbelievers lawful for them. Give back to the disbelievers what they have spent on them and it is no sin for you to wed them provided that you pay them what is due to them" (The Test 60:10), 48.

THE THUNDER / AR-RA'D

"Such as the symbol of the Heaven promised for the righteous beneath which rivers flow, its fruit and shade everlasting." (The Thunder 13:35), 124–125.

THE VALLEY / AL-HIJR

"He said, 'What is your mission, O messengers?' They said, 'We are being dispatched to evildoers. As for Lot's family, we will save them all except his wife whom we counted with the doomed'" (The Valley 15:57–60), 108, 118–119.

"And the people of the city came, rejoicing at the news. He said: 'These are my guests. Embarrass me not! Be fearing of God and shame me not!'" (The Valley, 15:67–68–69) 109.

"And we turned it upside down and rained upon them *sijjīl* rock." (The Valley 15:74), 119.

THE WALLS / AL-HUJURĀT

"O You who believe! Let not a people [qawm] deride other people, for they may be better than they. Nor shall any women ridicule other women, for they may be better than they" (The Walls 49:11), 105.

"O mankind! We created you from a male and a female, and made you into nations and tribes, so that you may know one another. The most righteous among you is the noblest in the sight of God. God is all omniscient and knowing" (The Walls 49:13), 101.

WOMEN / AN-NISĀ'

"Such wives you have enjoyed thereby, you must give them their wages" (Women 4:24), 59.

"Test well the orphans, until they reach the age of marrying; then, if you perceive in them right judgment, deliver over unto them their property" (Women 4:6), 123.

"The men get a share of what the parents and the relatives leave behind. The women too shall get a share of what the parents and relatives leave behind. Whether it is a small or a large inheritance, it is a definite share" (Women 4:7), 24, 25.

"And when relatives, orphans and the needy are present at the time of dividing up the inheritance, you shall give them therefrom and treat them kindly" (Women 4:8), 26.

"As for those women from whom you fear *nushūz*, first admonish them, then desert them in bed and beat them" (Women 4:3), 53.

"God decrees in the provisions regarding your children that the male gets twice the share of the female. If the inheritors are women, and more than two, they get more than the two-thirds of what is bequeathed. If the inheritor is one woman, she gets one-half of what is bequeathed" (Women 4:11), 28.

"If the deceased left children, his parents get one-sixth of the inheritance each. If he left no children and his parents are the only inheritors, the mother gets the one third. If he has siblings, then the mother gets the one sixth, and this after fulfilling any will left by the deceased and paying off all debts" (Women 4:11), 34, 35.

"It is God's law that you do not know who among your parents and children is the best and most beneficial to you. God is omniscient and most wise" (Women 4:11), 33.

"You have half of what your wives left behind, if they had no children" (Women 4:12), 35.

"If the deceased man or woman, having left neither parent nor child, has two siblings, male or female, each of them gets one-sixth of the inheritance. If there are more siblings, then they equally share one-third of the inheritance, and this" (Women 4:12), 38.

"Those who commit abomination among your women, you must have from among you four witnesses against them. If they do bear witness against them, then you shall keep such women in their homes until they die, or until God provides a solution for them" (Women 4:15), 103, 128n85.

"And as for those among you, who are guilty of committing it, have those both punished. And if they repent and straighten up, then leave them alone. God is ever redeemer and merciful!" (Women 4:16), 116, 128n85.

"O you who believe! It is not lawful for you to inherit the women nor should you force them to give up anything you have given them, unless proven guilty of abomination" (Women 4:19), 117.

"For if you dislike them, it may happen that you dislike a thing in which God placed much good" (Women 4:19) 54.

"If you want to replace one spouse with another" (Women 4:20), 54.

"Such wives you have enjoyed thereby, you must give them their wages. And lawful to you are all others beyond these. So, seek them with your money in wedlock, not prostitution" (Women 4:24), 59.

"Those among you, who cannot afford to wed free believing women, may wed the believing slave women your right hands possess. God knows best the faith of each and every one of you. You shall obtain permission from their guardians before you wed them and give them in fairness what is due to them in wedlock, not as prostitutes or secret lovers" (Women 4:25), 54.

"As for those women from whom you fear nushūz, first admonish them, then desert them in bed and beat them" (Women 4:34), 53.

"And if you are ill, or on a journey, or one of you has finished answering nature's call, or you have touched women, and you find no water, then seek clean earth and wipe your faces and hands therewith" (Women 4:43), 56.

"And you will not be able to be equitable between your wives, however much you see to it" (Women 4:129), 77.

"They ask you for a ruling. Say: God imparted to you of His divine ruling regarding the inheritance of distant kindred. If one dies and leaves no children, and he had a sister, she gets half of what he left behind. If she dies first and has no children, he inherits all of her wealth. If there were two sisters, they get two-thirds of what he left behind. If the siblings are men and women, the male gets twice the share of the female," (Women 4:176), 28, 38.

"Forbidden to you are your mothers, daughters, sisters, the sisters of your fathers, the sisters of your mothers, the daughters of your brother, the daughters of your sister, your nursing mothers, the girls who nursed from the same woman as you, the mothers of your wives, and the step-daughters on your lap from the wives with whom you have consummated the marriage. If the marriage has not been consummated, it is not sin to wed them (the step-daughters). Also forbidden to you are the women who were married to the sons of your own blood. Also, you shall not be married to two sisters at the same time, except for what has already occurred in the past. God is most forgiving and merciful. And forbidden to you are all married women save those slave women whom your right hands possess. These are God's commandments to you" (Women 4:23–24), 94n8, 98n147.

"And keep an amicable companionship with them" (Women 4:19), 96n65.

"Men are in charge of women because of that with which God has distinguished one of them over another and because they financially provide for them" (Women 4:34), 99n193.

Appendix B

*Index of Hadiths (Even Those Disputed)
and Historical Accounts*

A ا

It was a charitable penance for a man to sexually approach his wife, 118.

"The obligation to fulfill that which gave you lawful access to a vagina is the highest of obligations," 50.

"Verily, what I fear most for my nation is the deed of the people of Lot," 121.

"If a man calls his wife, she must answer him even if in labor," 57.

"If a man calls his wife to bed and she refused to answer him, the angels will curse her till the morn," 57.

"When a man rides a man, God's throne is shaken," 121.

"Islam does not decrease, it increases," 27.

In another story, Aysha mentions what the Qur'an said in regard of those orphans who are girls: "This is about the orphan girl who lives with her guardian and shares his wealth. Because he has no desire to marry her and hates that another suitor marries her and has a stake in what has been so far his wealth, the guardian would imprison her. So God forbade them to do that," 78.

"Give anyone what is due to him and to the closest of males the rest," 35.

[. . .] Thābit Ibn Qays's wife visited the Prophet, peace be upon him, and told him: "O Prophet of God. I am not accusing Thābit of lack of religion or morals, but I cannot stand him. He said: Return to him his garden. She said: Yes," 54.

The wife of Sa'd Ibn Rabi' went to the Prophet, Peace be upon him, and told him that Sa'd had died and left behind two daughters and a brother who set out to take everything he left behind as inheritance, and a woman is married only for her wealth. He did not answer her during that meeting. When she came back, she said: "O Apostle of God! And Sa'd's two daughters?" He replied, Peace be upon him, "Call on his brother." When he arrived, the Prophet said: "Pay the two thirds to his daughters, the one eighth to his wife and to you the rest," 29.

"Heaven consists of that which no eye has ever seen and no ear has ever heard, with no harm done to the human heart," 125.

Aws Ibn Thābit al Ansāri died and left behind three daughters and a wife. The two men to whom he bequeathed his wealth—known as Suwayd and 'Arjafa on his paternal family side—came and took over everything. So, Aws's wife went to see the Prophet, Peace be upon him, and told him the story of the two male trustees who did not pay anything to either her or her daughters. So the Prophet, Peace be upon him, said: "Go home until I see what God will decide about your case." This is when this verse was revealed to the Prophet, Peace be upon him: "The men get a share of what the parents and the relatives leave behind. The women too shall get a share of what the parents and relatives leave behind. Whether it is a small or a large inheritance, it is a definite share," 29.

"Benī Hishām Ibn al Mughīra requested my permission to marry their daughter to 'Alī Ibn Abī Tālib. And I won't allow it, and I won't allow it and I won't allow unless Ibn Abī Tālib wants to divorce my daughter and marry theirs. She is a piece of me. What upsets her upsets me and what harms her harms me," 79.

"If a lūtī were to die without repentance, he is transformed in his tomb into a pig," 121.

"Some people, who were friends to the Prophet, peace be upon him, sat together one day with a Jewish man. So, some of them said: I come in unto my wife when she is lying. The other said, I come in unto her when she is standing. Another said, I come in unto her when she is lying on her side. The Jewish man said, 'You are like donkeys. We come in unto women only in one way.' So, God revealed his statement, 'Your women are a tilth for you,'" 68.

"These middle-aged women in your trust are of the same station as a slave or prisoner of war," 58.

"She, who dies and her husband is pleased with her, shall enter paradise," 80.

B ب

"Your wife says, 'spend on me or divorce me' and your slave says, 'spend on me or sell me,'" 58.

C ث

"The third is much. Leaving your heirs well off is better than leaving them a burden begging people," 25.

J ج

A woman is said to have visited the Prophet, peace be upon him, and told him that she was married to Rifā'a, but he divorced her three times. After him, she got married to 'Abdul Rahmān Ibn al Zubeyr. And pulling a piece of cloth from her djellaba, she said to the Prophet of God that he had nothing but a similar piece of cloth. This was said, according to the person who transmitted the hadith, in the presence of Abū Bakr who was sitting with the Prophet, peace be upon him, and Ibn Sa'd Ibn al 'Āç, who was at the door waiting to be let in. Then, Khāled started shouting at Abū Bakr asking him to restrain this woman for what she dared to say in front of the Prophet, peace be upon him. The Prophet could not stop laughing. Then he said to her that perhaps she wished to return to Rifā'a so that they could taste each other's honey," 52.

H ح

This is echoed in the following account by Aysha who attended the Prophet's explanation, peace be upon him, of the following two verses, "We have created them anew and virgins we made them" (The Event 56:35–36). He said, peace upon him: "The word "*atrāban*" means people who are of similar or equal in age. Every time a husband comes in unto his spouse, he finds her a virgin. When Aysha, peace on her, heard that from the Prophet, peace be upon him, she said, 'Oh! It is so painful!' And he said, peace be upon him, there is no pain," 73.

KH خ

"Take it from me that God has made a last recourse about them. The maiden is flogged and the non-virgin is stoned," 116.

"When the Prophet asked for Aysha's hand from Abū Bakr, Abū Bakr said to him: I am your brother. He said: You are my brother in God's religion and Book and I am allowed to marry her," 70.

S س

"A man had asked the Prophet, peace be upon, about coming in unto women in the anus. The messenger said it is halal. When the man came back, he called him and said to him how he put it, in what two orifices, openings, or slits. If it is from front to front, it is yes. If it is from back to front, it is yes, but from back to anus, it is no. If it is from front to front, it is yes. If it is from back to front, it is yes, but from back to anus, it is no. God shies not away from what is righteous, 'Do not come in unto women in the anus,'" 67.

"'Urwa asked Aysha about this verse and she has said that the verse is about the orphan girl who lives with her guardian and shares his wealth. Her wealth and beauty may tempt him to marry her without giving her an adequate *mahr* (dowry) which might have been given by another suitor. So, such guardians were forbidden to marry such orphan girls unless they treated them justly and gave them the most suitable *mahr*; otherwise they were ordered to marry any other woman," 78.

"Seven kinds of people God shall avert his eyes from on Resurrection Day. He will deny them His grace and they shall not be with those who are saved. They will be the first to enter Hell unless they repent, for God gives repentance to those who seek it. These are: He who has sex with his hand; he who initiates fornication; he who is seduced into fornication; he who is addicted to alcohol; he who beats his parents until they cry for help; he who harms his neighbors until they curse him; and he who has sex with the lawful sexual partner of his neighbor," 89.

Q ق

"The Prophet, peace be upon him, said: The best marriage is the easiest. And he told a man: Do you consent that I marry you to this particular woman? When she said yes, the man married her and consummated the marriage without giving her a dowry or anything else," 49.

"People said after the descent of the verses on inheritance: "A woman (wife) is given the one-fourth and the one-eighth, the daughter the half, and the child is also provided while none of them fights in battles or takes possession of bounty? Be silent over this statement in the hope the Prophet, Peace be upon him, forgets or we ask him to change it," 31.

A man is said to have stood and said, O Prophet of God! What is the *'iddah* of a young one who has not menstruated yet? And so came the revelation, "and those who have not menstruated as yet," 71.

"I said, O Prophet of God, that I was a young man who fears the sin of fornication, yet I could not find any woman to marry. He remained silent. Then I said something similar and he remained silent. Then I repeated my question a third time and he remained silent. In the fourth, he said, O Abū Hurayra! The pen has run dry after writing about what you are going through. Either castrate yourself, or sow your seeds," 89.

K ك

"Only an adult male used to inherit, neither a male child nor a woman could. When the verse on inheritances was revealed in the sūra of Women, it was hard to bear by people who said: 'How come the child and woman alike, who neither make money nor provide, inherit just as any man who works for a living?' And they wished and waited for a revelation to come from above. When nothing happened, they said: 'if this was allowed to happen, it could only be a binding law,'" 31.

"We were fighting with the Prophet, peace be upon him, and we did not have women. So we told him, O Prophet of God! Should we get ourselves castrated? And he prohibited it," 89.

L ل

"People from two different faiths do not inherit from each other," 27.

M م

"What shares of inheritance are left behind, they go to the male relatives," 35.

"'It is the duty of a Muslim who has money to bequeath to not let two nights pass without writing a will about it.' This hadith, too, shows my absolute freedom to write a will," 24.

"I did not consult with the Prophet over anything as much as I did in regard of al kalāla and he had never spoken to me as rudely as he did over this matter. Pointing his finger at my chest as if stabbing me, he said: 'O Umar! Isn't it enough that you have the summer verse, i.e., the last verse in the sūra of Women?'" 38.

"When Sa'd became seriously sick in Mecca, he said, the apostle of God came to see him. He said: "O! Apostle of God! I am very wealthy and I have no heirs, just dependents. Should I entrust to them my entire legacy? He said: No," 25.

"He who is delighted that the Great and Almighty God will serve him wine in the afterlife, let him leave it in this worldly life. And he, who is delighted that the Great and Almighty God will clothe him in silk in the afterlife, let him leave it in this worldly life," 123–124.

"He who is found having sex with a female donkey, he and the female donkey shall be put to death," 120.

"Whoever you find doing the action of the People of Lot, execute the one who does it and the one to whom it is done," 120–121.

N ن

"We the Prophets are not a folk to give as inheritance what we left behind as charity," 27.

W و

"The child belongs to the marriage bed, and the adulterer gets the stone (i.e., nothing)," 63.

W ي

"O' Young People! Whoever among you is able to afford marriage let him be married. And whoever is not able to get married, he should fast, for fasting curbs sexual desire," 88.

"'O Prophet of God! If this is the servant, then how about He who is served?' He replied, 'I swear by God, who holds in His hand Muhammad's soul that the supremacy of the one being served over the one serving is like the supremacy of the full moon over other stars,'" 122.

Selected Bibliography

'Alī, Jawād. *Al Mufassal fī tārīkh al 'arab qabl al Islām.* Beirut, Baghdād: Dār al 'ilm lilmalāyīn/maktabat al nahdha, 1970.
Ibn 'Arabī, Abū Bakr. *Ahkām al Qur'an.* Matba'at al bāb al Halabī, 1986.
Ibn 'Arabī, Muhieddīne. *Tafsīr al Qur'an al Karīm.* Beirūt: Dār al Andalus, 1981.
'Asqalanī, Ahmed Ibn Hajar al. *Fath al Bārī.* Beirut: Dār al Ma'rifa, 2004.
Ben 'Āchūr, Muhammad Tāhar. *Al Tahrīr wa al Tanwīr.* Tunis: Al dār al tūnisiya li al nashr, 1984.
Benslāma, Rajā. *Bunyān al Fuhūla: Abhāth fī al mudhakar wa al mu'anneth.* Tunis: Dar al Ma'rifa li al nashr, 2006.
Bouhdiba, Abdelwahab. *La Sexualité en Islam.* Tunis: Cérès, 2000.
Bukhārī, al. *Sahīh.* N.p. Dār Matābi' Asha'b, n.p.
Butler, Judith. *Trouble dans le genre, pour un féminisme de la subversion.* Paris: Editions la Découverte, 2005.
Chaboudez, Gisèle. *Rapport sexuel et rapport des sexes.* Paris: Denoël, 2004.
Didier-Weil, Alain. *Les trois temps de la loi.* Paris: Seuil, 1995.
Dolto, Françoise. *Tout est langage.* Paris: Vertiges du Nord Carrere, 1987.
Grāmī, Amāl. *Al Ikhtilāf fī al thaqāfa al 'arabiyya al islāmiyya.* Beirut: Al Madār al Islāmī, 2007.
Ghazālī, Abū Hāmid al. *Ihyā 'Ulūm al Dīn.* Beirut: Dār al ma'rifa, n.p.
Haddād, Tāhar al. *Imra'atuna fī al Sharī'a wa al Mujtama'.* Tūnis: Dār al Tūnusiyya li al nashr, 1989.
Hamon, Marie Christine. *Féminité et mascarade.* Paris: Seuil, 1994.
Ibn Sa'd. *Kitāb al Tabaqāt al Kabīr.* Beirut: Dār Sāder, n.p.
Kathīr, Ismā'īl Ibn al. *Tafsīr al Qur'an.* Dār al Tayyiba li anashr wa al tawzī', 1999.
Kishk, Muhammad Jalal. *Khawāter Muslim fī al Mas 'ala al Jinsiyya (Meditations of a Muslim Regarding the Issue of Sexuality).* Cairo: Maktabat al turāth al Islāmī, 1992.
Munjid, Muhammad Ben Sālih al. *Muharramāt Istahāna bihā kathīrun mina ennās.* Saudi Arabia, 1993.
Moslem. *Sahīh. Dār Ihyā al kutub al 'arabiyya,* 1955.
Naysābūrī, Abū al Hassan al Wāhdī al. *Asbāb al Nuzūl.* Beirut, Dār al Kitāb, 1986.
The Personal Status Code. Ed. Muhammad Habīb Cherif. Tunis, Sousse: Dār al Mizān li al Nashr, 2004.
Qurtubī, Abū 'Abdullah al. *Al Jāmi' li Ahkām al Qur'an.* Cairo: Dār al Kutub al Misriyya, 1964.
Qutb, Sayyid. *Fī Dhilāl al Qur'an.* Beirūt. Al Qāhira: Dār al Shurūq, 1988.
Rāzī, Fakhr al Dīn al. *Mafātīh al Ghayb.* Beirūt: Dār al Fikr, 1985.

Rusāfī, Ma'rūf al. *Kitāb al Shakhsiyya al Muhammadiyya*. Köln, Germany: Manshūrāt al jamal, 2002.

Suyūtī, Jalāl al Dīn al. *Al Itqān fī'Ulūm al Qur'an*. Beirut: Dār al Ma'rifa, n. p.

Tabarī, Abū Ja'far Ben Jarīr al. *Jami' al Bayān fi Ta'wīl al Qur'an*. Beirūt: Dār al kutub al 'ilmiya, 1968.

Tabarsī, Abū al Fadhl 'Alī Ibn al Hassan al. *Mujma' al Bayān fī tafsīr al Qur'an*. Beirūt: Dār al Ma'rifa, 1986.

Ibn Taymiyyah, Ahmed. *Al Fatāwī al kubrā*. Beirut: Dār al kutub al 'ilmiyya, 1987.

Tīfāshī, Shihāb Uddīn al. *Nuzhat al Albāb fīmā lā yūjadu fī kitāb*. Ed. Jamāl Jumu'a. Riyādh al Rayes li al kutub wa al nashr: London-Cyprus, 1992.

Youssef, *Olfa. Weak in Mind and Religion*. Tunis: Dār Sahar, 2003.

———. *Al Ikhbār 'an al Mar'a fi al Qur'an wa al Sunnah*. Tunis: Sahar, 1997.

Vasse, Denise. *L'Autre du désir et le Dieu de la foi: Lire aujourd'hui Thérèse d'Avila*. Paris: Seuil, 1991.

Zamakhsharī, Abū al Qāsim Jār Allāh al. *Al Kashāf 'an Haqāeq Attartīl wa 'Uyūn al Aqāwīl aqāwīl wa fī wujūh atta'wīl*. Beirut: Dār al Ma'rifa.

Zarkashī, Badruddīn Muhammad Ibn 'Abdullah al. *Al-Burhan Fi 'Ulūm al Qur'an*. Beirut: Dār al Jīl, 1988.

Index

About the Author

Olfa Youssef is distinguished professor in Arabic letters, gender studies, and applied Islamology at the University of Manouba, in Tunisia. She earned her B.A. degree in Arabic from École Normale Supérieure of Sousse. Upon graduating in 1987, she received President Habīb Bourguība's Award for her oustanding academic achievement. In 2002, she became Docteur d'État in Arabic Letters and Civilization at the Faculty of Arts of Letters of Manouba. She published over ten books in Islamic feminist studies, the most famous of which are *Women Weak in Mind and Religion: Chapters in the Hadiths/a Psychanalytic and Psychological Approach* (2003), *The Multiplicity of Meanings in the Qur'an: A Study of the Foundations of the Multiplicity of Meaning in Language through the Science of Interpreting the Qur'an* (2003), *A Debate Between Lexicography and Linguistics Among Contemporary Arab Linguists* (1997), *Narrating about Women in the Qur'an and the Sunna* (1997), *Perplexity of a Muslim Woman: Over Inheritance, Marriage and Homosexuality* (2008), and *Desire: A Reading of Islam's Foundations* (2010). After the 2011 Tunisian Revolution, she published *The Male is Not Like the Female: On Gendered Identity* (2013) and a series of books called *Allahu A'lam* (*God Knows Better*). She also has a scholarly monograph in French titled *Le Coran au risque de la psychanalyse* (2007). Considered Tunisia's child prodigy throughout her educational career, she also served in key important administrative positions, namely the director of the Higher Institute for Children's Executives in Carthage (2003–2009) and the director of Tunisia's National Library Beit al Hikma (2009–2011). She also hosted several literary and educational programs on national TV. She is a prominent member of the new psychoanalytic school of Islamic feminism of Tunis. Her most important contribution is her introduction of the methodology of modern scholars in psychoanalysis, Saussurean linguistics and Arabic lexicography, to the traditional interpretations of the Qur'an and the hadiths.

ABOUT THE TRANSLATOR

Lamia Benyoussef is a Tunisian-American academic living in the United States. She is currently an assistant professor in Arabic Studies in the Department of Modern Foreign Languages at Birmingham-Southern College. She holds a BA in English from L'École Normale Supérieure of Sousse in Tunisia and an MA and a PhD in English from Michigan State University. Her areas of specialization are post-coloniality, feminist theory, and African literature with a specific emphasis on the Maghreb. Prior to coming to UAB, she taught British, American, and postcolonial literature at the University of Carthage and the University of the Center (Sousse) in Tunisia. Her current research projects are: the Holocaust in North African literature and Tunisian women during WWII. She is author of *The Production of the Muslim Woman: Negotiating Text, History and Ideology* (2005). She published a number of articles such as "Anne Frank Goes East: The Algerian Civil War and the Nausea of Postcoloniality in Waciny Laredj's *Balconies of the North Sea*" (2010), "Teaching about Women and Islam in North Africa: Integrating Postcolonial Feminist Theory in *Foreign Culture Pedagogy*" (2011), and a book article "Is it the End of State Feminism? Tunisian Women During and After the 14 of January Revolution," in Fethi Mansouri's *The Arab Revolutions in Context: Socio-Political Implications of the Middle East and Beyond* (Melbourne University, 2012). In 2013, she published a co-authored article on Islam in Tunisia in Oxford Encyclopedia of Islam Online and made two contributions to The [Oxford] Encyclopedia of Islam and Women. Her poems "Milk of the Ogre" and "The Beautiful Widow of the Green Mountain" appeared in 2013 in *Contemporary African Women's Poetry*, an anthology compiled by Juliana Makuchi Nfah-Abbenyi and Anthonia Kalu. Her most recent article, "Year of the Typhus: Operation Torch through the Eyes of Tunisian Women, or How to Make the Holocaust an Arab Story," appeared in the forum section of *The International Journal of Francophone Studies*.